FAREWELL TO PEASANT CHINA

Studies on Contemporary China

Studies on Contemporary China

FAREWELL TO PEASANT CHINA

Rural Urbanization and Social Change in the Late Twentieth Century

Edited by

GREGORY ELIYU GULDIN

with a Foreword by Walter Goldschmidt

 An East Gate Book

M.E. Sharpe
Armonk, New York
London, England

An East Gate Book

Copyright © 1997 by M. E. Sharpe, Inc.

Chapter 2 and 4 appeared in *Chinese Sociology and Anthropology*,
Vol. 28, No. 2 (Winter 1995–96); chapter 3 appeared in *Ethnology*,
Volume 25, No. 4 (Fall 1996); chapters 5, 7, 8, and 9 appeared in
Chinese Sociology and Anthropology, Vol. 28, No. 4 (Summer 1996).

Library of Congress Cataloging-in-Publication Data

Farewell to peasant China : rural urbanization and social change in
the late twentieth century / edited by Gregory Eliyu Guldin.
    p.   cm.—(Studies on contemporary China)
        "An East Gate book"
    Includes bibliographical references and index.
ISBN 0-7656-0183-4 (cloth : alk paper).—ISBN 0-7656-0089-7 (pbk. : alk. paper)
        1. Urbanization—China.
        2. China—Rural conditions.
        I. Guldin, Gregory Eliyu.
            II. Series
        HT384.C6F37   1997
    307.76′0951′09045—dc21
            97-16297
                CIP

Printed in the United States of America

The paper used in this publication meets the minimum requirements of
American National Standard for Information Sciences—
Permanence of Paper for Printed Library Materials,
ANSI Z 39.48-1984.

∞

BM (c)   10   9   8   7   6   5   4   3   2   1
BM (p)   10   9   8   7   6   5   4   3   2   1

Contents

Part I. Introduction

Part II. Urbanizing China

Part III. Regional Patterns

Part IV. Social Dimensions of Rural Urbanization

Part V. Conclusion

Foreword: The End of Peasantry

Walter Goldschmidt

Reading the essays in *Farewell to Peasant China* makes me feel like Rip van Winkle awakening from a long sleep. To appreciate its impact on our understanding of rural life in China we must look at the peasantry there and in the world over as it was when I was doing research on rural America and on peasant communities. It will be useful to see this in terms of the rural-urban dichotomy in social theory.

This distinction has played a large role in sociology. The difference between rural and urban life caught the attention of many pioneers in sociology, especially those influenced by anthropology or cross-cultural perspectives as, for instance, Émile Durkheim and Max Weber. It was, however, most clearly expressed by Ferdinand Tönnies (1957, [1887]) in his distinction between *Gemeinschaft* and *Gesellschaft*, the former referring to the community as a traditional social unit (*Gemeinde* = commons, commonality) and the latter to the groupings created to structure city life (*Gesellschaft* = company, both as business and as social gathering).

In this country early in the century, the empirical orientation of the "Chicago School" of sociology used that brash city as its great laboratory to document the nature of urban existence and what it did to those who came there as, for instance, expressed in the essays in the classic, *Gold Coast and Slum* (Zorbaugh 1929). The best definition of urbanism I know is Louis Wirth's essay, Urbanism as a Way of Life (Wirth 1938). The city is defined as a large dense concentration of heterogeneous people. They are ethnically heterogeneous because cities always are created by in-migration and are diverse in occupation because their existence depends on the division of labor and occupational specialization. These characteristics have several significant consequences for social behavior. The large population means that people are surrounded by strangers and that much social interaction is therefore impersonal and mediated through economic relations rather than personal ties. The heterogeneity means that people share neither the same life style nor the same traditions and values, so that formal rules must be created and these must be enforced by persons in formal roles of authority rather than by the mere force of custom. The result is a great disparity in personal life circumstances and differential access to power, leading to a class society. Rural life, by contrast, was seen as involving small aggregates of people with common background and similar economic activity who all know one another personally, share common values and live their lives according to customary rules with little distinction in power and privilege. These are, or course, "ideal types," but they have—or had —a good deal of face validity.

Professional ethnography began at the Bureau of American Ethnology and was fully developed by Franz Boas and his students at the turn of the century. it focused on the cultural practices of tribal peoples. Between the two great wars, however, anthropologists largely turned away from them and began to make "community studies" of peasant villages around the world and of towns in America. Robert Redfield, also at Chicago and with close ties to the Sociology Department (indeed, he was married to the daughter of one of its leaders), pioneered the study of village life in 1928 with his classic investigation of Tepoztlán, Mexico (Redfield 1930), a penetrating, if idealized, view of peasant life. The study of peasant villages grew throughout Latin America and in Asia, and expanded rapidly after the war in the era of economic aid to "under-developed" countries and even to Europe. Thus emerged a large empirical literature on peasant village life.

Inspired largely by the classic study of "Middletown" by the sociologists Robert and Helen Lynd (1929), for which the anthropologist Clark Wissler wrote the Introduction, anthropologists began also to study communities in the United States. Lloyd Warner, freshly back from studying the Murngin of Australia gave the greatest impetus to such research, starting with the study of Newburyport, "Yankee City," in Massachusetts (see Warner and Lunt 1941). After, interestingly, taking a post at Chicago, he instigated research by his students of a number of rural towns and cities throughout the United States and Canada. These studies, like the peasant village studies overseas, tended to treat the community as if it were a tribe; that is, as being largely self-contained rather than dependent on the nation-state of which it was a part. It also treated them as if they were representative of the nation or, at least, the region, as implied by such pseudonyms as Middletown, Yankee City, Deep South and Plainville. Not all students of American communities were associated with Warner; not, for instance, Hortense Powdermaker (1939), Carl Withers (1945), nor I, though it was the tradition to which my early research belonged—of which more later. Thus there came into being a large corpus of empirical research on community life; it grew without any clear central purpose and only vague theoretical implications, but the studies of peasant villages and modern small towns gave us detailed empirical documentation of the rural side of the rural-urban dichotomy, a counterpart to the empirical work on cities inspired by Chicago.

Throughout the "underdeveloped" world, wherever *latifundia* or other plantation-like land control had not reduced the rural population to serfdom, the farming practices of peasants had hardly changed, or seemingly hardly changed, from patterns that went back to the very beginnings of nationhood and urban life: family labor, ox-drawn plows with simple iron shoes, broadcast sowing by hand, sickle and scythe for harvesting, animal and human manure, the tools and artifacts of daily life made by the farmers and their wives themselves or other local craftsmen. In all this, their social life was very like that of "primitive" peoples of anthropological tradition and therefore fit its own romantic predilections.

Peasants differ from tribal peoples in that by definition they exist within a nation-state. This is a simple but important and highly intrusive matter, making things quite different from being surrounded by other tribes. For one thing, the village cannot go to war with its neighbors or expand its territory at their cost, as tribal people can and frequently do. This, in turn, insures a shortage of land and presses the villagers into poverty. Though the state hems the community within its boundaries it offers, in compensation, an urban escape for those who cannot make it locally or who chafe at the constraints of village life.

The nation-state has two other major influences on peasant village life: it promulgates laws to which that life must be accommodated; and it establishes a monetary system and sets market conditions and determines the money locally available by control of rents, taxes and/or prices. Despite these external controls of governance and markets, however, the peasant is free to live out his life according to local customs and it is such activities that occupy his energy, thought and emotions. These are the things that captured the attention of the anthropologists and have been recorded for each of the dozens of villages throughout the world that they studied and wrote about.

Of all such studies of life in villages, none appeals to me as much as Martin Yang's book (1945) about Taitou, Shantung Province, China, described in loving detail out of the memories of a childhood that go back to the 1920s. I prefer it to such more sophisticated descriptions by Fei and Hsu precisely for its innocence of a theoretical outlook, which would have impeded his recording the little dramas of everyday life in which one sees the true dynamics of peasant existence. We learn of the flag that used to be raised proudly to proclaim a son who had passed the Imperial Examinations (but not, with just the slightest hint of resentment, for the son who merely got a Ph.D. from Columbia). We learn that the peasant, when the potential bride's parents are to make a call, ties his neighbor's bullock so as to seem to belong to him and fleetingly wonder if he could have learned this from the Irish peasant who, according to Arensberg (1937), engages in the same little cheat—or if this does not reveal something more important about what we used to call "human nature." We not only learn that the ideal is a three-generation family, but that it is preserved by arranging the marriages and that this is not always pleasing to the sons, whose freedom of choice is impaired, but especially unpleasant for the daughters, who are forced into subordination to mothers-in-law who treat them like scum in a family that is alien to them, at least until they supply a son and heir. (A few years ago in a Japanese village, I met such a daughter-in-law, then in her seventies, who still chafed at the treatment she had received as a bride, further stung by the fact that modernization had deprived her of the opportunity to retaliate on her daughter-in-law.)

It was the description of Taitou and the remarkably similar details of the Irish village described by Arensberg (1937) that led me to examine the general character of peasant society. Evalyn Michaelson and I studied a world-wide sample of peasant studies, coding aspects of social life and belief from 46 villages that met our definition of peasantry, namely traditional agricultural production of independent peasants living in a community within a nation-state. (Goldschmidt and Kunkel, 1971; Michaelson and Goldschmidt, 1971, 1976). While each community is individual and shows influence of the nation to which it belongs, we found that it was possible to draw a profile of the typical peasant society. These uniformities showed little respect for differences in the nation, the kind of crops grown or the Great Tradition (in Robert Redfield's classic phrase) to which they belonged.

Not surprisingly, since we limited peasant society to those communities devoted to agriculture, the central focus was on land: its uses, husbandry and ownership. The very nature of peasant existence makes for land scarcity, as I have already noted, and therefore those who own more land have greater standing in the community, and the acquisition of additional land or the loss of holdings is the central concern of all. The social institution designed to keep land together is the three-generation household, which is usually the ideal, if not the norm. To preserve this family structure, marriages are arranged by the parents and brides brought into the usually patrilineal and patrilocal enterprise. A strong sense of age deference is part of the culture, and the leader of the farm is the senior man of the oldest generation, whose sons and grandsons he directs in their "cooperative" activities, often with no little resentment from the young. It is in this context that one must appreciate the relation between bride and mother-in-law that Yang described and I glimpsed in Japan. Religious belief, whatever the doctrinal theology, sacralizes both land and family. Social standing rests on the public image of a harmonious and effective household cooperating in the husbandry of its land. The emphasis on seniority reenforces traditionalism and frugality; this means making do with what one has and preserves traditional craftsmanship. Underlying all this is the sense that the village is a largely self-contained universe, subjected to the legal and fiscal control of the nation state but itself controlling the values, and the social standing of its own citizenry. A trip to the local town, let alone the city, is a major event and one to be avoided. We would be wrong to idealize this way of life; it has its virtues and its flaws; clearly it plays into the hands of the men and the elderly at the expense of women and the young; it serves those who like the security of a closed community rather than those who prefer excitement and novelty.

America never had a peasantry. The manner in which our land was settled rendered the local population heterogeneous from the outset, and our farm enterprise has always been heavily into commercial production. Even Plainville, in pre-war "backward" Ozarks, could not be seen as traditional peasantry. The only true peasants to be found in the United States live in the remote villages in the valleys of northern New Mexico settled by Spaniards from Mexico in the eighteenth century and all but forgotten. Even by the thirties, the mules had everywhere largely given way to tractors, the agricultural agents had taught modern methods of farming and had sold the farmers on chemical fertilizer while their wives decorated the farmhouses out of the Sears and Roebuck catalog. But it was a community; the farmers and their hired hands and the local tradesmen formed towns toward which they felt strong loyalty. This American commercial farming was a pattern of life that lies between the peasantry that the settlers had left when they emigrated from the Old World and the industrial agriculture that emerged in California in the nineteenth century and is now rapidly spreading throughout the United States.

It is this industrialization that I studied. In 1940 I went to the town of Wasco in California to make a "community study," in the tradition described earlier (Goldschmidt 1942, 1947). This and a later study (Goldschmidt 1946), showed that the California agriculture was industrialized. This was made possible by the rich farmland, equable climate and land ownership practices inherited from the Spanish and was by then already spreading through what is now called the "Sunbelt." Industrial farming is not traditional; indeed, it is anti-traditional. It tends to be large scale, is highly dependent upon an underclass of seasonal labor, and is capital intensive in the use of the most modern machinery, chemical fertilizers, pesticides and herbicides. The enterprise is dominated by the profit motive. It does not foster social relationships but creates wealth; it exists to make a profit and it must make a profit to survive. Social standing is based on income and wealth and not upon personal qualities. Family operation tends to give way to corporate control.

I found California farm communities to be more like cities than villages: from industrialized agriculture one reaps urban life, as expressed in the title *As You Sow* (Goldschmidt, 1947). This urbanization involved the creation of larger towns, the impersonalization of social relationships, the erosion of tradition, the development of a rural proletariat with virulent antagonism between the social classes. The strong and direct influence of the outside world on the social life of the community is a major factor. Corporate representatives with headquarters in San Francisco, Los Angeles and more remote cities dominated the community. The local head of the branch of the great banking chain, Bank of America, was called "mayor," and was just the most powerful of the many corporate representatives and their wives who filled the civic organizations that set the tone of social life and made public policy. These leaders are directly dependent upon the outside for their income and their social rewards and expect to move elsewhere as they advance in the corporate structure; they therefore understandably have limited loyalty to the town. Industrial agriculture blurs the border between town and country and renders the urban-rural dichotomy meaningless. The laborers in the field remained a class apart.

The anthropologists' custom of writing cultural descriptions in what they call the "ethnographic present" leaves their communities frozen in time, rendering them history rather than sociology. I have been roused from the nostalgic reverie they create by the essays in this book, as I said at the outset. China has seen an eon's worth of change in the years since Yang's youth: the growing power of the Kuomintang, the Japanese invasion, the communist accession to power and Land Reform, the impact of the commune era and the decade and more of post-1979 reforms. These events and processes constitute the more obvious forces of change that have brought the villages throughout the land into the mainstream of Chinese life.

Zhou Daming and Zhang Yingqiang, in their essay on urbanization in the Pearl River Delta, summarize some of these changes in the village of Lujiang, which has long since been encircled by Guangzhou. They write that in 1940 Lujiang was "a self-contained economy relying on the land. In social system, kinship played an extremely important part. The major form of kinship was the clan organization . . . A person's name decided his or her economic and social status and peer group. The family was the site of economic, religious, educational and recreational activity as well as the basic unit of production and consumption." They describe how the encroaching city changed the population structure. "Land requisition was compensated by hiring and change of household registration status" with the result that the people "became state employees and [legally] urban residents although they continued to live in the village." By the 1980s little cultivable land was left and the area completely engulfed by the city. They conclude their discussion by saying "Lujiang now has all the basic characteristics of urbanization: (1) a big population of high density, . . (2) a high degree of heterogeneity . . . turning Lujiang into a pluralistic community; (3) a relatively high degree of occupational differentiation; and (4) universal spread of mass media."

Lujiang, lying close to a sprawling city, is perhaps further along this path than most villages, but more general statistics suggest that all are well along it, certainly beyond the point of no return. We are given data from various areas showing the increase in crop diversification and cash sales of produce and involvement with industrial production. We learn also about the peasants' increased mobility and frequent trips to Guangzhou and Hong Kong and their involvement with modern radio and TV. For instance, Shi Yilong's data on Caitang Village shows the purchase of modern clothes and other consumer goods. Even in Duilongdeqing County in the remote Tibetan region Gelek and Li find that one can "see that rural Tibetans had gradually departed from self-sufficiency to reliance on cities and industry."

Implicit in these essays is the sense that all this is good, that this is progress. Gelek and Li tell us that the rural Tibetan girls can escape the dreary life of the village and get "dream husbands" from the cadres or the billeted soldiers. They end by pointing up the changes over the past "short dozen years," where urban lifestyles have replaced traditional ones integrating rural with urban that gave birth to "a new, more ideal type of culture." They are aware that these changes have been disruptive but conclude that "the positive side of urbanization no doubt outweighs the negative."

We also see the changes that took place when the commune system was abandoned in the early 1980s. Gelek and Li tell us that peasant strategies once again emphasize capital accumulation while some try to increase their production (now more for market than for consumption) by sub-contracting for the use of land that had been allocated to their neighbors. Guldin, Shi, and Zhou, in their separate essays, show that the line between village and city is now so blurred that many peasants still living in the villages engage energetically in commerce, construction or transportation. But the exodus from peasantry is perhaps the major dynamic; from Dalian in the north to Yunnan in the southwest and Fujian in the southeast, peasants are increasingly involved in the industrial and commercial activities of China.

While I am aware of the limitations and difficulties of peasant society, I do not see that the positive sides outweigh the negative in the urbanization process—certainly not with respect to the United States. The sense of community and the social solidarity of traditional life is lost to a depersonalized pattern of urban social interaction and material values take precedence over social ones. In America, urbanization has been spear-headed by industry, not by governmental sponsorship. It has led to a class of underprivileged rural labor engaged in back-breaking toil and all but prevented from social advancement. Perhaps in a communist country with its centralized control of the economy, urbanization can take place without such discrimination. This remains to be seen.

References

Arensberg, Conrad M. 1937. The Irish Countryman. Gloucester Mass: Smith

Goldschmidt, Walter. 1942. *The Social Structure of a California Rural Community*. Ph.D. Thesis. Berkeley CA: University of California.

———. 1946. *Small Business and Community—The Effect of Scale of Farm Operations on Community Life*. Washington: Committee on Problems of American Small Business, U.S. Senate.

———. 1947. *As You Sow*. New York: Harcourt, Brace and Co. (Also, Glencoe: The Free Press.)

———. 1978. *As You Sow; Three Essays in the Social Consequences of Agribusiness*. Montclair, New Jersey: Allenheld, Osmun (Reissue of *As You Sow*, and *Small Business and the Community*.)

Goldschmidt, Walter and Evalyn Kunkel. 1971. "The Structure of the Peasant Family." *American Anthropologist* 73(5):1058–1076.

Lynd, Robert S., and Helen M. Lynd. 1929. *Middletown: A Study in Contemporary American Culture*. New York: Harcourt

Michaelson, Evalyn Jacobson, and Walter Goldschmidt. 1971. "Female Roles and Male Dominance Among Peasants." *Southwestern Journal of Anthropology* 27(4):330–352.

———. 1976. "Family and Land in Peasant Ritual." *American Ethnologist* 3(1):87–96.

Powdermaker, Hortense. 1939. *After Freedom: A Cultural Study of the Deep South*. New York: Viking.

Redfield, Robert. 1930. *Tepoztlán, A Mexican Village: A Study of Folk Life*. Chicago: University of Chicago Press.

Tönnies, Ferdinand. 1957 [1887]. *Community and Society (Gemeinschaft und Gesellschaft)*. Charles P. Loomis, tr. & ed. East Lansing: Michigan State University Press.

Warner, W. Lloyd, and Paul S. Lunt. 1941. *The Social Lie of a Modern Community*. New Haven: Yale University Press.

Wirth, Louis. 1938. "Urbanism as a Way of Life." *American Journal of Sociology* 42:403–509.

Withers, Carl [James West, pseud.]. 1945. *Plainville, U.S.A.* New York: Columbia University Press

Yang, Martin C. [Mou-Ch'un]. 1945. *A Chinese Village: Taitou, Shantung Province.* New York: Columbia University Press

Zorbaugh, Harvey W. 1929. *Gold Coast and Slum: A Sociological Study of Chicago's Near North Side.* Chicago: University of Chicago Press.

Acknowledgments

Primary acknowledgment goes to Professor Zhou Daming of Zhongshan University's Anthropology Department in Guangzhou, the People's Republic of China. Professor Zhou has been my major collaborator on numerous projects, most recently this jointly directed project on rural urbanization. Professor Zhou organized the field site visits and coordinated personnel, budget and administrative logistics. He was also invaluable with helping craft our methodological and theoretical approach to the project. Those literate in Chinese would do well to consult his edition of a Chinese language report on this project entitled *Zhongguo xiangcun dushihua* and published in 1996 in Guangzhou by Guangdong Renmin Chubanshe.

Gratitude is also felt towards Professor Huang Shuping, then chair of the department at Zhongshan, for her support and encouragement, as well as to Dorji Tseten at the China Tibetology Research Center and Chen Guoqiang at Xiamen University, and department Chairs Lin and Ma at Yunnan and Xiamen Universities respectively. Sabbatical year support from Pacific Lutheran University was also a crucial element of this project, as has been the consistent secretarial support of Sharon Raddatz.

Finally, a word of thanks to Sydel Silverman of the Wenner-Gren Foundation for Anthropological Research and to David Vikner at the United Board for Christian Higher Education in Asia, for their continuing support of our anthropological efforts to understand the changing Chinese social scene.

Tables and Figures

Tables

Figures

Contributors

Gelek (Ge Le)	China Tibetology Research Institute, Beijing, P.R. China
Guldin, Gregory Eliyu	Pacific Lutheran University, Tacoma, Washington 98447
Guo Zhenglin	Zhongshan University, Guangzhou, Guangdong, P.R. China
Hoffman, Lisa	University of California at Berkeley, Berkeley, CA
Lan Daju	Xiamen University, Xiamen, Fujian, P.R.China
Li Tao	China Tibetology Institute, Beijing, P.R. China
Liu Zhongquan	Dalian University of Technology, Dalian, Liaoning, P.R. China
Shi Yilong	Xiamen University, Xiamen, Fujian, P.R. China
Zhang Yingqiang	Zhongshan University, Guangzhou, Guangdong, P.R. China
Zhou Daming	Zhongshan University, Guangzhou, Guangdong, P.R. China

Part I

Introduction

1

The Anthropology of Rural Urbanization in China

Gregory Eliyu Guldin

The Topic of Research

This volume is comprised of a collection of field reports on the urbanization of rural areas in Guangdong, Fujian and Yunnan provinces in southern China, plus reports from Tibet in the west and Liaoning in the northeast. All of these reports, save for that on Liaoning, were part of a joint effort of a team of Chinese scholars and, intermittently, the American editor of this volume. Professor Zhou Daming of Zhongshan University was Project Co-Director along with Professor Guldin of Pacific Lutheran University. The field research for these chapters, funded by the Wenner-Gren Foundation for Anthropological Research and the United Board for Christian Higher Education in Asia, was conducted between spring 1992 and fall 1993, with each field stay lasting from one to several weeks, and some sites visited at least twice. The Liaoning field study, although it followed the same research guidelines as devised for the rest of the project, was conducted with separate funding and undertaken in early 1996.

The approach of the project is ethnographical and explicitly comparative, seeking to understand the multiple dimensions whereby "rural" areas are becoming increasingly influenced by the twin processes of industrialization and urbanization. Given China's depth and breadth, the project endeavors to cover a variety of sites, including some in the more prosperous coastal regions of Guangdong and Fujian as well as areas where the process has just begun, such as in parts of Yunnan and Tibet. The inclusion of non-Han nationality districts, two special economic zones, and three variant urban patterns in the northeast, is an attempt to broaden the comparison.

Before commencing the project, the participants came together in Guangzhou to hammer out a common research frame for the undertaking. Representatives from each of the engaged *danwei* (Zhongshan University in Guangzhou, Xiamen University in Fujian, Yunnan University in Kunming, and the China Tibetology Research Center in Beijing) as well as the editor agreed to explore how economic changes were affecting social and cultural life styles in their respective sites. Data was therefore gathered on changes in production, and on the flow of information, capital, and population. The intent was to emphasize the oft-neglected cultural dimension of China's reform process as more and more areas in China metamorphose into an urbanized society.

The "Reform Era" inaugurated in 1979 and 1980 with the dismantling of the commune system, the establishment of special economic zones and the move towards a Chinese-style market economy, led to rapid changes in the countryside. With farming contracted out to individual households, pressures rose to release labor from the agricultural sector; these laborers were then put to work in the expanding tertiary and secondary sectors, and especially in transportation and construction. Further expansion of the rural enterprises (*xiangzhen qiye*) helped absorb agriculture's surplus labor and, in turn, helped to boost the demand for such labor. Complex migration trails began to take shape, with implications for both receiving and exporting districts. Increasing flows of people, capital, goods and information have spearheaded an urbanization process which promises to radically transform the lives of the solid majority of Chinese citizens. These reports describe the multiple forms that urbanization is taking in China, and give credence to the prediction (Guldin 1992:230) that by the year 2000, if we consider not only those living in officially designated urban areas but in urbanized townships and villages as well, the majority of Chinese will be living urbanized lifestyles.

The Articles

The articles were all penned by Chinese and American scholars who consider themselves anthropologists (although Liu Zhongquan probably leans more towards a sociological self-description). Anthropology was revived officially in China during the early 1980s with the establishment of anthropology departments in Zhongshan and Xiamen Universities, and then later in the decade as a disciplinary major (*zhuanye*) within the History department of Yunnan University. All three of these danwei participated in the project. Furthermore, the director of the Tibetan section of the project, Dr. Gelek, received China's first in-country Ph.D in anthropology at Zhongshan University in 1986.[1]

Urban anthropology did not become a distinct subfield, however, until its inauguration at the First International Urban Anthropology Conference held in Beijing in 1989–1990 (Guldin and Southall 1993). Since then the China Urban Anthropology Association has been set up in Beijing under the auspices of the Nationalities Institute of CASS and the Ministry of Nationality Affairs, and an International Urban Anthropology Conference was held in Shandong. Research projects have taken longer to materialize. One problem has been the lack of explicitly urban-oriented materials, and another, the absence of senior scholars with urban field experience. To combat these deficiencies, training seminars reviewing urban anthropological theory and method were conducted in Guangzhou and Beijing by this editor for those scholars interested in this project. The fieldwork which then ensued and the results reported in this volume represent the first large-scale urban anthropological research project in the People's Republic.

The first article is written by Zhou Daming, Associate Professor in Zhongshan's Anthropology Department. As project co-director, Professor Zhou provides the background and sets the framework for the project by first reviewing the debate regarding rural urbanization in the Chinese literature and the political factions that support different positions. He also introduces us to the complexity of defining "urbanization" in the Chinese context. He cautions us in the use of the common but insufficient yardsticks for measuring basic data such as growth in the officially registered urban population, or an increase in the number of rurally-registered people who change to "non-agricultural registration status," that is, urban registered status (nong zhuan fei). His article is also interesting in that it is a comparison of different prosperous areas. This is an unusual undertaking as most studies of these areas analyze them in isolation. Anhai in Fujian and Humen in Guangdong make for an instructive contrast, not the least of which is their similar overseas/Hong Kong connections.[2] By also contrasting these areas with Yunnan, he is able to draw on a wider canvas for his classification of urbanization types.

The second article, by the editor, reviews the multiple rural urbanization venues of the project, and asks whether a new pattern of Asian urbanization, the desakota process described by the geographer Terry McGee of the University of British Columbia, is emerging in southern China. Like Zhou, Guldin revisits urbanization definitions (this time from folk and scholarly perspectives), but then calls for a distinction to be drawn between "townization" and "citization," as "urbanization" is too broad a category to accurately describe the varying processes underway in contemporary China.

The next section of the book highlights regional and local patterns. The first article in this segment, co-authored by Zhou and his colleague Zhang Yingqiang, focuses on the process of urbanization in one area in the prosperous Pearl River Delta. The authors show that even there there is no single mode of urbanization, but rather four distinct patterns. In their analyses they adopt an applied anthropological perspective. After reviewing the problems which have arisen in each of the four patterns, they offer solutions as policy recommendations. Their comparative frame is refreshing, as is their emphasis on the human side of the economic changes experienced by both migrants and locals. Their description of the *mangliu* (the so-called "blind migrants") is particularly worth reading.

Shi Yilong, Associate Professor of Anthroplogy at Xiamen University, reports on his observations over a decade of the transformation of an agricultural village into an industrializing "suburb" of the Xiamen Special Economic Zone. He begins his article by critiquing demography-based definitions of urbanization ("concentrations of rural population in cities") which completely neglect the processes of rural urbanization. Professor Shi prefers a definition of urbanization that is more sociological, one that emphasizes the acquisition of urban ways of life. At times, though, he seems almost to be equating urbanization with prosperity and standard of living with lifestyle.

Rural urbanization is also a phenomenon in the northeast. Lisa Hoffman of the University of California at Berkeley and Liu Zhongquan of Dalian University of Technology analyze urbanization processes in the northeast and look at how local leaders are engaging reforms and the new economic policies. A study of three research sites—a village, a town, and a new form of farmer-initiated urbanization—reveals the critical importance of local leadership in determining *which* rural areas undergo urbanization first.

The next article, by Dr. Gelek and Li Tao of China's Tibetology Research Center, investigates rural urbanization processes in a suburban county outside of Lhasa, an area far removed from the coastal prosperity of Guangdong and Fujian. Here we see a relatively slow rate of increase in the proportion of the secondary and tertiary sectors in the economy, although the shifts have indeed begun. Out-migrant remittances back home to Duilongdeqing County have formed an investment capital pool that serves to jump-start the local economy, a pattern we saw in Hunan, Yunnan, and elsewhere. Gelek and Li note many lifestyle changes, including far more rural-urban economic ties than even a few years ago, leading them to conclude that rural urbanization has indeed commenced in Tibet as well. The trickle-down effects from the economic reforms of the 1980s have reached the Tibetan plateau, but it is clear that, at this point at least, rural urbanization is more a ripple than a flood. Interestingly enough, Gelek and Li also point to changes in food preferences (to vegetables, fruits, noodles, and rice) as indicators of "urbanization or acculturation" to the majority Han population. Probably both.

The next section looks at the social dimensions of rural urbanization. The first two articles focus on the migrant population. Lan Daju, a young researcher at Xiamen University's Anthropology Institute, worked with Professor Shi as well as Professor Chen Guoqiang in Caitang. Lan had great rapport with his migrant informants and buttressed the fairly unrefined questions utilized in his survey with keen observations. His article is noteworthy, especially for the segment on migrant self-perception. He reports that they were unclear whether they were rural or urban workers and then tells us that "actually they [the migrants] were little bothered by such things; all they knew was that they were out to earn money, and that was enough!"

Zhou Daming's study of migrant (odd-job) workers sites his "hamlet" within the great metropolis of Guangzhou. He takes the "urban village" approach to his investigation and explores the dynamics of social life in this migrant "ethnic neighborhood." He delivers fine ethnographic detail and shows us the quality work that part-time, off-residence Chinese fieldwork can accomplish.

In the last article, Zhou teams up with his Zhongshan University colleague, political science department researcher Guo Zhenglin, to assess the changes to the rural social security system that rural urbanization has brought about. As a companion piece to Zhou's chapter above on rural urbanization in the Pearl River Delta, this article helps explain how setting up rural social security systems in the postcommune era's rural townships has helped to narrow the gap between "rural" and "urban" dwellers' lifestyles significantly. The authors also alert us to the emergence of a new "shareholders" pattern of distributing social security benefits, a pattern that promises to establish a "socialist social security" pattern without hindering the growth of the market or of capital accumulation. Finally, the article points out the continuing importance of the collective sector in prosperous areas.

In both of these last two articles, the authors also demonstrate the strongly applied emphases of Chinese anthropology when they make specific policy recommendations. In the former, Zhou argues for comprehensive and equitable treatment for the odd-job workers, while in the latter, Guo and Zhou make the case for improving the social security system, call for better job safety precautions, and appeal for better treatment of both rural migrants in cities and migrant laborers in the countryside. With these suggestions, they follow the tradition of Chinese ethnographers and scholars making useful social contributions.

Terminology and Translations

Certain terms are hard to translate precisely from the Chinese. How should "*nongmin*" be rendered in English? The traditional translation as "peasant" is inappropriate in a non-feudal context, as the standard usage of the English term refers commonly to societies in which agriculturalists have little decision-making authority over production and marketing. If this was true during previous eras before and after the Communist Revolution, it is certainly not true today. The term might thus today be more accurately given as "agriculturalist" (or farmer) in some contexts, and "village resident" in others. In this volume we avoid using "peasant" altogether, other than in the hybrid term "peasant-workers" (*min-gong*).

Wailairen ("outsiders") or *wailai renkou* ("outsider population") refer to people not native to a locale. As used in Guangdong, they refer both to people from elsewhere in the province as well as *waishengren,* those from other provinces. We translate the former pair as outsiders and the latter as migrants.

Some other terms are best rendered in their Chinese original with occasional English versions given for variety's sake. Thus we use *danwei*/unit, *lianheti*/multi-family enterprise, *hukou*/household registration, and *getihu*/individual entrepreneur. The articles also make frequent reference to the oft-changing and perpetually confusing hierarchy of administrative towns, cities, counties, and local districts. For help with this, we point those interested to Ma 1992, whose article helps make sense of the differences between designated and undesignated towns (*jianzhi* and *feijianzhi zhen*).[3] For the Zhang and Zhou article specifically, the reader should note that Dongguan County has become Dongguan City and that we refer to the old county seat as Dongguan Municipality to distinguish it from the county-wide Dongguan City.

We also use the standard abbreviations GVIAO and GVIO, to stand respectively, for Gross Value Industrial and Agricultural Output and for Gross Value of Industrial Output. Furthermore, whenever Zhou and Zhang refer to a *wenming cun* ("civilized village"), the reader should know that they are referring to villages judged to be more educated and more cultivated, and more in adherence to administrative rules and regulations.

Notes

1. Xiamen's Anthropology Department, however, was forced to close its doors in the early 1990s when the university leadership, citing financial pressure, transferred faculty and staff elsewhere on campus.

2. Zhou's discussion of Anhai and Humen's historical development also display a characteristic of Chinese anthropology—its inclusion of the historical perspective as an integral part of the anthropological approach; what the late Professor Liang Zhaotao referred to as anthropology's "fifth field."

3. See Kam Wing Chan (1994) for a further discussion of urbanization definitions in the People's Republic.

References

Chan Kam Wing. 1994. *Cities with Invisible Walls.* Hong Kong: Oxford University Press.

Guldin, Gregory Eliyu. 1992. *Urbanizing China.* Westport, CT: Greenwood Press.

Guldin, Gregory Eliyu and Southall, Aidan W. (eds.). 1993. *Urban Anthopology in China.* Leiden: E.J. Brill.

Ma Rong. 1992. "The Development of Small Towns and Their Role in the Moderniza-tion of China," in Guldin and Southall (eds.), *Urban Anthropology in China,* Leiden, pp. 119–153. E.J. Brill.

Part II

Urbanizing China

2

On Rural Urbanization in China

Zhou Daming

Rural urbanization is an issue put squarely before us by China's rural development over the past dozen years. It is a question that greatly concerns both practical workers and the academic community. My research paper "Comparative Study of Urbanization in South China"[1] discussed it from the rural perspective, in the writing of which rural urbanization was the object of this author's extensive ruminations. This chapter lays out the results of my thoughts, which I present to my colleagues for reference.

How the Question of Rural Urbanization Was Raised

Originally, urbanization was urbanization. Any process of urbanization necessarily touched on rural-urban interaction. So what exactly does "rural urbanization" mean? In this author's view, the raising of the question itself reflects China's special characteristics and has to do with China's given cultural ecology. Specifically, it reflects the contradiction between, on the one hand, the reality of the existing dualistic structure separating urban and rural areas and, on the other, the ideal of coordinated urban-rural development in which the three big gaps (gap between workers and peasants, town and country, mental and manual labor) have been eliminated. The root cause of this contradiction was lack of coordination in the process of integrating China's hoary cultural traditions with Marxist thinking from the West. As this is a very broad issue, this chapter will limit itself to the aspect pertinent to urbanization.

One characteristic of China's long-established culture was an "uneven or differential configuration." In it, each individual or group had a given position, a position that was inherent and inherited, not competitive. China's urban areas definitely reflected this configuration. A look at the history of urban development in China shows that the political function of cities had

13

been consistently reinforced to the exclusion of other functions. Cities at every level were bases of control in a network of centralized political control. The political status of a city determined its size. This configuration broke down after the Opium Wars, when the colonialist empires built up a number of Chinese commercial ports into cities. But these cities, too, were quickly absorbed into the centralized political network. Chinese cities therefore never did possess the relative autonomy enjoyed by European cities but were inextricably bound with the political system.[2] The country's political orientation was the single most important factor determining the development of cities.

The founding of the People's Republic of China in 1949 did not change this tradition, but brought the cities even closer into the political system. A more complete city hierarchy was established. Its characteristic was the combination of multilevel administration and an uneven, "injection-type" of investment under a centralized system. The higher a city's level of administration, the more investments it obtained and the faster the development of its economic, social, and spatial scale. All cities currently with 1 million or more people are either centrally administered, provincial capitals, or separately listed under the State Council's plan. In this uneven configuration, rural areas are at the bottom. Many counties have larger populations and stronger economies than cities located in them but are administratively under them. They have become natural "blood banks" for the latter.

Besides this configuration which gives the cities the advantage over the rural areas, a set of policies loom like barriers between them. Such policies not only cannot eliminate the town-country gap or promote coordinated development, but exacerbate their differences and slow down the development of both. These policies are the fundamental reason urbanization was unable to make any headway over a long period of time.

China's dualistic urban-rural structure is a widely acknowledged fact, although different perspectives assess it differently. In his article "On China's Dualistic Social Structure," Mr. Liu Chunbin pointed out that this dualistic structure comprised a series of concrete systems, 14 of them to be exact. These were the systems of household registration, grain supply, nonstaple food and fuel supply, housing, supply of means of production, education, employment, medical treatment, pension, labor protection, talent, military service, marriage, and child-bearing. In all but the last named, cities had the advantage over rural areas.[3] Summing up Mr. Liu's ideas and that of others, this author has come to the conclusion that the following three systems are crucial in this dualistic structure:

1. The household registration system. This system divides Chinese citizens into two major categories: Those households which are registered in

"rural areas" and those registered in "cities." Each category can be subdivided into several grades. Cities are divided into super-large cities—large cities—small and mid-sized cities—townships. Rural areas are divided into city suburbs—county suburbs—township suburbs—ordinary rural areas— remote areas. Each individual's status is decided at birth—he or she is registered at one of the above grades. Apart from going on to school or promotion to official status elsewhere, people have virtually no chance of changing their registration status. Change of location is strictly controlled. The few cases approved are usually downward moves. This system not only separates cities from rural areas but also cities from other cities, villages from villages, *danwei* (work units) from other *danwei,* and even members of the same family. It has become the basis of other dualistic policies and has shown no fundamental improvement to date. In acceptance to colleges, for instance, the order of priority is based on where the applicant's household is registered. Colleges in Guangzhou follow the policy of "giving Guangzhou first priority, then Guangdong Province. In principle, no one from border and remote areas will be accepted." (Furthermore, applicants who are originally registered in Guangzhou are given priority in remaining in Guangzhou, followed by people registered in Guangdong. Students from border and remote regions, no matter what their scholastic performance, cannot stay in Guangzhou.) Several million civilians from other provinces have been working in the Zhujiang (Pearl River) delta for a long time now, but because their registration states they all belong elsewhere, they are still considered "outsider population" (*wailai renkou*) in the delta.[4] The household registration system is now showing a commercialized tendency—registration status can be bought at prices corresponding to the grade. To buy a Guangzhou registration status, for instance, costs an adult 10,000 *yuan* RMB and for a child under 18, half that amount.

2. The social security system. Social security includes the social welfare, retirement, labor protection, health and medical systems. These systems reflecting the superiority of socialism are implemented only in the cities. Rural populations are excluded. In cities, these benefits are also graded: State functionaries—employees in units belonging to the whole people—employees of large collective units—employees of small collective units—individual householders. The higher the grade the better the benefits. Thus, if the registration system decides the natural status of a person at birth, then the social security system reinforces the "differential configuration" in occupation.[5]

3. The land system. There are currently two types of land ownership. Urban land belongs to the state and rural land to the collective. Land use is under the unified control of the State Land Administration. For cities to

expand or for new cities or factories to be built, land must be requisitioned from the rural areas. The state has established a set of policies in regard to land requisition including payment of land requisition fee, compensation fee, relocation fee, as well as norms for hiring cadre and for changing household registration status (for peasants). Usually the requisition process is a smooth one, as there seems to be little conflict between the two land ownerships. In this author's view, however, the different land systems geographically separate urban and rural areas, making cities and factories isolated islands in a rural sea. From investigation carried out in urban border areas, we have discovered the relationship between factories and their surrounding villages to be an extremely delicate one. The real cost is far higher than mere requisition fees.[6] This is because the factories' water supply and drainage, power and transportation systems all have to go through surrounding collectively owned land and waste gases through the collective's air. If the collective's demands are not met, the rival dwellers may have to take further steps.

Because of the two land systems, new urban-rural barriers have arisen. In the past, peasants longed for urban registration status and were willing to pay for it. Now, the situation has reversed in richer rural areas. Many who have settled down in the cities are asking to come back, going so far as to buy rural registration status. The main reason is that registered rural households are allotted land for dwellings. At a time when real estate prices are skyrocketing, one's own house and land in city outskirts can be a major source of income. Since, in the cities, land is state-owned, no individual or unit has any right to use it on one's own; land is a business monopolized by local governments and real estate companies. They requisition rural land at low cost to expand city boundaries, and once that happens, the price of the land appreciates hundreds of times. With high land prices comes high commercial housing costs beyond the purchasing power of ordinary residents. Consequently, many city residents have inadequate housing while buildings remain empty. This is another reason peasants working in the cities have not been able to settle down. These people build houses in their villages that they cannot utilize, while their whole families crowd into one room in the city.

The three systems described above are the chief factors for town-country separation. They will continue to be restrictive factors in future town-country relations. The world in the past century has undergone a wave of urbanization. Urbanization is a revolution that affects the entire social system. In China, however, because of dualistic policies in regard to town and country, urbanization has two parts, namely, the further urbanization of cities and the urbanization of rural areas.

Some people say that these dualistic policies were formulated under the given circumstances of the past, the then underlying theoretical premise being: When a country's economy was relatively underdeveloped, urban and industrial development must be given priority, and once cities became developed, they would promote rural development. Eventually, there would be coordinated urban-rural development and elimination of urban-rural gaps. This ideal is not necessarily infeasible, the trouble being that things got on the wrong track and urbanization got slowed down because of the endless political movements putting "class struggle as the key link" as a result of "left" interference.[7]

In our view, aside from problems deriving from political movements, the dualistically structured policy itself is harmful to both urban and rural development.

The registration system not only prevents urban-rural population flow but also impedes the population flow between cities, between *danwei* and between enterprises in cities. Thus an enterprise or unit becomes a relatively independent and isolated organization where close relatives congregate. For a time, a system of offspring succeeding parents in their jobs was in effect in order to solve the younger generation's employment problem; that is, parents were allowed to seek early retirement and have their children take over their jobs. Some retired at age forty-five. Thus large numbers of skilled workers and key technical personnel left their jobs to be replaced by young people (some under sixteen). A similar problem existed in academic and scientific research units. Talented people were overly concentrated in large cities and large state-owned enterprises.

Because the social security system has not been socialized, the state only pays for the benefits of state functionaries while all other enterprises and undertakings pay for their own employees' benefits. The work units are thus "running society" (instead of the other way around). Each unit is responsible for its employees in the cost of childbirth, aging, illness, and death (including birth and maternity care, children's day care, schooling and employment, retirement and illness of the elderly, medical treatment, and death and funeral expenses), as well as living arrangements including housing. This expenditure is constantly snowballing and is one of the work unit's heaviest burdens. In some units, the retirement number has reached over 50 percent without cutting down on expenses, because the pensions and medical expenses of the retirees alone amount to a huge figure. This is one of the reasons state-owned enterprises are in a sorry state. Some township and village enterprises, as well as towns and villages themselves, are now emulating state enterprises in setting up similar social security systems, and sometimes they provide even better terms. Although these may be state funded, the implementation of the system of financial responsibility has caused these huge social security benefits to become a heavy burden on their budgets.

Despite the priority given it, urban development has suffered because of the erroneous direction of urban economic development. First, there was an overemphasis on industrial development, especially heavy industry, to the neglect of the tertiary sector. Services and commerce were wrongly considered an industry that did not create wealth or engage in production and even viewed as "capitalistic" and cut. Consequently urban transportation, energy, telecommunications, and water and gas supply lagged in development and financial and commercial services shrank, making cities pools of stagnant water. From the perspective of employment alone, heavy industry is highly organized and absorbs large investments but it does not employ many people. This plus the shrinking of urban services has greatly reduced urban employment opportunities. That is why, despite city residents tightening their belts and getting minimum wages so that the state could put more funds into industry, industrial development and employment opportunities have grown slower than the natural increase in urban population. Cities are finding it tough to absorb the cost of its own labor power, not to speak of surplus rural labor power.

And the rural areas? For the longest time, the rural areas were considered a "vast world" capable of absorbing all sections of the population without danger of unemployment. Whenever cities felt a crunch in population and unemployment, people were shunted off to the rural areas. This, in addition to an incorrect population policy, caused the rural population to swell and per-capita farmland to drop drastically. Currently, average per-capita farmland in the nation is only 1.4 *mu* while that in coastal areas is less than 1. During the period of collectivization, there was a surfeit of nonproductive labor (engaged in capital construction of the land, political movements, etc.) as well as a lack of efficiency, so that peasants were busily occupied despite an excess of manpower as compared to land. They had no say in management, even to what crops should be planted. Dominated by the policy of "grain as the key link," grain crops were given priority and cash crops restricted. Under the leadership of the ultra-left line, handicrafts and other sidelines were prohibited. Orchards were cut down to build "Dazhai-type fields"; the farmers' vegetable plots were taken back so that they were even deprived of home-grown vegetables. This author had once visited a peasant family which was held up as a typical "capitalist tail." They kept a pig, had a few fruit trees in the yard, and showed fine vegetables growing in their plot, and for these reasons they were criticized. Such were the conditions that impoverished the rural areas. Many peasants toiled the year round without earning enough food to supply the family. The value of one day's work points came to 8 fen (the price of one pack of "Economical" cigarettes).

After institution of the output contracting system in 1979, the basic livelihood of the peasants was assured. With the rise in production yields, however, the hitherto covert problem of unemployment surfaced. How large was the actual size of surplus rural manpower? According to investigations, the average surplus rate was 40 percent, or 220 million out of the 550 million total social labor force. A World Bank survey predicted that from 1980 to 2000, the Chinese labor force would increase by 10 million people yearly. Chinese sources put the increase at 12 or 13 million. 70 percent of this number are in the rural areas. Such an enormous number of jobs could hardly be expected to be found in the rural areas alone.[8] Under the double pressure of decreasing farmland and rural job opportunities and increasing rural population and development of nonfarming industries, rural industrial enterprises are concentrating in the townships and residents are living in compact communities to save land. This trend will push urbanization, a push much more powerful than the limited absorption rate of cities. On the other hand, cities also have their pull.[9] "Rural urbanization" was the product of this push and pull.

Theoretical Exploration of Rural Urbanization

Many expressions have appeared reflecting rural urbanization, such as "town-country integration," "coordinated urban-rural development," "big efforts to develop small towns," and "speeding up development of township enterprises." The concrete content is the same, which is the following: local shifting of surplus rural manpower and prevention of a rush to the cities, especially large cities; urbanization to be motivated by development of township enterprises; and the road to urbanization being the building up of small towns.

The academic community has responded eagerly to the question of "rural urbanization," the majority holding a positive attitude toward it. Mr. Fei Xiaotong expressed great warmth for the idea of developing small towns and rural industry. He called this "the peasants' road to prosperity with Chinese characteristics." He actually caused an upsurge in the study of small towns. Some scholars found a theoretical basis for this idea from Marx. We quote the two following paragraphs:

> Contemporary history is the history of rural urbanization, not urban ruralization as in ancient times.[10]

> To enable existing cities and villages to gradually evolve into new social entities possessing the characteristics of both cities and rural areas, where citizen communes work in both industrial and agricultural production, combines the advantages of the urban and rural way of life and avoids the biases and defects of both.[11]

Rural urbanization is one of today's concrete issues that needs no quotes from Marx. Having found this "golden shield," however, in addition to the buildup by theoretical workers and the response of practical workers, development of township enterprises and towns has been able to proceed smoothly. Despite its use in warding off political interference, the "shield" also had an unfavorable effect on free academic discussion. People opposed to "rural urbanization" also used quotes to prove the above interpretation to be incorrect. Their interpretation was: "Contemporary history is the history of the infiltration of urban relations into the villages, not the infiltration of rural relations into the cities as in ancient times."[12] With this weapon, opponents of rural urbanization pitched themselves into the opposition.

In discussing rural urbanization, the first question is that of concept. Different concepts imbue the process with different content and course of development. Mr. Fei Xiaotong declared:

> The major changes overtaking rural China today is essentially a process of industrialization. Yet another aspect of putting factories in the rural areas is the urbanization of the rural areas, that is, the spread of cities to the rural areas. This may be a characteristic of Chinese industrialization. We are not taking the course of concentrating the peasants in cities to develop industry, but that of letting the peasants bring industry into the villages in order to get rich and leave poverty behind. This is a choice made under given historical conditions. This choice decides that peasants must integrate with existing cities, thus generating current new town-country relations.[13]

His central point was that "industry goes to the rural areas" (which he had also mentioned in other works) in order to effect the shift of surplus rural manpower locally, the site of the shift being small towns.

Some people interpret "rural urbanization" literally, claiming that it means turning the broad rural community into cities. They then criticize their own misconception and called it a "utopia that cannot be realized at the present stage."[14]

Some scholars divide the process into two phases based on the history of world urbanization. In the first phase, industrialization is effected by sacrificing agricultural development and shrinking the rural economy and congregating rural populations in the cities. "Rural urbanization is the second phase, in which urbanization deepens and overall urbanization is achieved.

The difference between this and the first phase is that the dominant element is not the shift of rural production factors to the cities, but the shift of the advanced production factors of cities and factories to the rural areas. This includes the shift of overly concentrated urban industries and a part of the urban population to promote rural industrialization and modernize agriculture, and, on this basis, accomplish rural urbanization, integrate town and country and form a modern urban system consisting of large, mid-sized, and small cities and towns." Urbanization in developed countries is accomplished in two phases, but in China, it should be combined in one phase. "Rural urbanization should not be effected after completing industrialization and urbanization. We should elect the process of dual development of urbanization and rural urbanization in the course of industrialization and urbanization. Simultaneous with urbanization through developing large, mid-sized, and small cities, small towns should be actively developed in a planned way and made to function as cities."[15]

A different view is that "rural urbanization is the dynamic process of concentrating rural industry in the cities, relocating peasants who have turned from farming to nonfarming production in the cities, continuous expansion of existing cities, and the building up of rural communities into new cities." This author also opposes making township enterprises and small towns the final target mode of China's rural industrialization and urbanization. He claims such a theory leads to the "rural disease."[16]

The above shows some unanimity of approach toward rural urbanization, the difference being in the interpretation of urbanization, which led to a divergence of appraisal of the road to rural urbanization. In China, urbanization concepts have been strongly colored by the views of geographers and demographers. Geographers emphasize the spatial structure and urban system of the urbanization in rural areas whereas economists emphasize changes in the economic structure in the transition from agricultural to nonagricultural economy. Demographers emphasize the extent of the rural population's concentration in the cities. An influential definition is this: Urbanization is the process of the growth of urban population, or, more specifically, the process whereby the agricultural population changes into nonagricultural population and congregates in the cities.[17] The influence of this definition is shown not only in the above discussions, but also in the following views. The author of the book *Unbalanced China* defines the concept thus: "Urbanization generally refers to the concentration of population in the cities or urban areas, that is, the gathering of agricultural population near nonagricultural population and that of rural population near urban population. Such a process of concentration is reflected in both the increase of urban numbers and the ceaseless expansion of urban population. The mark of urbanization is the proportion of urban population in the total national population" (see note 15).

Guided by this concept, discussions on the road of rural urbanization revolve around the concentration of population. Differences lie in that some advocate development of small towns and concentrating population therein, some advocate development of county towns into cities, and some advocate development of large cities. In short, most consider the concentration of rural population in cities or towns indispensable. The dispute is on the evaluation of "rural industry" and "small towns" and can roughly be divided into the following three schools:

One school is represented by Mr. Fei Xiaotong, whose slogan is "town-country integration and coordinated development," or "town-country unification." The major ideas are the following:

1. Vigorous development of rural industry, including township enterprises at every level, thus increasing peasant incomes while allowing agricultural population to turn into nonagricultural population.

2. Development of small towns, including small towns at different levels. This is the only way for rural urbanization. Small towns can link up cities and villages and produce results corresponding to scale while avoiding the evils of the big city.

3. Enhancement of mutual infiltration between town and country. Guided by the above theory, this school has designed a system whereby cities administer counties and townships administer villages.

A second school is the reverse of the above. It considers town-country integration "empty utopianism." It opposes development of small towns, the main arguments being the following:

1. Development of small towns is consistent with the old dualistic structure theory of "shifting rural population locally" which separates town and country.

2. Small towns generally lack public facilities and utilities such as water, power, ventilation, gas, recreation, and drainage.

3. Economic results are poor in small towns. Economic results are significantly better in large, mid-sized, and small cities, especially large and mid-sized ones.

4. Small towns lack construction funds.

Its road to Chinese rural urbanization is to develop county towns and gradually turn them into cities. Members of this school also object to development of rural industry, pointing out its defects as follows:

1. Serious wastage of land. Rural industrial enterprises, sprawling across the land, take up a lot more space than normal standards for industrial-use land.

2. Inefficiency in use of resources. More than 10 million rural enterprises are dispersed in tens of thousands of small towns. This makes it hard to obtain results corresponding to size. Uneconomical size makes waste of valuable resources unavoidable.

3. Environmental pollution is hard to eliminate due to dispersion of the small factories, making costs to control pollution beyond each's means.

4. Investment environment is poor.

5. Industrial and commercial civilization is hard to cultivate. The majority of rural enterprises are particularly lacking in the aspect of industrial civilization pertaining to product quality and in developing the beliefs attendant to commercial civilization.

6. Production factor markets are hard to establish. Industrialization needs swift and effective concentration of funds, but investment for rural enterprises comes from small communities and labor power can only be provided locally.

Their solution is this: Rural China needs to go through an industrial revolution with the emphasis on large industry. The present configuration of rural industry must be fundamentally changed. It must be adapted into the national industrialization process, that is, become urban industry. They fail to explain how the industrial revolution should come about or what type of a revolution it would be.

The third school advocates development of large, mid-sized, and small cities including both existing cities and development of new cities in the rural areas.[18] They criticize the road of developing township enterprises and small towns, claiming that "with the development of township enterprises and small towns, a 'rural disease' more dangerous than 'city disease' is quietly spreading." They sum up the symptoms of this "disease" as follows:

1. Rural industry becoming "localized," causing it to be overly dispersed.

2. Farming being superseded by sidelines, because the nonagricultural population would not give up their right to contract the land. In developed areas, farming itself would become a sideline. This is unfavorable to the modernization of agriculture.

3. Rural ecological environment worsens. Because of dispersion, rural industry leads to pollution over wide areas, causing far greater harm than urban industrial pollution.

4. Small towns develop in a disorderly fashion.

5. Rural population which have left their homes become "amphibianized." Peasants who are now working in industry or business are unable to get urban resident status. They are neither peasants nor city residents and have hence become "amphibians."[19]

Because of these factors, this school maintains, urbanization in China cannot rely on development of small towns and rural industry, but must go the way of developing urban industry, especially big city industry. The major reasons cited are as follows:

1. In developed countries, modernization all took the road of the establishment of large cities with concentrated populations, such as New York, Tokyo, Paris, and Los Angeles.

2. Economic results are far better in big cities than in small ones.

3. Large cities have greater radiation and role model effects. That is why areas with relatively developed township enterprises are all backed up and supported by big cities. Jiangsu, for instance, developed because of the support and radiation effect of modern industry in Shanghai.[20]

If forced to select among these three roads, this author would choose the first theory of development of rural industry (including tertiary sector) and small towns. Actually, nobody is saying that existing cities should stop development or that existing small towns are the final urbanized product.

This author also feels some of the basic characteristics of rural China need emphasizing. First, the population is dense and land scarce, and total dependence on agriculture would never extricate it from poverty. In the past, people often talked about China's "scissor's gap" policy, artificially keeping down purchasing prices for farm products to develop cities and industry. Actually, no matter how farm prices are raised, products will be limited because of limited land. In the coastal regions, rural per-capita land is less than 1 *mu*. Such paucity of land will never feed the huge rural population. The reason that rural commune or brigade enterprises in coastal areas had been able to survive was because of this "unprecedented" high-pressure policy. The rural areas contain a large potential army of the unemployed. There are only two ways out for them: Either they are absorbed by local nonfarming industries, or they move to the cities.

The second basic characteristic is that Chinese peasants must emancipate themselves and improve their livelihood through their own efforts. They must not depend on the cities, because the latter are now so overburdened they have a tough time taking care of themselves. Even during the most difficult times in the past, the state had stressed that "peasants should stay in situ and help themselves through developing production" and not "blindly" flow into the cities. The output contracting system started in 1979 is more the beginning of the peasants' self-emancipation than the result of policy. The many different types of nonfarming production now going on in the rural areas are all the result of spontaneous peasant action.

Rural industry does have many problems, just as has been pointed out above. However, in China's rural areas with their large population and little land, especially on the southeastern coast, rural industry is the only way to go. In the final analysis, without rural industry, unemployment cannot be resolved and rural livelihood cannot improve. Agriculture and the tertiary industry cannot develop and rural modernization and urbanization would be impossible. As they develop, township enterprises will continue to improve and become stronger in order to survive. Actually, on the southeastern coast, many township enterprises have already reached international standards in size, equipment, and product quality. The situation is now entirely changed. In the country as a whole, the gross industrial production value of township enterprises in 1990 was 950 billion *yuan* RMB, making up 25 percent of the total output of society and 60 percent of the total rural social output. Township enterprises handed in 41 billion *yuan* of taxes to the state, making up 12.63 percent of total national revenue. Half of the net income of all peasants in the country come from township enterprises.[21] Township enterprises really took off after 1990; they are already a mainstay of the Chinese economy. In Jiangsu Province, the gross production value of developed township enterprises has already exceeded the urban industrial gross production value. This can chiefly be attributed to a market economy and rural industry, and the fact that small towns have become a competing ground for the development of the tertiary industry.

Development of small towns and rural industry is synchronous. If rural industry promotes reform of urban industry, small towns promote expansion of existing cities. Table 2.1 shows the chronological process of urbanization.

From Table 2.1, we can see that in the first period, 1952–57, there was a slight increase in the number of cities and an increase in urban population. The number of designated townships (*jianzhi zhen*), however, decreased drastically. [*Jianzhi zhen* constitute the lowest rung in the official urban administration hierarchy, which excludes *un*designated towns such as county and *xiang* towns.—Ed.] In the second period, 1957–65, cities as well as incorporated townships decreased. The third period, 1965–78, was the time of the Cultural Revolution. Designated townships continued to decrease but a few cities were added. According to some estimates, the number of designated townships in the nation was down to 2,000. The fourth period was 1978–90. The number of cities rose from 192 to 467. Metropolitan cities increased especially fast. Many small cities expanded into mid-sized cities and counties turned into cities. This last made census-taking difficult, because the areas of entire counties' territories were included. The number of small towns grew rapidly; designated townships increased five times. This was also the period when rural industry started and developed. As described above, the speeding up of urbanization in China can be attributed to the success of rural reform and develop-

Table 2.1

Urban Development in China (1952–1990)

	1952	1957	1965	1978	1990
Metropolitan cities (over 1 million people)	9	10	13	13	31
Large cities (0.5 to 1 million)	10	18	18	27	28
Mid-sized cities (200,000 to 500,000)	23	36	43	60	119
Small cities (under 200,000)	115	114	97	92	289
Designated townships (*Jianzhi zhen*)	5,400[a]	3,621[b]	@3,000	@2,600	12,000
Total population (million)	574.82	646.53	725.38	962.59	[c]
Total urban pop. (million)	71.63	99.49	130.45	172.45	[c]

Source: This table is based on figures in the *Chinese Statistical Almanac.*
[a]1954 data.
[b]1956 data.
[c]Because of changing census formats, it was not possible to obtain comparable figures from the census (household registration statistics could not be used).

ment of township enterprises. That is why we say that in China, rural development promoted urban development, and not vice versa. Rural urbanization also promoted urbanization of the entire society.

Some Comparative Case Studies

We surveyed four provinces (including one autonomous region), namely, Guangdong and Fujian on the southeastern coast and Yunnan and Tibet in the southwest. The former are Han districts, whereas the latter are nationality areas. ["Nationality areas," or *Minzu qu,* refer to areas populated by the non-Han minority nationalities.—Ed.] As China has extremely complex geographical and social conditions, the pathways rural urbanization treads are necessarily divergent. The comparative study of the above four areas will help us get an in-depth understanding of the issue.

First, let us consider Fujian and Guangdong. We selected three locations for study in southern Fujian: Caitang village on the outskirts of Xiamen city, Anhai township under Jinjiang city, and Shancheng village in Nanjing County. Caitang can roughly be compared to Guangdong's Nanji village; Professor Shi Yilong's chapter and the chapter I have co-authored with Zhang Yiqiang will discuss both villages exhaustively. I will therefore not repeat their analysis. Limited by space, I will only compare Anhai and Humen.

Selection of Anhai and Humen for comparative study was purely coincidental. It was I who chose Humen and colleagues from Xiamen University who chose Anhai. After researching the two locations, I found them appropriate for a comparative study because of similarities in size of population, chief economic goals, cultural background, and geographic environment.

1. Anhai township

The township belongs to Jinjiang County under Quanzhou municipality and covers 67.66 sq km of land. It administers 36 villagers' committees (83 natural hamlets), 4 residents' committees, and 115 enterprises and undertakings. In 1990, its population was 107,904 (of which 25,219 were nonagricultural) from 21,285 families (of which 5,152 were nonagricultural) and total cultivated land was 39,543 *mu,* making per-capita acreage for the agricultural population 0.48 *mu.* The people are mostly Han, but the township also has people from 16 nationalities (*minzu*) including Hui and Miao. From the township, 12,064 people have settled in different Southeast Asian countries and 3,397 in Taiwan, Hong Kong, or Macao. Many of those places have established Anhai townspeople associations (*tongxianghui*).

In ancient times, the area was called Wanhai—so named for its uneven shorelines. In the sixth year of the Kaiyuan reign in the Tang dynasty (A.D. 718), Jinjiang established the designated county system (*xianjianzhi*), and Wanhai came under Jinjiang County. During the Kaibao reign under the Song dynasty, An Lianji a descendant of the famous Tang mandarin An Jinzang moved to Wanhai and changed its name to Anhai. In Song times, in the local organizational system whereby *xiang* (district) administered *li* (neighborhood), Anhai came under Jinjiang County Kaijian *xiang*'s Xiuren *li* and was called Anhai city. At its peak, overseas trade was so developed that "merchant ships in Anhai port flew the colors of the world and foreign traders rubbed shoulders with residents." In the second year of Yuanyou's reign in the Song (A.D. 1087), Quanzhou set up the Sibo subdistrict and "Shijing Crossing" to collect customs duties. In the fourth year of the Jianyan reign under the Southern Song (A.D. 1130), "Shijing township" was established with Zhu Song, father of Zhu Xizhi, appointed the first township head. This was the earliest time Anhai township was adapted into the organizational system. In the Yuan dynasty, *xiang* and *li* were changed into *du* (subdivision of the county), and Jinjiang was divided into seventeen *du*. Anhai belonged to *du* No. 8 and continued to be called Shijing township. Under the Zhizheng reign, the township system was abolished and the Xunjian subdistrict established. Subsequently, the Ming dynasty carried on the Yuan system and Anhai continued to belong to the No. 8 *du* of Jinjiang County under Quanzhou, its name now changed to Anping township. In the Qing dynasty, the old name, Anhai township, was restored. Later on, Anhai became a subcounty. At the end of the Qing, it had a customs *lijin* (tariff) agency. After the Revolution of 1911, Anhai was still a subcounty, but later changed into an auxiliary county. In 1919, Anhai *xian* (county) was established, and this was changed into a district in 1933. In 1944, the district was abolished and a *xiangzhen* (rural township) established. Anhai and its surrounding villages merged to become Anhai township. After Liberation in 1949, Anhai was a district, and in 1955, was restored to a designated township. In 1958, a people's commune was set up there. In 1961, the Anhai People's Commune was divided into two communes, Anhai and Neidang. In 1965, reorganization divided the area into Anhai township and Anhai Commune, which merged again in 1970. In 1980, it again separated into Anhai township and Anhai Commune. In 1984, Anhai Commune became a *xiang* and Anhai township was changed into the Anhai Township People's Government. In 1985, Anhai township and Anhai *xiang* again merged into Anhai township and remain so until today.

Before 1978, Anhai's economic structure was chiefly characterized by county-run, state-owned industry and collectively-owned industry. Its concentration of technology and overall labor productivity ranked first in the county. Enterprises run by the township itself were weaker. Before 1978, there were only seventy-four township enterprises, most of them of small sizes and engaged in traditional handicrafts, with the total yearly output at only 15.47 million *yuan*. Eighty percent of the township population worked in agricultural production, of which 74.93 percent engaged in crop-planting,

24.12 percent livestock-breeding, 0.09 percent fishing, and 0.86 percent forestry. Total agricultural output was 11.02 million *yuan*. Per-capita income was only 74 *yuan*.

Starting in the 1980s, township enterprises developed swiftly and by 1990 the number had increased to 532 and the number of employees expanded from 4,200 to 25,000. Comparing 1990 to 1978, the number of township enterprises had increased 6.18 times, labor productivity 8 times, per-capita wages 2.3 times, and per-capita tax paid to the state 10 times. By 1992, the number of enterprises had grown further to 736. Besides absorbing over 50 percent of the local labor force, they also attracted large numbers of workers from outside, amounting to an estimated 10,000 to 30,000 people.

In 1990, the gross value of industrial and agricultural output (GVIAO) was 199.48 million *yuan*, of which that from industrial enterprises was 182.60 million *yuan* (not including state-owned and collectively-owned enterprises) and that from agriculture, 16.88 million. Per-capita income was 900 *yuan*.

In 1992, GVIAO tripled to 609.14 million *yuan* and total social output value was 1,113.46 billion *yuan*, ranking first in the province. Industrial output was 560.12 million, an increase of 118.32 percent over the year before, ranking third in the province. Tax paid to the state amounted to 30.32 million *yuan*, of which the township received 8.04 million. Urban and rural per capita income averaged 1,885 *yuan*, also ranking third in the province. In 1992, 35 joint, cooperative, or foreign-owned ventures with a total investment of 500 million *yuan* were established, with a median of 5.49 million *yuan* per project. Altogether 60 projects have gone into production with a total output of 280 million *yuan*. Total tax and profit created was 20.69 million *yuan* and foreign currency earned from exports equivalent to 880 million *yuan*, an increase of 102 percent and 220 percent, respectively, over the year before. The biggest contract signed was a steel works with 98 million *yuan* investment covering 500 *mu* of land. When the first and second phases go into production, 300,000 tons of steel products will be manufactured worth nearly 1 billion *yuan*. In 1993, agreements were signed for another 24 such enterprises. Among joint, cooperative or foreign ventures, 20 are entirely foreign-owned, 10 are cooperative, and the rest are joint ventures. Chinese capital input averages 15 percent. Foreign investors come from Singapore, the Philippines, Taiwan, Hong Kong, and Macao, with 60 percent from Hong Kong. (The chief reason for this is the large number of mainlanders who had moved to Hong Kong before and during the Cultural Revolution, and who have come back to invest.)

Anhai's tertiary sector is also growing fast. Businesses and services are already of some scale, especially restaurants, karaoke and dance halls, and communications and transport. In 1987, this sector provided only 20 percent of the total social output, but by 1992, it rose to 34.8 percent and was making 387 million *yuan*. Total agricultural output makes up only 8 percent of the total industrial-agricultural output, and occupies an even smaller percentage in total social output.

With economic development, the township's downtown area has expanded rapidly. Before 1980, the downtown area was six sq km. There was one main street of some ten meters in width and a few smaller streets. In 1990, it expanded to twelve sq km. Three thoroughfares were built, each twenty-six meters wide. In 1992, it had grown to eighteen sq km, with the main streets expanded to forty meters. The plan is to further expand it to twenty-five sq km by the year 2000, or the size of a small city. A business district has now formed on the major streets. Parks and cultural palaces have been built.

2. Anhai and Humen Compared [For details of the situation in Humen, please see pages 84–91, below.—Ed.]

Anhai and Humen have several similarities. First, both occupy important geographic positions and have well-developed transportation facilities. Anhai is located not far from Xiamen on the road to Quanzhou and Shishi. It has a port backed up by a wide hinterland. Anhai is the gateway to the Minnan and Minbei areas of Fujian. ["Minnan" and "Minbei" refer to the distinct cultural and geographical regions surrounding Xiamen in the southern and Fuzhou in the northern areas of Fujian, respectively.—Ed.] Humen is situated in the geographic center of Guangzhou, Hong Kong, and Macao. By land, it is the middle point between Guangzhou and Hong Kong. By water, its Taiping Harbor makes Pearl River access easy. Currently the Humen Bridge linking the eastern and western banks of the Pearl River Delta is under construction, and this will make Humen a key transportation node.

Second, both are well-known homes of Overseas Chinese. Many Hong Kong and Macao compatriots invest there. Beginning in the 1990s, development of joint, cooperative or foreign ventures has been rapid (mainly Hong Kong investment), and these have acted as a big impetus to local economic growth. Making a start with Hong Kong investment, Humen set up in 1979 its first company engaged in *sanlai yibu* (processing, assembling, and customized manufacture of goods from materials supplied by foreign customers, and compensation trade). By 1991, there were 435 such companies which paid the state HK$180 million in revenue. Such investments, besides the direct benefits they bring, also bring up-to-date technology, equipment, talent, and management skill to the locality.

Third, both have long histories and a wealth of tourist attractions. In

Anhai are such historical sights as the Anping stone bridge built in the Song, the Shijing Studio where Zhu Xi of the Song had lectured, the famous Longshan Temple, the Baoan Temple, the White Pagoda, and Mt. Loyuan. After the rebuilding of the Longshan Temple, crowds of followers have visited it from Fujian and abroad. In addition, Anhai residential dwellings possess a unique style and religious beliefs are varied, providing a fine site for observing Minnanese traditions. Humen was known to the world since Lin Zexu [known traditionally in the West as Commissioner Lin Tse-Hsu.—Ed.] burned opium there during the Opium War and major historic sites of that war have been preserved including the Shajiao Fort, the Weiyuan Fort, the "Golden Key" and the "Bronze Pass." Humen has made the most of its heritage to develop its tourist trade by restoring ancient sites and erecting a museum dedicated to the Opium War, the Lin Zexu Park, and the Lin Zexu monument. It receives a million visitors each year.

Fourth, both have been exposed to outside cultural influences relatively early, have well-established trading traditions and are not afraid of taking risks in opening to the world. Both being port towns and the native places of overseas Chinese, town residents are experienced in trading and familiar with outside cultures. At present, residents learn about world events directly through television, Anhai mainly through Taiwan television and Humen through Hong Kong television.

Both Anhai and Humen have taken full advantage of their assets. Besides bringing in large amounts of outside investment, both have extremely well-developed tertiary sectors, a result of utilizing their advantages in transportation, tourist attractions, and commercial experience.

Because of different concrete conditions, however, their process of development and extent of urbanization do differ.

First, judging from pre-1978 foundations, Anhai was better off than Humen. Anhai was the industrial center of Jinjiang County and had a fairly large number of county-run state enterprises and collective enterprises. It thus possessed a certain technological capability and a body of technical workers. Anhai's urban area was already fairly large at six sq km; it had many nonagricultural residents and some foundation for doing business. Its cultural and education foundations were good and residents' cultural level was high. The surrounding areas had always been prosperous and occupied a paramount position in the Jinjiang region, even to the point of looking down on Qingyang (the Jinjiang county seat) and Quanzhou.

Compared to Anhai, Humen lagged far behind. It had no industrial foundations and a dearth of technical personnel—in 1980, it had only eight specialized technical workers with secondary or vocational education. Its urban area was 1.2 sq km. It was, in fact, a deserted little town. Then, even transportation was inconvenient. Before Shenzhen became a hub, Humen's land route to Guangzhou involved crossing several rivers (by ferry). The county to which Humen belonged, Dongguan, was considered a poor county in the Pearl River Delta and relatively backward economically and culturally.

Despite their different foundations, because of their differing paces of economic development, by 1990 Humen's overall economic capability was stronger than Anhai's. Anhai's economic takeoff took place only in the 1990s, with GVIAO doubling every year. Large amounts of foreign capital flowed in, and some large projects were started. Humen had its start with *sanlai yibu* enterprises, which were locally called "store in front and factory in the back" enterprises; that is, Hong Kong merchants invested funds, equipment, raw materials, and technology and took care of all sales. The local side only provided factory buildings and low-cost manpower, for which the Hong Kong side paid rent and wages. They were necessarily in the labor-intensive industries such as toys, garments, and electronics. Although the Hong Kong side earned the lion's share, they provided a way out for surplus rural manpower and helped Humen accumulate the necessary funds, equipment, and technology to make its own start (at the end of the agreed-upon term, the locality gets the equipment).

Second, as far as economic structure is concerned, industrial output is absolutely dominant in Anhai, making up 92 percent of the total, while agricultural output makes up only 8 percent. The tertiary sector in Anhai is extremely developed and may eventually overtake industry. In Humen, industrial output only makes up 70 percent of the total and agricultural output 30 percent. The proportion of the tertiary sector, especially real estate, is mounting. In 1991, agriculture still brought in 152.7 million *yuan* and created US$11.92 million's worth of foreign currency. The reason for this is that the population-density is higher in Anhai, where per-capita land now comes to only 0.43 *mu*. Humen has a smaller population and more land. It is closer to Hong Kong and Macao and can directly supply its farm produce to their markets. In addition, Humen transportation improved at a faster rate. Because its position became increasingly important, it was able to attract foreign capital in real estate development. Anhai has no such advantages.

Third, development of township enterprises has shown that they form the backbone of township development. The major characteristics of Anhai's township enterprises are the following:

a. Different economic sectors developing together. Anhai relies on different economic sectors to develop its enterprises. It encourages and supports self-financing by the residents to set up factories. In township industry, besides the state-owned and collective economic sectors and joint, cooperative, and foreign-owned ventures, there are also enterprises run by the township, villages, and neighborhoods, enterprises run jointly by a number of families or multihousehold enterprise collectives (*lianhe qiye*), and private enterprises. Of fixed assets, 50.5 percent are owned by the latter two.

b. Emergence of villages engaged in specialized lines. Because of historical and existing conditions, many such specialized villages have formed, including the Zhuangtou foodstuffs village, the Yangnan hardware village, the Qinbing plastics village, the Anqian and Sucuo construction materials villages, the Qiaotou and Xingta machine parts villages, the Kemu tanning village, the Shuitou, Xibian, and Houdi *mifen* (vermicelli) villages, and the Wushan and Xishe casting villages. There is no division of labor and coordination among these villages. Each village is a single large production unit.

c. Township enterprises are backed up by state enterprises. The machine parts and plastics industries of Xingta, Qiaotou, and Qinbing were started by technical workers from township factories. Some machinery and electrical machinery factories were manufacturing parts for the Xiamen Engineering Machinery Plant and the Eastern Fujian Electrical Machinery Company.

d. Development of multihousehold enterprises has been swiftest. Beginning in 1983, their output has climbed by 50 percent yearly, and this has become the fastest-growing economic sector. By 1987, their proportion in township industrial output had reached 60 percent, the net profit they made had reached 80.5 percent of total profit made by township enterprises, and they were paying 50 percent of the total taxes paid to the state.

In Humen, although many economic sectors are also represented in the township enterprises, township-run enterprises, and collective enterprises belonging to the management districts ["Management Districts" (*guanli qu*) are the new titles given for the previous *xiang* (subcounty) administrative units. Dongguan County has also become Dongguan City.—Ed.] have remained dominant. *Sanlai yibu* enterprises were put in the industrial district at the management district level while the township invests in high-grade, technology-intensive enterprises. Since 1990, it has successively invested and built such key, externally oriented factories as the Dongguan CDC Cable Plant, the Nanfang Glass Fiber Plant, and the Humen Canning and Cement plants in an effort to change into technology-intensive industries. It also encourages cooperation with other provinces and cities in setting up new enterprises.

Fourth, from the perspective of urbanization, Anhai took the road of concentrated development, that is, expansion on its former foundations. Anhai streets, like extending antennas, grew increasingly wider in chronological sequence. The problem it faces is that urbanization has been too rapid, leaving basic facilities and management behind. Water, power, and road shortages are getting serious. Such a manner of development may have something to do with Anhai people's concept of urbanization. They seem to think that, with continuous development of the downtown area, the township will naturally turn into a city. It plans even greater expansion by the year 2000.

Humen took the road of nonconcentrated development and divided its urban area into three districts. Roads and bridges will link up the three districts in the future. It has also built a satellite township each on its eastern, southern, and northern sides so that population would not be over-concentrated. Humen people take Hong Kong and Guangzhou as models for their urbanization: To their mind, a city should have skyscrapers, wide streets, and shopping malls. They have set high sights for urbanization. An eighteen-story commercial building is completed, and taller ones are under construction. Traffic lights have been set up at street corners and traffic cops are directing traffic. Environmental sanitation services are available.

The reason Humen was able to avoid Anhai's problems is chiefly because the township and management districts have economic capability. They are able to plan and build public facilities. Humen township's 1991 revenue exceeded 40 million *yuan*, while Anhai's 1992 revenue was just 8–plus million. Although 80 percent of Anhai's industrial output were made by multifamily enterprises, these enterprises only paid 50 percent of the taxes, with the difference pocketed by individuals. That is also why private dwellings in Anhai are tall and beautiful, but their neighborhoods are in such bad condition that pedestrians find it hard to pick their way through.

Fifth, from the perspective of changes in way of life, both Humen and Anhai are still designated by the state as rural market towns (*nongcun jizhen*), although production and life have changed drastically from the days when they were truly rural. The following changes are similar:

1. Agriculture. This is no longer dominant. Very few people do farming. The majority of the labor force are in industry and the tertiary sector.

2. Food. The greater part of the rural families now buy grain, nonstaple foods, vegetables, and fuel. Their eating habits are no different from city people.

3. Clothing. In both places, the habit of making one's own clothes is gone with the wind. Everybody buys clothes from the stores. The younger generation follow Hong Kong and Taiwan fashions.

4. Housing. Peasants care most about their dwellings and spend the greater part of their savings on housing. In both places, villagers have built two- or three-story houses. Anhai dwellings are especially well built with wide, spacious rooms. For residents of both, their houses are their pride and

joy and they feel they live better than city dwellers. Homes are well decorated and furnished with purchased furniture. Newer houses have bathrooms and bars.

5. Transportation. Since many are working in nonagricultural occupations, villagers go out to work or travel. People in commerce and transportation are frequent travelers. Major means of transportation are the bicycle and motorcycle. Motorcycles are often used to carry passengers. When asked "What is the major difference between city dwellers and you?" most answer that the difference is that they own some land and their own houses. That is another reason peasants here are unwilling to change their rural household registration into urban residence registration.

Anhai and Humen have each taken its own road of industrialization and urbanization based on its own conditions. Anhai started with individual and multihousehold economies where the scale of industry is small, investment low and risks minimal. Many enterprises began as "mom-and-pop stores" and developed into firms employing two dozen employees. The products of such enterprises are small parts or components, which are indispensable but ignored by larger enterprises. Family enterprises may be small, but when ten or even a hundred households join forces, they become much larger. The many specialized villages in Anhai were formed this way. They also absorb large numbers of labor from outside. Development of such enterprises increase individual and township incomes and stimulate local commerce. The large amounts of foreign investment brought in and the appearance of joint, cooperative and foreign enterprises beginning in the 1990s will give a powerful impetus to the local economy. Anhai had a lot of problems in its process of urbanization, such as inadequate urban facilities and a poor environment. But Anhai residents are aware of these problems and are trying to resolve them. The author feels that only Anhai residents themselves can improve their environment.

Humen got its start through *sanlai yibu* enterprises. Hong Kong investors were the first to set up factories there. Such enterprises pose no risk for Humen but can absorb a big part of its surplus rural labor power while giving it startup capital and free training. Because of its proximity to Hong Kong (90 km), its farm produce can be marketed there to earn foreign currency. This helped in commercializing and specializing Humen's agriculture. Because of rapid capital accumulation, Humen was able to develop its own industry and tertiary sector and plan urban development and improvement of investment environment at an early date.

The radical changes that have taken place in the way of life and economic structure of the two localities did not come about at the expense of agriculture. Agriculture developed in pace with the secondary

and tertiary sectors. The two areas' agriculture is characterized by the following features:

1. Diversity. High-quality, high-income produce is selected.
2. Commercialization. Farm produce is market-oriented.
3. Centralized management in a dispersed mode; that is, families engage
   in production while companies process and market their products.
4. Land management is steadily moving from dispersed to large-scale as
   more and more specialized households emerge.

The author considers the above to be changes in agriculture brought
about by rural urbanization.

3. Eshan County and Ruili City

Now let's consider Yunnan and Tibet. These are both minority areas far
from the political centers of China. Both are situated on high plateaus.
Yunnan Province averages 800 meters above sea level and Tibet even
higher, at 3,000 meters. Their economies are relatively backward and their
degree of urbanization is low.

In Yunnan, we chose the Eshan Autonomous County of the Yi Nationality and Ruili, a border trade city. Though a mountainous province, Yunnan
has surprisingly good transportation facilities. This is said to be the result of
the many airports and highways built during the Anti-Japanese War when
the province was built up as a rear base. These the province has rebuilt and
expanded in recent years. Kunming, the capital, now has direct flights to all
towns on the provincial borders. Several expressways are open to traffic.
One, the Kunming-Yuxi Expressway, makes it only a two-hour trip from
one city to the other. The free-flowing traffic allows speeds of up to 120 km
per hour. Yuxi city is known as Yunnan's "cash cow" because of the fine
tobacco it produces. The Yuxi Tobacco Plant is the biggest tobacco plant in
the country, providing half the total provincial revenues in taxes and profits.
The expressway is flanked by hundreds of kilometers of tobacco fields and
drying sheds. People say that local elevations of 500 to 800 m. are especially suitable for tobacco growing, in addition to long hours of sunshine
and absence of extreme cold. Yunnan tobacco is known for its high quality
and output and the industry is a mainstay in the province.

Eshan County is fifty kilometers south of Yuxi and has an elevation of
twelve hundred meters. From Yuxi to Eshan County town is a drive of
one-and-a-half hours. The county has a population of 100,000 and occupies
1,800 sq km of land. It is chiefly inhabited by the Yi nationality, but also
has inhabitants of the Jingpo, Han and Hui nationalities. As an autonomous
county, it is exempt from paying taxes and remitting profits and instead

receives annual state appropriations. The county has two townships, one the county seat Eshan, the other Xiaojie. Eshan town is neatly laid out and has many stores. It has a brisk night life with all the shops, video stores, and movie theaters open after dark. Karaoke has arrived in town but, being new, is watched by many but participated in by few. The food street is the busiest, open until the wee hours. Eshan town is on the road from Kunming to Xishuangbanna and other places, so many cars pass through, especially freight convoys. It has a number of hotels, restaurants, and a new market, as well as trading companies specializing in native and mountain produce. Local government agencies have also started to do business; each government bureau has at least one company. The town does not have too many enterprises but is chiefly the site of government agencies and schools and has some service facilities. It has a fairly large post office and bookstore. It is also the site of a nationalities middle school. In-town county government cadres have the habit of wearing suits and ties; some have also begun just wearing ties, without the jacket. Other residents dress fairly like Kunming residents. Male villagers who come to town like to wear army caps; women still wear their nationality costumes. Most people can speak the Han language (as spoken in Kunming), but more Yi is spoken. We were told by natives that the Han and Jingpo were the poorest while the Hui the richest and the Yi have the highest status. Yi head agencies at every level. Hui are good traders. Jingpo live in the remote mountains. As for the Han, historically, they were slaves of the Yi. Current national benefits policy favors national minorities, which do not include the Han. Eshan used to be extremely poor, but with the growth of commerce and trade in 1979, it began to grow rich.

The focus of our survey was Xiaojie township's Civilization Office (*wenming banshiqu*) and Gaoping *xiang*. Set up in 1991, the Civilization Office is in charge of two villages mainly inhabited by Hui. The total population is more than fourteen hundred. Two local mosques belong to different religious sects, one the Shiye sect to which 90 percent of the Hui belong. The mosque is big and there is also an Arabic-language school, remodeled in 1985. The other sect's mosque is newly built with contributions deriving from the twelve-odd village households in the sect. Though it does not occupy a lot of land, this mosque's buildings are only slightly smaller than those of the other one. All doors and windows are built of chromium, tinted glass, and concrete. People estimate the cost to have been at least half a million *yuan*. This alone shows the wealth of the villagers. Most of the dwellings here are of two stories, surrounded by walls. The architecture and decoration are Islamic. The Hui love cleanliness and all yards are tidily kept. Living spaces are wide and extended families live together. Women generally do not work out of the home while men spend most of their time doing business outside. The Civilization Office itself runs a transport business and other businesses. The Hui are traditional traders. Before 1949, the male villagers all worked in caravans transporting goods from Kunming to Burma and Thailand. Beginning in 1978, many returned to long-distance trade and transportation. They are a people who stick together and are not afraid of taking risks. They go in for all kinds of business and make a lot of money fast. With money they buy tractors and trucks and specialize in transportation. Seventy percent of the families now have automobiles, some two or three. A "civilization truck convoy" has been set up which has virtually monopolized long-distance transportation in the county. Some families also run mid-sized buses and vans. Cars parked in people's backyards are all privately owned. Each car can earn some 10,000 *yuan* a year. Before 1978, farming was the chief occupation, but now very few people farm. They let a neighboring Han village, or other villagers, use their farmland. In 1991, the area was designated as part of the township, and neighborhood offices were established. Television sets are common, although no other recreational facilities are available mainly because of Islamic customs. Religion is the center of life and all males at home spend time in the mosques (only males are allowed). Every family has the Koran and hang Islamic calendars. Every year, some villagers make the pilgrimage to Mecca at their own expense. Owing to a quota system, there is a long waiting list.

Entering a neighboring Han village, one feels as if one has entered a different world. Village homes are built of mud or mud bricks, the latter relatively new, showing that these homes were recently built. There are no concrete roads and the place is relatively untidy. On the north side of the village is a newly built area where two-story, mud-brick buildings stand. This village used to be a farming village, specializing in planting paddy rice. They have now started to plant tobacco, which has given them a new start. Seed and technology are provided by the Yuxi Tobacco Plant, which also undertakes to buy all its products. However, much experience and skill is needed in planting and drying tobacco, and the better the skill, the higher the price of their produce. We visited our driver's uncle's house. He is a successful tobacco farmer and his crops are growing better than those in neighboring fields. He could afford to build a new home. We found that he was a graduate of the agricultural technical school. Most other villagers are not as successful because they keep to the traditional ways of planting tobacco and are not receptive to new techniques. A catty of good quality tobacco leaves can sell for 8 *yuan*, while that of inferior quality has no buyer and has to be self-consumed. One *mu* of high-yielding land can produce 200 to 300 catties.

Gaoping *xiang* is about thirty kilometers southwest of the county town and was newly established in 1985 when two other *xiang* each gave it a few villages. In the words of the *xiang* party secretary, it was given what the others did not want. The *xiang* has the highest elevation in the county, some villages rising 1,800 to 2,000 meters above sea level. The total population is more than three thousand. It is divided into five villages. The *xiang*'s administrative building is not far from the highway and in the center of town is a central elementary school, a clinic, and a couple of snack shops and grocery stores. According to the party secretary, he plans to even out the road in front of the administrative building and turn it into a commercial district. Major industries are quarrying and mining. Farming in the past was mainly corn-growing, but has now diversified. The *xiang* runs a tea farm from land the party secretary organized residents to reclaim and plant with tea bushes. Tea crops can already be harvested on part of the farm. Because of the high elevation, tobacco growing was not feasible in the past, but they have now found a new strain that can be planted at elevations of 1,200 to 1,400 meters. All villages have therefore taken up tobacco growing, which has become their major source of income. In 1992, the money paid to the *xiang* by the tobacco growers alone amounted to over 200,000 *yuan*, which it used to buy a Santana sedan (220,000 *yuan*) made in Shanghai. This was the first passenger car in the *xiang* and is used only to drive to the county town and Yuxi city. The car is washed after every use and covered with tarpaulin. Jeeps are used to go to the villages because of the mountainous roads. It takes three hours to reach the farthest Jingpo village.

Shenguo village is in charge of three "natural villages" (*ziren cun*), two of them inhabited by Yi and one by Jingpo. The latter, with three hundred inhabitants, is the farthest from the *xiang* seat. Built against a hillside, all houses are made of mud and have flat roofs where grain can be spread out to sun. Inside the rooms are small and dark, but all have lofts where people sleep. This hamlet has no industry but cultivates around 100 *mu* of corn and rice. It also plants some corn on the slopes, where yields are very low. The hamlet has a lot of children, but most are dressed in rags. Pigs run freely in the streets. There is an elementary school on a flat piece of land with a basketball backboard. The hamlet has erected a satellite TV dish, no doubt for the one or two television sets the government had given it. In the mushroom-harvesting season, most villagers are in the mountains gathering mushrooms. A young fellow on a motorcycle comes from the county town to purchase their mushrooms. These and other mountain produce are packed into the trunk of a manual tractor. Some villagers do not like the low price the young fellow offers and would rather go to the county town themselves to sell their stuff. The walk, via mountain trails, is about three hours, quicker than by cars and tractors.

Zongguo village is in another direction from the Jingpo hamlet. It is a two-hour trip from the *xiang* seat. This Yi village is two thousand meters above sea level. Our ride there was not too rough, being much more comfortable than our trip to Shenguo. This is a larger village with a better appearance. It has a wide concrete road bisecting the village and in the center there is a solar energy-powered bathhouse as well as a satellite TV dish. Increasingly, more families have TV sets. Not a few of the villagers work in the county town. Another number of people have gone to work in Shenzhen's Nationality Customs and Cultures Village. [This tourist attraction is called "Splendid Village" in English.—Ed.] Although the houses are still in traditional Yi styles, construction materials have improved. Families install pipes to bring stream water right into their yards. Even in summer, because of the rain, fires are built in the homes to ward off the chill. Diets include sugar buns (*tang baozi*) (which is Han food). Breakfast is eaten at ten in the morning because people have the custom of eating only two meals a day. Our host explained to us that this was because fields were far, mostly under the foothills or on the slopes, so people went out early and returned late. Tobacco farming is the village's chief industry, with corn-growing running second. In slack seasons, everyone goes hunting. That is why every family owns hunting guns. People here dress much better than the Jingpo. On rainy days, villagers come out with colorful umbrellas alongside palm fiber rain capes. Most people can speak the Han language; the Han culture is fairly widespread.

Ruili city is chiefly inhabited by the Tai nationality. It has a population of more than 100,000. Besides Tai, there are also Jingpo and Han residents. All three languages are spoken, with Tai and Han being more common. Our driver belonged to the Tai nationality but spoke very good Han. The Han cadre who also accompanied us spoke Tai. With the development of border trade, the Han language is becoming more and more popular; of the villages we visited, most residents could speak Han (with a local accent). Ruili has an area of only 800 sq km, but its southern border faces Burma right across the river, for a distance of some three hundred *li*. In some mixed villages you have "one village, two countries," where people of the two countries live together. Every one has relatives across the borders, so there is a lot of traffic back and forth. In the past, when life was better in Burma, many residents sneaked across the border to Burma, this being especially frequent during the Cultural Revolution. Many educated youths settled across the borders. A lot of girls also married there. The situation has now reversed and many have returned. After reform and the open policy, religious worship has been restored. The Tai are Buddhists. In the past, all males had to become monks for a period of time. During the Cultural Revolution, many temples were destroyed and the career monks ran across the border. Now the villages are beginning to rebuild temples (called *zong fang* locally). Some villages have two or three temples. The temples are run by senior monks (*dafoye*) and have many lesser-ranking monks. Besides studying the sutras, they also work the fields and do other work. With living standards rising, the temples are getting more donations. New temples are bigger than before and are better furnished. All temples own TV sets, stereos, VCRs, and refrigerators. The senior monks seem to be living well.

Most of the Tai live on the plains, which stretch for a 100 sq km. The Jingpo live on the surrounding mountains, while the Han live in the city. Ruili's tropical foliage, religious edifices, colorfully dressed residents, and Tai dancing and singing provide the city's most important resource—tourism. After the borders were opened, domestic and foreign visitors have come in a steady stream. All hotels are booked during the Water Splashing Festival and in summertime. The Kunming-Ruili highway is being expanded because of too much traffic. Four flights leave Kunming daily to Yikou city (capital of the Dehong Tai and Jingpo Nationalities Autonomous Prefecture). Each Boeing 737 seats 180, but all seats are booked by the tourist agencies and individuals like us had a tough time getting tickets. From Yikou to Ruili is a matter of ninety kilometers, now taking three hours. Better highways are being constructed that will cut the driving time to one hour. Ruili is building an airport to link up with the Yikou air route. Many of the tourist groups we met spoke Cantonese. One group came from Foshan.

Two trade ports were built after the borders were opened. One port city had a street named "Sino-Burmese Street." Ruili's slogan is to become "The Second Shenzhen." The Burmese government cooperated by making its border city a special zone. The Sino-Burmese Street has one section built entirely in Burmese style where many stores are already open. A railway is being built to the Burmese border which would eventually link up with Rangoon. In the past, the Burmese border was full of soldiers in uniform, which made visitors apprehensive. Now the troops have retreated several dozen kilometers from the border and are rarely seen. [Local Chinese people from the border area need only arrange for a frontier defense pass and they can freely pass over to that Burmese border city.—Ed.] We did not get frontier passes but got across by paying 5 *yuan* at the checkpoint. 1.5 kilometers after the checkpoint, we hired a couple of pedicabs and rode to the border city. There happened to be a market fair that day, and the crowds, other than dressed differently, were no different from this side of the border. All goods were Chinese made and we found Chinese "Jianlibao" and "Qiangli" beer. The streets were full of garments and gold jewelry.

Most store owners could speak the Han language and Chinese currency could be used. One Chinese *yuan* exchanged for 8 to 10 Burmese *kyats* and store owners actually preferred Chinese currency. The city had some tourist spots, mostly large temples. Border trade has brought a lot of benefits to the Burmese on the borders. Many cars were parked in parking lots to be sold in China. Prices were written in Chinese currency units. One Toyota Crown was marked for 450,000 *yuan* RMB and a Nissan for 420,000 *yuan* RMB, both including license plates.

On the Chinese side of Sino-Burmese Street, a row of temporary buildings sell all kinds of tourist souvenirs. A street several times bigger than that in Burma is under construction. A bridge to Ruili has already been completed. Low land on the two sides of the wide road is being filled, and business buildings are rising. Currently, all visitors are from the Chinese side and there are no Burmese visitors. The Burmese government, however, is supportive and has made appropriations for construction. It has also made an exception in allowing Chinese construction units into Burmese territory to get soil for the landfill.

Ruili chiefly relies on beneficial policies to attract investors from other Chinese cities and provinces and from Hong Kong. The thrust of investment is the tertiary sector, including hotels, restaurants, transportation facilities, and energy. Guangdong is currently its largest investor, followed by Sichuan. The large numbers of investors, business people and tourists have turned Ruili into a very busy city. Construction is going on everywhere for commercial buildings, factories, and roads. The service trades have developed swiftly, especially hotels and restaurants. Crowds throng the 1–*li*-long business district day and night. All kinds of goods are sold, from gold and silver jewelry to daily necessities and electrical appliances. Many imports are sold, including liquors, perfumes, and cosmetics. Many types of transportation are available: pedicabs, taxis, mid-sized vans, and tourist buses.

Not only are there many workers from out of town, but also foreign people, roughly of the following two types. One are business people who sell gold, silver, and jade or are there to exchange foreign currency. Another type are workers, mainly in construction. The majority are from Burma and Pakistan (compared to the locals, they have darker skins and different facial features and are easy to distinguish). The latter earn 150 to 300 *yuan* monthly.

Living standards in Ruili have risen rapidly. The average wage is over 500 *yuan*. Girls like bright clothes. The consumer index is rising. Prices of hotels, restaurants, and other services are comparable with Guangzhou's (of comparable quality) and higher than Kunming's. Because of rising incomes, most families have TVs and many own cars and motorcycles. Hong Kong TV programs can be received.

Ruili's economy started to develop because of the opening of border trade and because of tourism. Farming consists chiefly of paddy rice planting plus tropical fruit such as lemons, bananas, and mangoes. The rice produced is of extra-fine quality and sells for a high price. Tai women are very capable and work in the fields, embroider, perform household chores, and conduct business.

The neighboring Mengmao township has two offices, each in charge of four villages. The eastern office has linked up with Ruili. They use their land to develop commercial and other urban buildings. Most people are in the service trades or transportation. Extra rooms can be rented out or turned into hotel rooms. They live a better life than in the cities. One-third of the population under the western office are still in farming while the remainder are in the city doing business or working in services or transportation. Vegetable-growing is the chief farm work along with paddy rice cultivation. Five years ago, farming was predominant in this township, but now it has become a sideline. Rural urbanization is rapid. New houses are built of bricks, although still Tai in style. There are windows on all four sides of the houses, with the living rooms and kitchens downstairs and the bedrooms upstairs. People take off their shoes when they go upstairs and sit on the floors. Every family has Buddhist altars, beside which are placed TV sets. Former bamboo buildings are now used to house cows, pigs, and poultry. The Tai are very neat and keep their houses extremely clean. New temples have risen in the villages; still others are under construction, demonstrating the important role religious life plays.

The Civilization Office of Xiaojie has taken another course. It started with business, mainly transportation, which has rapidly replaced farming. There, the process of rural urbanization has been completed. The reason for their success is the Hui's business traditions, which enabled the economy to take off early, develop fast, and bring them prosperity first.

Eshan's county town also developed on the strength of commerce and services. Their livelihood has improved a great deal. Market fairs are attended by people from several hundred *li* around. Many Kunming units and corporations also attend to buy mountain produce. That a mountain town receives thirty thousand to fifty thousand people on market days reflects its commercial prosperity.

4. Duilongdeqing County

The road to rural urbanization traversed by Tibet's Duilongdeqing (see Chapter 7) is a complex one. In the 1980s, the place set up village, township and county enterprises jointly with the interior [the interior, that is, of the People's Republic; i.e., more "central" or internal provinces—Ed.] under the policy of developing small towns and rural township industry. However, it lacks industrial raw materials and energy as well as management and skilled personnel. All enterprises eventually shut down without even paying back bank loans. Eventually, it decided on a course of development based on its own resources. One resource was farming. It replaced the former policy of grain-growing to the exclusion of everything else with a policy of diversification including vegetable-growing. Its second resource was its proximity to Lhasa, the capital of Tibet. Tourism and services developed very fast in Lhasa and large-scale capital construction needed a lot of manpower. Duilongdeqing exported its manpower to work in Lhasa's construction and service industries. Although most still farm in the busy farming seasons and only do other work in the off-seasons, labor export has already become an important source of revenue. Its third resource is its important geographic location. The Lhasa to Nepal defense highway passes through the county, and this stimulated its transportation industry including passenger and freight transport. Although its nonagricultural population is only 18 percent (not including people who both farm and do other work) and the urban population is not large, a commercial consciousness has taken root in Tibetan minds.

A similarity in the development of the two nationality districts cited above is the simultaneous spread of urbanization and of Han culture. In the past the government pushed the Han language usage without much success. With commercial development, people are learning to speak the Han language on their own to facilitate trading. Many people in Duilongdeqing are learning Han from TV programs. The popularization of the Han language is true of both Yunnan and Tibet. Ways of life, eating, and dressing habits are also changing. Apart from the Tai who have preserved their nationality costumes (chiefly among the women), the dress of the Yi and Tibetans are gradually becoming closer to the Han. In food habits, especially in restaurants, the Han influence is even more evident. Third, economic structures have also changed, whether in farming or services or the commercialization of farm produce. Increasingly closer ties have been formed between the nationality and Han areas. Ideologically, changes have also taken place. Ruili in Yunnan, however, has preserved strong ethnic flavor except in language. Architectural styles and food and beverage services are strongly Tai. This is because they feel their traditions and culture to be a major attraction to tourists.

Another common characteristic is the vigorous religious life both regions enjoy. The Hui under the Xiaojie Civilization Office are Muslims, the Yi have their folk beliefs, Ruili people believe in the Theravada form of Buddhism whereas the people in Duilongdeqing believe in the Mahayana form of Buddhism. Religion is an integral part of their daily lives and a major factor in preserving their nationality identity. With the commodity economy developing apace, religious holidays and edifices are also a major resource for tourism.

Different Roads

The road to rural urbanization differs between the nationality regions and coastal regions. On the coast, township industry leads the way and promotes commerce and development of small towns. There, rural industry plays a critical role. In the nationality regions, they have already learned that industry has failed.

In this author's view, the different roads reflect the different natural and human conditions of the regions. The coast lacks natural resources and are thickly populated, thus feeling the pressure of unemployment a lot more as compared to the nationality regions. At the same time, it has better commercial traditions and industrial foundations. Their choice of industrialization has proved to be correct. The nationality regions have sparse populations, vast land, and abundant resources, with the potential for natural resource and for tourism development. They have little problem with unemployment and lack industrial foundations. In fact, industrialization may undermine tourist resources. Their rural urbanization therefore does not necessarily have to be led by rural industrialization. The revenue created by commerce and tourism is no smaller than that from industry. Actually, in the coastal areas, because of one-sided emphasis on industrialization, some tourist resources may have been destroyed. It is therefore only right for the different regions to choose their own roads of urbanization based on their own conditions.

Notes

1. "Comparative Study of Urbanization in South China" was funded by the United Board for Christian Higher Education in Asia. Dr. Gregory Eliyu Guldin was in charge of the project overall and this author represented the Chinese side. Places surveyed included Guangdong, Fujian, Yunnan, and Tibet.

2. Rhodes Murphey, "The City as a Center of Change: West Europe and China," in P. C. Wagner and M. M. Midesell, eds., *Readings in Cultural Geography* (Chicago: University of Chicago Press, 1962), pp. 330–41.

3. Liu Chunbin, "On China's Dualistic Social Structure—Exploration of Impediments to the Progress of China's Rural Industrialization and Urbanization," *Shehui* (Society) 8 (1989): 20; "Positivistic Analysis of the Dualistic Social Structure," *Shehui* (Society) 9 (1989): 22; (1989) 10: 12.

4. Zhou Daming, "Study of the Outside Labor Force in the Pearl River Delta," *Shehuixue yanjiu* (Sociological Studies) 5 (1992).

5. Guo Zhenglin and Zhou Daming, "Study of Social Security in the Pearl River Delta's Rural Areas."

6. Zhou Daming, "On the Urbanization of Rural Communities on City Fringes," *Shehuixue yanjiu* (Sociological studies) 6 (1993).

7. Zhou Erliu and Zhang Yulin, *Study of Coordinated Urban-Rural Development*, (Jiangsu: Jiangsu People's Publishing House, 1991), pp. 9–19.

8. Research Group on the Movement and Transfer of China's Rural Labor Force, "Current Situation and Development of China's Rural Employment," *Nongye jingji wenti* (Agro-Economy) 7 (1989): 12–20.

9. Research Group on the Movement and Transfer of China's Rural Labor Force, "Some Relationships in the Transfer of China's Rural Labor Force," *Nongye jingji wenti* (Agro-Economy) 12 (1989): 40–42.

10. *Collected Works of Marx and Engels*, Vol. 3, pp. 24–25.

11. *Selected Works of Marx and Engels*, Vol. 1, p. 220.

12. In an article published in *Urban Problems*, no. 1 (1987), Chen Guangting stated that this passage has been mistranslated. The word *urbanization* first appeared in French in 1900. Marx and Engels had not used the term.

13. The postscript written by Fei Xiaotong to the book *Study of Coordinated Urban-Rural Development* (Jiangsu: Jiangsu People's Publishing House, 1991), p. 322.

14. Liu Fuyuan, "Some Questions of Understanding in Regard to Rural Urbanization," *Nongye jingji wenti* (Agro-Economy), no. 9 (1988).

15. "Jiangsu Province—Research Report on the Road to Rural Urbanization," *Shehengde Zhongguo* (Unbalanced China) (Hebei: Hebei People's Publishing House, 1990), pp. 214–15.

16. Gu Yikang, Huang Zhuhui, and Xu Jia, "Historical Critique of the Township Enterprise-Small Town Road," *Nongye jingji wenti* (Agro-Economy) 3 (1989): 11.

17. *Demographic Dictionary* with Liu Zheng as chief editor (People's Publishing House, 1986), p. 367.

18. Meng Lingwei, "The Dualistic Structure and Rural Urbanization," *Nongye jingji wenti* (Agro-Economy) 1 (1989): 46–47.

19. Gu Yikang, Huang Zhuhui, and Xu Jia, "Historical Critique of the Township Enterprise-Small Town Road," *Nongye jingji wenti* (Agro-Economy) 3 (1989): 11–14.

20. Wang Yiping, "The Road of Urbanization in China as Seen from Rural Industrial Development," *Shehui* (Society) 4 (1989): 2–5.

21. *Chinese Statistical Yearbook, 1991* (Chinese Statistical Publishing House, 1991).

3

Desakotas and Beyond

Urbanization in Southern China

Gregory Eliyu Guldin

China's fifteen-year economic boom has encouraged a rapid urban expansion as well as a significant transformation of its urbanization process. The number of urban places has increased, the number of people living in urban places has increased, and the number of people living urbanized lifestyles has increased. The dimensions of the rural transformation that have given rise to these shifts include a move out of agriculture into nonagriculture occupations (projected at 40 percent of the rural labor force by the year 2000), a demographic shift of villagers to towns, and the remaking of rurally oriented towns into more urban centers of production and communication (Lee 1992).

In some regions of the country, however, an even more significant change has begun: the age-old town and country chasm is disappearing as quickly as a gap between metropolis and small urban area appears to be taking its place. Such a process of change is facilitated by an urbanization process that can be conceptually divided into three distinct dimensions, all with awkward English labels inspired from Chinese-language discussions of these phenomena: deagriculturization, townization, and citization. The author apologizes for the infelicitous introduction of the neologisms and offers the rationale that "urbanization" as a conceptual frame is too broad to describe the urbanization process in China.

This chapter is reprinted with only minor modifications and with permission from *Ethnology* 35:4: 265–283 (Fall 1996). Grateful acknowledgement goes to the Wenner-Gren Foundation for Anthropological Research and the United Board for Christian Higher Education in Asia for research support. I also thank Lin Chusheng, Andrew Marton, and Wang Yaolin for their critique of an earlier version of this article.

To some analysts of Asian urbanization (Ginsburg, Koppel, and McGee 1991), such developments might reflect the emergence in China of a new pattern of Asian urbanization, the *desakota* process. Desakotas (the term is derived from the Bahasa Indonesian terms for "village" and "town") are transformed areas that are no longer clearly urban or rural areas but rather a blending of the two. Research throughout the continent, and particularly in Southeast Asia, has noted the spread of this phenomenon. If desakotas are becoming the dominant mode in China's late-twentieth-century urbanization transformation as well, then the world is witnessing a significant new path of human settlement and development.

Searching for the Essence of Urban

From the perspective of China, certainly, the dynamics of change unleashed in 1979 with new reform policies are historic and breathtaking, as the society with "the longest and largest continuous urban cultural tradition" in the world irrevocably industrializes and urbanizes (Southall 1993: 19). The rapidity of the above-mentioned social, demographic, and economic changes has certainly taken the Chinese by surprise and forms a crucial part of how Chinese view their society and its development. To the Chinese way of thinking (and indeed to the bulk of humanity as well) urbanization is defined at the folk level as many tall buildings, and folk comparisons of urbanization rates count tall buildings and the relative ubiquity of cemented-over areas. (One town official told me that city planning in the classic sense is absent when new buildings go up; people feel no need to leave green areas of trees and grass, considering them to be unnecessary rural elements intruding in an urban scene.) Urbanization is also viewed as improving sanitation, such as covering sanitation ditches and cutting down on dust ("like in Shenzhen, Hong Kong and in Tiananmen Square"), and as the spread of appliance and electronic goods ownership. As the images of rural poverty fade, one young woman in Guangdong put it: "Soon there will be no more villages, all will become industrialized districts. I hope it all gets industrialized: more people is good, there will be more jobs, and it'll be easier to make money!"

The folk view thus jumbles together conceptually distinct aspects of the changes swirling about: urbanization, prosperity, nonfarm work, and industrialization. This commingling of concepts is in fact quite understandable, as it represents the reality of the pre-1978, pre-reform era when rural household status did indicate the likelihood of a far lower income, an agricultural work assignment, and few opportunities to pursue an urban lifestyle. Rural/poor/farmer/agricultural were linked categories in contradistinction to urban/rich/worker/industrial (Beijing 1991: 2–3).[1] The emergence in the post-1978 period of amalgam categories—of rural urbanization, rural industrialization, the "million-*yuan* households" (and then "100 million-*yuan* households") of prosperous villagers—has yet to seriously affect popular thinking. If anything, another pair of opposites has been added, respectively, to the old lists—"traditional" and "modern." A calendar printed in Shanghai caught the mind-set well when it depicted the *modeng zhushi* (modern home style) for December's illustration: a woman covered in mink, in a European-style, ornately furnished room complete with piano, TV, stereos, and a kids' room with bunk beds and tennis racquets. And what are the comments of the cadre-turned-factory-owner and her son in whose room the calendar hangs? "That's modern because it's prosperous. Our home is not modern because our walls lack Italianate design, tiled floors, etc."

Bureaucrats and scholars are also likely to make the same facile and outmoded equations. One stressed that many people in Inner Mongolia and Qinghai who have urban *hukou* (urban household registration status) are not really urban since "their thinking is so feudal." Another explained his classification of one area as rural, even though he had discovered a profound urbanizing transformation in the local people's occupations and lifestyle, as owing to their preference for household items such as "traditional" carved furniture. By his and other people's reckoning, young people are more "modern" and thus more "urban" because of their perceived preference for nontraditional styles. Most of these urbanization specialists are economists and demographers,[2] and their urbanization studies and indices focus on easily observable and quantifiable items like occupation, population, and production statistics.

Official census and other standards make use of precisely these markers to define the urban hierarchy in China, with recognition conferred on four "city levels" (metropolises, large cities, medium-sized cities, and small cities [Ma 1992: 121]) and one "town level" (the "designated towns," the *jianzhi zhen* [Lee 1992: 13]). The latter may indeed represent the lowest level in the official urban hierarchy, but it does not accurately demarcate a sharp urban-rural divide in today's China. The urban sociologist Ma Rong advises us (1992) to distinguish among three categories of towns by separating out the *xian,* or county town, from other *jianzhi zhen* (the *xiang* or subcounty district towns) and recognizing the still smaller market town (*nongcun jizhen*) as also a discrete town form despite its odd official designation as an undesignated town (*feijianzhi zhen*).

Furthermore, if we view urbanization as an increasing flow of people, information, services, goods, capital, and property between rural and urban areas (Leeds 1980; see also Rondinelli 1983), then we are well advised to look toward the actual lifestyles of the inhabitants of the different levels of towns and compare them to those of villages and cities.

Ma (1992: 124) believes that from the perspective of the community study, the *xiang* towns are sufficiently similar to undesignated towns (the market towns) for both of them to form a category separate from that of the county towns that he, in turn, likens to small cities. In so separating the smaller *xiang* and market towns to form a "smaller township" category, Ma is inspired by his teacher Fei Xiaotong (1985: 10), who defined a small town as being different from rural communities in terms of size, area, economy, population, and environment but which nevertheless "keep[s] a close relationship with the surrounding rural community." Fei's definition is, in turn, merely the flip (town) side of earlier definitions of rural villages, such as Li's (1937), with its emphasis on lower population density, a common territory, agriculture as the main occupation, and a common lifestyle.

To a great degree, and like the folk definitions, Fei and Li's continuity in their sociological definitions of town and country reflects the pre-1978 realities of the People's Republic. Prior to reform, the rural-urban gap formed a social chasm wherein urban residents far outstripped their country cousins in terms of benefits such as the "iron-rice bowl," as well as income levels, prestige, and opportunities. During such times, the real differences between cadres and workers were dwarfed by far greater rural-urban differences (Beijing 1991: 5), and thus the difference between any village and even a small town marked the front line of the rural-urban contradiction as well.[3]

Basing his research on post-reform China, however, Ma (1992: 150) points out how small towns (the *xiang* and market towns) have evolved from being the weakest link in the PRC's urban system prior to 1978 to becoming a dynamic and growing segment of society. The differences between these small towns and villages are rapidly disappearing in the more prosperous areas of the country, such as in coastal Fujian and Guangdong, but the process has also begun in places like Hunan and Yunnan. Similarly, the increased flows of people, goods, information, and capital that reform has unleashed have also caused the differences between big towns (such as county towns) and cities to decrease.

Figure 3.1 charts these different village, town, and city levels as intervening points along an urbanization continuum and indicates the situation prior to 1978 in both administrative and lifestyle dimensions, while Figure 3.2 indicates conditions emerging in the early 1990s. The urbanization of China during the past fifteen years has caused the entire spectrum to become more citylike, but such generalization masks great diversity and complexity. Some areas, for example, remain with an urbanization continuum fairly sim-

Figure 3.1 **PRC Urbanization Continua: Pre-1978**

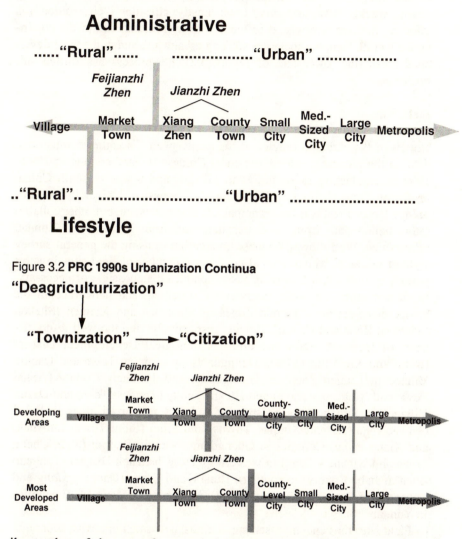

Figure 3.2 **PRC 1990s Urbanization Continua**

ilar to that of the pre-reform period (Figure 3.1), while others (perhaps most?) reflect the continuum indicated in the upper half of Figure 3.2.

Underpinning these processes of rural urbanization is the deagriculturization of the countryside whereby many people give up farming but stay on in the villages and the rural areas. (Others, of course, may continue farming or working in sideline agricultural pursuits, at least for a portion of the year). A second dimension is this rural population's engagement with town enterprises and activities, leading to a general townization of both them and their village and giving rise to the many reports of decreasing differences among village, market town, and *xiang* town. Lastly, citization ("city-ization") is affecting the county towns as influences flow from that end of the continuum. Overall, then, the society is shifting urbanward, and in the most developed areas (the lower half of Figure 3.2), the process has shifted still further.

Field Sites

Not all of the nation is moving at the same speed. To gather comparative data on the process, I joined a team of Chinese researchers during 1992–1993 in conducting field studies in villages and towns in south China. Professor Zhou Daming of Guangzhou's Zhongshan University Anthropology Department was my principal Chinese colleague, but other collaborators hailed both from his department and from Xiamen and Yunnan universities. We followed Chinese convention in using the general survey style of research, which aims at covering a number of field sites in short periods of time, with follow-up visits conducted as possible or necessary. In such manner, I visited, interviewed, observed, and networked in the prosperous Special Economic Zones of Shenzhen and Xiamen (Shekou Industrial Zone and Caitang Village, respectively) and the well-to-do districts of Huangpu Economic and Technological Development District (Nanji and Xiji Villages) and Dongguan City (Taiping Town and Daning Village in Humen Zhen) in Guangdong, and Jin Jiang County (Anhai Town and Xingchu Village) and Huian County (Zongwu Town and Dazuo Village) in Fujian. Less prosperous and less urbanized areas included Gaoyao (Nan An and Xinqiao Towns) and Sihui (Sihui Town, Luoyuan, and Xiabu *xiang*) Counties in Guangdong, Nanjing District (Shan Cheng Town and Xibian Village) in western Fujian, Chenzhou District (Tangcun Zhen in Jiahe County) in southern Hunan, and Eshan (Gaoping *xiang* and Shuangjiang Town) and Ruili (Deng Hang Nong and Mang Mau) counties in Yunnan.

Field sites thus encompassed small cities, new satellite towns, economic development zones, county towns, *jianzhi* towns, *xiang* towns, villages, and the metropolitan research bases of Guangzhou, Xiamen, and Kunming. Multiple visits were made to selected sites, and I chose Dongguan and particularly the Daning Village as my area of concentration. Research facility was eased by my fluency in Cantonese and Mandarin, while my colleagues ably helped me clear the many bureaucratic, financial, cultural, and political barriers to good fieldwork, and for these efforts I am most grateful.

Townizing Villages

Deagriculturization[4] is proceeding apace in the continuing wake of decollectivization and emphasis on developing town economies. One study of ten widely separated counties in the eastern two-thirds of China found about one-fourth of villagers (16 percent of females, 38 percent of males) currently engaged in non-farm occupations (Parish, Zhe, and Li 1994: 5), while predictions for the next century foresee hundreds of millions of peasants leaving the farm and agriculture within a decade or so. For 1991, the Chinese were officially reporting that 19.45 percent of their total population was nonagricultural in terms of household registration (Zhongguo 1992: 87), but fully 40 percent were nonagricultural as reckoned by occupational distribution among the workforce (Zhongguo 1992: 98). Clearly, many of those retaining rural official status are no longer farming, despite what their household records might indicate.

The developing districts show this evidence all around. In the Huangpu District, villagers declared, "There are no longer any farmers here, the [Guangzhou] Open Development District has taken all the land!"[5] Other districts are not equally "de-farmed"; moreover, one factory manager in a town in Gaoyao explained that whether one has an agricultural or nonagricultural household registration status is no longer important. What matters now is how important nonagricultural activities are to individual households, indicating that supposedly agricultural households have access to many nonagricultural employment opportunities, all without changing official status labels. In the relatively poor Eshan District of Yunnan, although the total nonagricultural population remains low, it is increasing rapidly (up 37.5 percent between 1991 and 1992). A complex mix of possibilities has thus arisen: some households have left agriculture entirely, some households have different members pursuing agricultural and nonagricultural pursuits, and others have the same individuals alternating between agricultural and nonagricultural activities.

Furthermore, not only is the population leaving the land but farmland is disappearing. Throughout the Pearl River Delta and much of coastal Fujian it is common to see bulldozers, trucks, or wheelbarrows filled with dirt (often obtained through leveling nearby hillocks), which are dumped into rice fields and onto other prime agricultural land. The land cleared and leveled is used for factories, housing, and commercial properties. Local villages and villagers are often paid substantial *anzhi fei* (resettlement fees) to compensate for their loss of land, and it is often the prospect of such disbursements that encourages many peasants to keep rural household status and thus their entitlement to these payments.

Despite this massive shift toward nonagricultural pursuits, agriculture has remained a significant industry and even a booming occupation in some regions of the country. Wang (1995) reports consistent farm production increases for the villages he studied in the Shenyang-Dalian corridor in Liaoning in the northeast, even as the area was rapidly urbanizing (undergoing townization, in our parlance). In the Pearl River Delta to the south, furthermore, Chinese researchers also report a new type of agricultural production that mimics the agribusiness management techniques of North America. Large-scale farming profitably supplies the large urban markets that surround the delta, and thus agriculture continues to co-exist with manufacturing and service occupations in creating part of that mixed rural-urban feel that permeates the area (Lin, pers. com.). The ever-increasing share of humanity living in such districts questions vigorously the conventional dichotomy of rural and urban settlement for an increasing section of the globe.

Much of this transformation occurs at roadside. In Fujian, for example, there are numerous examples of town-to-village roads (especially once paved) stimulating dual-banded real estate development. In some cases (such as Xibian Village near Nanjing and Xinchu Village near Anhai), the town has expanded along the roads and then absorbed the villages it encounters. In the Xiamen Special Economic Zone (the Caitang Village area) and elsewhere, local village industrial zones are merging to form industrialized bands of development. This tendency to physical and functional integration is abetted by reform-era moves toward the decentralization of administration and government control and a weakening of policies that supported clear countryside and urban boundaries (Beijing 1991: 3).

Not all villagers welcome the townization of their birthplaces. People in Xingchu Village (officially 1 km from Anhai Zhen) made it clear that there was a major social gap between them and the new people moving in and around their village. Of the 3,500 people in the village area, about 2,000 were village people (*nongmin weiyuanhui*), the rest belonging to Anhai Zhen's neighborhood organization (*zhumin weiyuanhui*). Some of the approximately 1,500 nonvillagers were originally villagers who changed their registration status to nonagricultural (*nong zhuan fei*) to gain some advantage (e.g., to get their children into town schools or to be able to work in town), but may have no connection whatever to the villagers.

Villagers living farther away often find that towns are coming to them in other ways, as, for example, when villages become more self-sufficient in the goods and services once only available in the towns. Villagers outside Taiping Zhen, for instance, report that they actually visit the town less frequently than before because their villages now stock most goods previously available only in town. A sole movie theater in Taiping served the entire district before 1978. Now, people in villages see films on screen or video, or they can travel to Guangzhou or elsewhere by long-distance buses or one of the ubiquitous motorbikes.

Mobility by bus, bicycle, motorbike, and automobile allows villagers to spend more time in town working, purchasing, and playing, and such village commuters are a key conduit for the townization of the countryside. As a cadre in Sihui County said of them, "They build houses in the city, work in the city, but they are still called peasants! It's easy for them to become citified."

People in these areas are conscious of these changes. One village factory worker in the Daning Village area observed that, "Administratively we're still considered a village but actually we're a small city. The countryside still exists because we still have farmers." This folk view equating farming with rural status was mirrored in the analysis of one of our team researchers, Shi Yilong, who felt that Xiamen's Caitang Village was more accurately described as a suburb. Why a suburb and not an urban area? "You can see it from its still-extant green areas. People also are doing a complex mix of economic and occupational activities, not just farming. In 1984, this area was one-third nonagricultural, but by 1991 it was two-thirds nonagricultural. Factories are replacing fields and roads are connecting the urbanized areas, but you can see from its streets that it's still not a city." *Suburb*, here, is used to denote a rural-urban mix—that is, townized villages. Thus Professor Shi's comments help us refine the picture of such areas as locales with the physical structure of villages but having an urban lifestyle.

The old contrasts and determinants of preferable living areas are thus breaking down. By all accounts (Zhu and Selden 1993: 5; Beijing 1991: 5), urban living conditions were universally better than those of the countryside prior to the reform era, but now the balance sheet is being readjusted in every Chinese county and district. In some, no doubt, the old verities of urban opportunity versus rural boundedness (if not stagnation) endure. But this is no longer true nationwide. There is a growing recognition that in some areas the countryside offers benefits over urban living. Housing and land availability, as well as the opportunity to raise two children, were the key rural advantages mentioned repeatedly in our interviews. By contrast, urban areas are valued as places where one can select from a wider array of goods and where children can obtain a superior school education. Urban dwellers, however, have to put up with more regulations (Beijing 1991: 6).

The less well-off areas have changed the least, and there one still finds major lifestyle differences among villages, towns, and cities. In such places the farmer-worker gap still obtains, with the fixed work and eating sched-

ules of town residents contrasting sharply in peoples' minds with the un-
clocked timing of people on the land. What impresses farmers in Gaoping
Xiang in Yunnan about town life is the ability of the people to eat three
times rather than twice per day. This difference in schedule and the fact that
people in the *xiang* only take in about 70 percent of the income of Shuang
Jiang residents are measures of the relative lack of urbanization and development. The last five years, however, have seen the beginnings of an upturn
in economic activity even in poor areas, such as in Eshan County in Yunnan
and Jiahe County in Hunan, and for these areas townization is not far
behind.

In moderately prosperous areas, where the process is much further advanced, there is a more mixed folk assessment of town and country differences. People say that farmers would still go to live in the urban areas if
they could, where one can earn far more, and that urban life is more sophisticated; for example, outside Anhai Zhen, villagers said that town people
used a lot more *la jiao* (chili sauce), had more telephones, and perhaps had
better sanitation. Yet there are also indications that the greater attractiveness
of towns is diminishing. If workers earn more, they also live in dormitories,
while farmers build their own houses. People in towns and villages have
similar tastes in consumer goods and young people in both places dress the
same. In Xingchu Village, people point to the end of foodstuff supplements
for many town dwellers and the provision of tap water to the village in the
mid-1980s as items that narrowed the gap greatly in local eyes.

Significantly, villagers no longer covet urban registration permits as
much as they once did. In Gaoyao's Xinqiao Zhen area, many villagers
continue to want to move to town, but others, particularly those without
special skills, no longer do. The people who most want a town *hukou*
(household registration) are usually those who feel they have the wherewithal to make money and who feel town life will free them from village
entanglements.

Contrasting sharply with this ambiguity are the perspectives of those
living in the most prosperous areas. To them, living in the countryside is no
longer the punishment it was in the past, but is an often highly desirable
situation. Villages like Caitang have greater freedom from outside regulations on making money. Furthermore, the increase in rural incomes (household and collective) has led to rising living standards and an improvement
in the physical conditions of villages. In prosperous Humen Zhen of
Dongguan City, the local *guanli qu* (management districts—that is, the old
xiang) are being redesigned for new roads and schools; one district's new
primary school was clearly superior to its town counterparts.

One Daning Village worker said,

The countryside is much better because you can receive the *fenpei* [commu-nal payments distributed to those with official village residence], get free schooling, medical *butie* [subsidies], and old age pensions. We also now have all our roads paved with concrete and have good television to watch. . . . We have everything they have. In the past, peasants envied city dwellers because peasants could only earn work points; now villagers, like city dwellers, have salaries. Fifteen years ago there was a big difference in cultural level, but now we have good schooling in the *guanli qu*. Nowadays, some people say "*noong chuen ho gwoh seeng see*" [villages are better than cities].

Citization

Despite the improvement in village living in some areas, for many villagers, and especially those in less well-off districts, towns still have the edge—for example, more cultural activities, better sanitation, and perhaps something as elemental as tap water. The villagers moving to towns have caused a major expansion in China's town population, which increased 40 percent within eight years, rising from 6.1 percent of the national population total in 1982 to 7.6 percent in 1990 (Zhongguo 1991: 32; Zhongguo 1992: 80). The *xiang* towns we visited have been a part of this explosive growth. In Gaoyao's Xiqiao Town, 3,000 villagers moved to town in the 1987–1991 period, boosting Xiqiao's population to over 8,000, while Sihui's Luoyuan saw its population treble from 1978 to 1991. Even so, with under a thou-sand inhabitants Luoyuan is the smallest town in the county (which led the town mayor to joke that you could hit a gong at one end of the town and everyone in the town would come in response). But not for long—the county planning bureau estimates that Luoyuan will be host to a few thou-sand more people by the decade's end.

County towns like Sihui are also experiencing rapid growth. Already abutting yet another administratively separate town, Qing Tang Zhen, Sihui's actual town sprawl comprises an area and population far greater than the official 4.89 sq km and 75,000 people that it held in 1992. The planning bureau estimates that the town will encompass 9.3 sq km and 100,000 by 2005. (One town planner unofficially predicted that number would be surpassed by 1997.)

This county town is thus on its way to becoming a small city as light industry absorbs the population flowing in from the countryside and as the town core is rebuilt to the same seven- and eight-story standard common to county towns and small cities in the Pearl River Delta. County town Anhai Zhen in Fujian is likewise poised to become a small city within the decade, but Humen's Taiping Zhen will have a hard time making the official leap into city status. In Dongguan, with the former county itself counted as a city, the emergence of cities from among its over two dozen towns and *qu* will be difficult, local officials believe, because of their proximity to Dongguan City proper (in Humen's case only 20 km). City status would give local cadre greater autonomy and would decrease one level of bureaucracy above them, as cities report directly to the provincial government. Undaunted by this bureaucratic blockage, Humen city planners nevertheless are sketching out a future Taiping City-Town with "skyscrapers" over ten stories high so as to create a "middle-sized city" early in the twenty-first century.

Such expansion moves towns along the urbanization continuum, sometimes with significant changes in lifestyle, other times with less dramatic effect. Thus, in Guangdong's Gaoyao County, people report minimal differences between villages and *xiang* towns like Xinqiao, Dawan, and Nan An,[6] but a big gap separating them from a medium-sized city like Zhaoqing: "Between them there's an economic and cultural gap of fifteen years," said one cadre. "Similarly," he went on, "Zhaoqing is twenty to thirty years behind Guangzhou." People in Jin Jiang's Anhai Town also feel that the town has moved far from its rural roots (and thus part of the rural urbanization process), and that life there is substantially similar to that of Jin Jiang, the county capital. This lifestyle evaluation would confirm that the citization process of Anhai is well along. Townspeople in Zongwu Town up the coast in Huian County report a similar phenomenon.

Citization of towns means that the old equation of large cities with more opportunity and a more desirable standard of living is also being recalculated. Many Anhai people believe their fashions to be "more stylish than in Xiamen," while others maintain that even Anhai's standard of living is higher than that of a medium-sized city like Quan Zhou. One former Quan Zhou resident compared the two locales and declared that people in Anhai "eat breakfast out frequently and are more likely to drink tea rather than merely boiled water." Residents of Pearl River Delta towns do not necessarily covet a Guangzhou address, given that city's high prices and crowded living conditions.

Yet the gap remains between smaller and larger cities, as between Zhaoqing and Guangzhou. Metropolitan districts are universally recognized as being in a league of their own, with entertainment and life opportunities perceived as far richer. Thinking is said to be the "most open" there and they do things unencumbered by the obstacles encountered in lesser places. One worker asserted, "Here in Zhaoqing they're building a pedestrian bridge and it's taking months, whereas in Guangzhou it'd be done in two, three weeks!" This reverent view of the big city persists even when people feel that the actual standard of living (in terms of consumption and housing) is not superior in the metropolitan areas. Life in big cities is "prettier" because of all the things to see and do. In Yunnan, residents of Yuxi District averred that life was quite similar in Yuxi City (a small city) and Eshan County's Shuang Jiang (a county town), but there was no comparing the two to Kunming City, the great provincial metropolis. Ma Rong's advice to place small cities and county towns into a single category seems well founded. They are indeed a place apart, both from the townizing country-side and from the large cities.

Even such an urbanized place as the Shekou Industrial Zone in Shenzhen, by population considered in the county town category (Shenzhen 1991: 50),[7] displays this same respect for the large metropolitan locale. When people from Shekou go to Shenzhen City proper (with a population of nearly 750,000), they say they're going to *ru cheng* (enter the city) and they will mockingly call Shekou a *nong cun* (village) or a *nongcun chengshi* (rural city) or even a *Xianggang jiaochu* (Hong Kong suburb). Why the snide remarks? What indeed does Shekou lack? As a planned industrial adjunct to the Shenzhen Special Economic Zone, Shekou grew rapidly in the 1980s, but retail services and leisure activities were paid scant attention as the economic infrastructure commanded nearly all investment funds. By so creating what some call a "cultural desert," Shenzhen's planners helped starkly outline the gap that still remains between the small and large cities of China. In terms of amenities, as well as occupational and entertainment possibilities, large cities differ dramatically from county towns and smaller cities.

The primacy of Shenzhen and other large cities in a cognitive urban hierarchy would not be gainsaid by residents of the metropolitan districts themselves. Discussions with mini-van riders in Guangzhou and Kunming invariably revealed that permanent residents feel that these cities are good places in which to live: "Why else would all the *waishengren* [out-of-province people] and countryfolk want to move here? Why would a factory worker stay home to earn 150 *yuan* per month when he could come here to Guangzhou to make 300?"

Village Views of Urbanization

Discussion with villagers regarding the desirability of urban versus village living reveals a wide variety of attitudes. In richer areas, the pride of the villagers in the improvement in their living standards over the past decade or more is striking ("like city people, 80–90 percent of we Xiji Villagers now cook with gas"), leading some to exaggerate the similarity of their lifestyles with those living in cities and towns. Still others claim, as we have seen, that countryside life is now better than life even in the once-coveted metropolitan areas. One middle-aged woman declared that in Guangzhou, "They all close their doors in the city, unlike our open doors in the country-side. When I go to Guangzhou, I don't even want to spend one night there." A man in his mid-forties who has spent much time both in Guangzhou and in his natal village said, "Life in Guangzhou used to be twice as good as ours; now it's better in Xiji Cun [in Huangpu District] than in Guangzhou. The whole [Pearl River] Delta is like this." One Daning farmer explained that people no longer want to live in Guangzhou or Taiping Zhen because "you can become a worker while living right here in Daning. And if you moved there, you'd give up your local benefits [the *fenpei* and the other funds accruing from sale of village lands to industrial enterprises]." The classic push-pull of forces steering villagers to urban areas has thus slack-ened considerably in these more well-off areas.

Prospering villages in Fujian, such as Caitang in Xiamen's suburbs, also claim their lifestyles to be the same as those of Xiamen. In the past, they used to provide their urban cousins with farm produce when they visited; now few raise pigs or any other animals. Some consider Caitang to be "more urban than Xiamen because even the poorest own their own house. And our new houses are all in Western style, with three or four stories." Judging urbanization by standards of prosperity, these villagers estimate that they are only three years "behind" bustling Jin Jiang, the city (erstwhile county) district capital.

Visiting relatives and friends in the big city, these newly prosperous villagers compare their home life favorably with that of their urban hosts. The villagers emphasize that their living standards are getting closer to that of the big towns and cities, even while some might readily admit that their lifestyles are still different. Thus one village leader in Xiji Cun claimed that his friends in Guangzhou lived no better off than he ("We eat better than they do and our housing is superior, and prices are about the same"), but he acknowledged that night life in the village is hardly as lively as in town. Similarly, women in Daning claim villagers observe lunar holidays such as Qing Ming and the Mid-Autumn Festival far more regularly than city dwellers, while older villagers are much less likely to spend their *yuan* at the teahouses in the morning than the elderly in towns.

Yet even in these prosperous zones, not all agree that village life is always superior to or at least the equivalent of urban life. Residents of relatively poorer districts in these prosperous zones are far more likely to desire urban life, especially if some of the benefits of townization (im-proved sanitation, housing, education) have passed their village by. Resi-dents of the least-developed village in the Daning *guanli qu* preferred to live in Taiping Town even as they acknowledged that they could probably earn more money by working in Daning; in Daning, factory salaries were equal to those in town or higher, while expenses were lower. Still, people in the village preferred to go to Taiping if given the chance.

Young people in these rich districts also are attracted to town and city life, but their elders lack their enthusiasm for the greater variety of night attractions in town. Daning's middle-aged letter carrier pointed out, "There's no real difference between life here and there. In fact, in town they don't have as good welfare benefits like here in Daning. There you work hard and live for no purpose. The city looks pretty, but it's not better than the countryside; there's just more to buy. So now we say *noong chuen ho* [rural villages are good]." His sons nodded agreement, but privately said, "It's true that Taiping is not much different than Daning, but I'd live there if I had the chance."

Thus, for a good time, young villagers go to town, where they learn urban ways. Xibian Village young people go to Xiamen a few times a year "to play," while they make it to Zhangzhou even more often. "We just can't dance and sing karaoke as well as them." But this "karaoke gap" may not last for long. Although some of their elders believe young people want to try living in the big city so as to avoid hard work, most youth are simply fascinated by the fads and lifestyles of large towns and cities. One villager remarked, "Nowadays village youth are getting more and more like town youth. Step by step, as the old die, we have more and more one culture."

Less prosperous districts are less keen on the advantages of the countryside life and correspondingly more attracted to urban areas. In moderately developed districts such as Gaoyao County and Nanjing District, people are more likely to see urban folks as more refined and urban living in some ways preferable to village life. Yet even there, they will respond that nowadays village life is vastly improved over a decade ago.

The contrast with the poorer districts we visited in Hunan and Yunnan is striking. In Eshan County people were constantly decrying local conditions as lagging far behind other places (*"Zheli hen cha!"*), looking covetously on what they perceived were the more secure lives of city dwellers whose retirement pensions, educational opportunities, and environmental conditions seemed to place them in a world apart. This otherworldliness of the big city was vividly impressed on me during my stay in Yunnan. On our way back toward Kunming, two teenage girls from Shuang Jiang Town excitedly came along for the ride. Although they were just accompanying the driver for the round-trip of three or so hours each way, for them it was their first chance to catch sight of the provincial capital. Their faces were pressed to the windows as soon as we arrived in Kunming, no time more so than when we stopped for a light and they stared long and hard at the new Holiday Inn; *"nemme piaoliang!* [so pretty!]." When we asked them for their impressions of Kunming, they just repeated *"Kunming hao!* [Kunming is OK!]."

Chinese Desakotas?

The folk evaluations of desirable places to live closely follow both the reality and the perceptions of economic prosperity. As areas become richer, townization and citization proceed apace; villages become more like market and *xiang* towns, and county towns and small cities become more like large cities. This in turn dampens the ardor of people in villages and *xiang* towns to move to county towns, and so on up the line, even when people continue to recognize a higher "cultural level" in cities.[8]

The urbanization process unfolding is thus caused not only by a stream of rural-to-urban migrants but also by urbanization in place—that is, entire districts become more urbanized at all levels of the rural-urban continuum. At the lower, townization level, some Chinese have conceptualized this town-village blending as *chengxiang yitihua* (urban-rural integration [Zhang 1989]). Are these, in essence, Chinese desakota zones? As we have noted above, the desakota process posits that a new form of settlement—the desakota—has emerged in Asia generally, a form neither rural nor urban but a blending of the two wherein a dense web of transactions tie large urban cores to their surrounding regions. Does this describe the Chinese situation? To some degree it does, particularly at the village–*xiang*-town level, as a result of the townization process. Elsewhere in Asia, desakotas emerge without large-scale migration, but large-scale migration is certainly happening in China. Furthermore, with citization simultaneously transforming county towns and small cities in some areas of China, we see urbanization occurring along with desakota creation, creating truly dense urban zones. If desakotas are arising in China, then they are desakotas with Chinese characteristics.

Yet another dimension of these Chinese developments worth pondering is their rural grassroots dynamism. Whereas elsewhere in the world (Gottman 1961), in other parts of Asia (Ginsburg et al. 1991) and in India (Dandekar 1986), urbanization has been fueled by the vibrant expansion of large cities through suburbanization or the collapse of agriculture, in China rural vitality has jump-started this process. The decollectivization reforms of the early 1980s led to a countryside economic turnaround that powered major social transformations, including urbanization. Contrary to traditional theoretical constructs of urbanization which begin "with the assumption that processes of regional transformation extend *from* the city *into* the country-side," the Chinese experience provides good evidence that rural industrialization and rural urbanization have been at least as important as big cities in these processes (Marton 1995: 12, 28).

As noted, these transformations have proceeded more afield in some areas than others. Chinese desakotas have thus arisen in some areas, but not in others. Zhou's (1995) analysis of urbanization in the Pearl River Delta has pointed to four separate but interlocking processes:

1. Urbanization of rural-urban boundaries
2. Urbanization of small towns
3. Urbanization of villages
4. Establishment of economic and technological development districts

All of these involve townization. Thus in this Chinese region at least we can see townization working to create what could accurately be designated a desakota-like zone.

The emergence of this new type of settlement pattern has been recognized at the scholarly and folk levels, as, for instance, in popular discussion with reference to the Pearl River Delta. In the past, the delta meant the three counties of Nanhai, Xunde, and Panyu, plus immediately adjoining areas to the southeast like Dongguan. Now people refer to this as the Little Delta, with the Big Delta expanding to include all areas that have become prosperous (and urbanized) in the vicinity, including once-marginal Sihui County to the northwest.[9] Some also argue that Hong Kong, Macao, and the Special Economic Zones of Shenzhen (including Shekou) and Zhuhai should also be considered part of the delta.

This vibrant area is not only relatively prosperous but also relatively urbanized. Dongguan's Humen District is a case in point. Not only have its villages, such as those in the Daning *Guanli qu,* become townized but the once-rural district outside of Taiping Zhen has become urbanized as government and office buildings, residential quarters, and factories have been constructed on former cropland. Taiping Zhen and Humen District, once separate administratively, have been combined into one bureaucratic entity, and in the transforming countryside, Daning Qu now has an invisible townlike border with adjoining Longyan Qu, where once green fields marked their boundary. Commented one Daning cadre, "With this type of development, we're no longer countryside. In many of our districts there has been both a taste of urban and a taste of rural. Now many feel that the taste is mostly urban. And our twenty-year planning document looks toward a city and town administration in the near future."

If the "taste" is becoming mostly urban in the heart of the Delta, then perhaps the desakota pattern will only prove transitory, as citization replaces townization as the key aspect of urbanization. For much of the post-reform era, Chinese geographers and other urban analysts have argued over the relative merits of encouraging rural townships and small cities on the one hand, or large cities and metropolitan areas on the other, as the nodes of Chinese rural development.[10] Ironically, it appears that with townization and citization in full swing, both processes are proceeding apace.

Conclusions

The Fourth Population Census of 1990 had two standards of analysis for urbanization. The first version (*diyi koujing*) counted as urban all populations of administrative districts dubbed *shi* (city). Since Guangdong is now divided into nineteen *shi,* this standard sees Guangdong as totally urbanized! An alternative interpretation of the statistics (*dier koujing*) divides locales in a province into three levels: *chengshi* (*shi qu,* or city district), *zhen* (town), and *xian* (county).[11] This standard reveals a more modest figure of 36.8 percent urban, up from the 12 percent in 1953, 18.3 percent in 1964, and 19.3 percent in 1982 (Guangdong 1991: 105).[12] The quick rise in the 1980s, nearly doubling within eight years, is the fastest rate of urbanization in all of China (Banister 1991: 15), and has led some demographers in the province to cast doubt on the 36.8 percent 1990 estimate. However, our field experience has shown that if one looks at actual lifestyle and occupational structure instead of focusing on household registration status (that is, if one considers the townization process), then perhaps the official statistics, in their bureaucratic wisdom, are fairly good indicators of urbanization. Xu Xueqiang (pers. com.) estimates that perhaps 40 percent of the province is indeed urbanized, based on occupation, lifestyle, and "thinking." Similarly, the nonagricultural population is in the range of 40–45 percent. Perhaps those responsible for adjusting the definitions of urban places in China in the late 1980s either stumbled onto or consciously recognized the emergence of a new type of town and city pattern.

Banister (1991: 15) tells us that for China as a whole, the urban population increased from 21 percent in 1982 to 26 percent in 1990, and that these are conservative estimates. The figures include villages located within formal city administrative zones—villages likely to have undergone some degree at least of townization, as in Guangdong—while at the same time they exclude all *xiang* towns. The latter, certainly, is a major omission, causing a serious underestimation of China's urbanizing population. Furthermore, this quantitative approach to understanding China's urbanization may not be the most insightful. If what we are seeking to comprehend are processes of deagriculturization, townization, and citation (all aspects of Chinese urbanization), then how can these be reduced to a single figure? How much does it tell us to be told that Liaoning grew from 42 percent urban in 1982 to 51 percent in 1990, and Heilongjiang from 40 percent to 47 percent? What does this mean for the nature of changes in people's lives? It seems clear that the effort to produce a single urbanization-rate figure is a fool's errand. We could just as well, and more accurately, attempt to estimate percentages of the population undergoing deagriculturization, townization, and citation. Combining these figures skillfully with the number of people in officially recognized spaces in the formal urban hierarchy would yield a more valid urbanization rate (or rates).

Moreover, other problems arise with the same statistics. They tell us, for example, that some provinces have ostensibly "recorded no increase in urbanization" (Banister 1991: 15). Can it be true that Fujian, Jiangxi, Henan, and Guizhou underwent no expansion in city-influenced patterns during the 1980s? No, for other researchers working in Guizhou (Huang and Gong, pers. com.), as well as our own field observations in Fujian, reveal the ongoing townization of village life and the citation of county towns and small cities. Because these changes are occurring in those areas not officially recognized in the urban hierarchy does not mean they should be ignored in analyses. The urbanization rates given for the provinces of Guangdong (36.7 percent), Fujian (21.3 percent), Hunan (18.2 percent), and Yunnan (14.6 percent) would undoubtedly be higher if this broader definition were used (Zhongguo 1991: 32).

China's urbanization is thus proceeding along a continuum of townization and citation, where the rates of urbanization may differ between north and south, coast and interior, and prosperous and less developed areas. The changes of the post-1979 reform period with its rural urbanization and rural industrialization have already caused epochal change in China's rural-urban balance. Since the Han dynasty 2000 years ago, historians estimate that the urbanization rate for the country as a whole has never exceeded the 20 percent range, perhaps representing an agriculturally based societal urbanization ceiling (Guldin 1992: 229). By any reckoning, this urbanization ceiling has been shattered forever. The countryside's emerging desakotas may represent only the first step on the road to a fully urbanized China in the twenty-first century.

Notes

1. Prior to 1978, the richest quintile of the population was completely urban, while the poorest was all rural. By 1990, the poorest quintile had remained rural, but the richest was split between rural and urban residents (Beijing 1991: 3)

2. Professor Xu Xueqiang of Zhongshan University estimates that these two fields alone account for 70 percent of urbanization researchers in the country, with the rest in urban planning, geography, or sociology (pers. com.).

3. For excellent overviews of urbanization processes and policies in China since 1949, see Chan 1992 and 1994.

4. Villages on the outskirts or in the hinterland of cities and county towns also undergo urbanization. Initial data from our study in Yunnan indicates that cities may quicken the urbanization rate.

5. Of course, there is probably some hyperbole here and elsewhere when villagers claim that "no one farms anymore!" They might simply be trying to impress the outsider with how modern or prosperous their area has become.

6. Nan An and Gaoyao used to fall under the jurisdiction of adjacent Zhaoqing City. With the administrative independence of Gaoyao, Nan An, a *xiang* town, was elevated to county-town status as the center of Gaoyao's local government. Socially, however, Nan An remains *xiang* townlike.

7. The population of the zone was 43,437 in 1991 and the population of the adjoining Shekou Town area was 20,271. The combined total was still below the official city threshold of 100,000 (Shenzhen 1991: 50).

8. Prostitution increases further down the urbanization continuum the more prosperous an area becomes, and the density of sex workers can act as a barometer of development and urbanization: the more prosperous an area is, the more likely whores will find lucrative employment, first at the county-town and then at the *xiang*-town levels.

9. As an indication that Sihui is moving in the same direction as the delta as a whole, consider that demographers in Guangzhou estimated the nonagricultural population of the delta at 40–45 percent in 1991, while Sihui's nonagricultural population was given as 28.9 percent in 1991 and estimated to reach 40 percent by the year 2000.

10. See Marton (1995: 20–29) for a good overview of this debate.

11. *Chengshi* is in turn divided into three sublevels: *da chengshi* (or *zhi xia shi,* those cities directly under control of the provincial government), *di ji shi* (district-level cities), and *xian ji shi* (county-level cities).

12. The four *Renkou Pucha* (Population Censuses) of 1953, 1964, 1982, and 1990 are felt by many analysts to be the best vehicles for understanding urbanization and migration numbers. Using these censuses also avoids the anamolous 1984 redefinition of city and town, which the 1990 census corrected.

References

Banister, Judith. 1991. "One Billion and Counting." *China Business Review* (May-June): 14–18.

Beijing University "Social Differentiation" Research Group. 1991. "Cong chengxiang fenhuade xin geju kan zhongguo shehuide jiegouxing bianyi." *Shehuixue Yanjiu* (Sociological studies) 2: 2–14.

Chan Kam-wing. 1992. "Post-1949 Urbanization Trends and Policies: An Overview," in Gregory Eliyu Guldin (ed.), *Urbanizing China,* 41–64. Westport, CT: Greenwood Press.

———. 1994. *Cities with Invisible Walls: Reinterpreting Urbanization in Post-1949 China.* New York: Oxford University Press.

Dandekar, Hemalata C. 1986. *Men to Bombay, Women at Home: Urban Influence on Sugao Village, Deccan Maharashtra, India 1942–1982.* Ann Arbor: Center for South and Southeast Asian Studies, University of Michigan.

Fei Xiaotong. 1985. *Xiaochengzhen siji* (Four articles on small towns). Beijing: Xinhua Press.

Ginsburg, N., Koppel, B., and McGee, T.G. (eds.). 1991. *The Extended Metropolis: Settlement Transition in Asia.* Honolulu: University of Hawaii Press.

Gottman, J. 1961. *Megalopolis: The Urbanized Northeastern Seaboard of the United States.* Cambridge, MA: Harvard University Press.

Guangdong tongji nianjian 1991 (Statistical yearbook of Guangdong 1991). 1991. Guangdong Tongji Chubanshe: Guangzhou.

Guldin, Gregory Eliyu. 1992. "Urbanizing China: Some Startling Conclusions," in G.E. Guldin (ed.), *Urbanizing China,* pp. 157–184. Westport, CT: Greenwood Press.

Huang Shuping and Gong Peihua. 1993. Personal communication.

Lee, Yokshiu F. 1992. "Rural Transformation and Decentralized Urban Growth in China," in G.E. Guldin (ed.), *Urbanizing China,* pp. 89–118. Westport, CT: Greenwood Press.

Leeds, Anthony J. 1980. "Towns and Villages in Society: Hierarchies of Order and Cause," in *Cities in a Larger Context, Southern Anthropological Society Proceedings* 14: 6–33.

Li Jinghan. 1937. *Zhongguo nongcun wenti.* Shanghai: Commercial Press Limited.

Lin Chusheng. 1995. Personal communication, May 26.

Ma Rong. 1992. "The Development of Small Towns and Their Role in the Development of China," in G.E. Guldin (ed.), *Urbanizing China,* pp. 119–154. Westport, CT: Greenwood Press.

Marton, Andrew M. 1995. "Restless Landscapes: Spatial Economic Restructuring in China's Lower Yangzi Delta." Ph.D. dissertation, Chapter 2. University of British Columbia, Department of Geography.

Parish, William L., Zhe Xiaoye, and Li Fang. 1994. "New Work Opportunities in the Chinese Countryside." Paper presented at Association for Asian Studies annual meeting, Washington, DC, March.

Rondinelli, D.A. 1983. *Secondary Cities in Developing Countries: Policies for Diffusing Urbanization.* Beverly Hills: Sage.

Shenzhen City Fourth Population Census Office. 1991. *Shenzhen shi disici renkou pucha shougong huizong cailiao* (Shenzhen city fourth census manual of collected data). Shenzhen.

Sihui Urban Planning Bureau. 1992. Unpublished office materials.

Southhall, Aidan. 1993. "Urban Theory and the Chinese City," in Greg Guldin and Aidan Southall (eds.), *Urban Anthropology in China,* pp. 19–40. Leiden: E.J. Brill.

Wang Yaolin. 1995. "Invisible Urbanization in China: Case Study in the Shenyang-Dalian Region." Paper presented to Western Division, Canadian Association of Geographers, March.

Xu Xueqiang. 1993. Personal communication.

Zhang, L.J. 1989. *Chengxiang yitihua zhilu* (The path towards urban-rural integration). Beijing: Rural Reading Materials Press.

Zhongguo disici renkou puchade zhuyao shuju (Major figures of the fourth national population census of China). 1991. Beijing: Zhongguo Tongji Chubanshe.

Zhongguo tongji nianjian 1992 (China statistical yearbook 1992). 1992. Beijing: Zhongguo Tongji Chubanshe.

Zhou Daming. 1995. "On Rural Urbanization in China." *Chinese Sociology and Anthropology* 28 (2): 9–46. [Reprinted as chapter four, this volume.]

Zhu Ling and Selden, Mark. 1993. "Agricultural Cooperation and the Family Farm in China." *Bulletin of Concerned Asian Scholars* 25 (3): 3–12.

Part III

Regional Patterns

4

Rural Urbanization in Guangdong's Pearl River Delta

Zhou Daming and Zhang Yingqiang

Since 1978, urbanization has made rapid headway in China. The dualistic configuration in which cities and rural areas were separated has broken down and a new era of coordinated urban-rural development has arrived. China is a large agricultural country in which the farming population remains predominant even today. In discussing Chinese urbanization, rural urbanization is thus a necessary topic. As to the road of rural urbanization, it is still being *hotly* debated in the academic community. This article will explore the issue with rural urbanization in the Pearl River Delta as the case study.

The Pearl River Delta is situated in the south central part of Guangdong province and faces the South China Sea. It is an open economic zone encompassing twenty-eight municipalities and counties, one open city—Guangzhou; and two Special Economic Zones—Shenzhen and Zhuhai. The delta has caught much attention because it was one of the first areas to engage in reform and the open policy and is, today, an area with one of the highest degrees of urbanization. Twenty-six million people (including more than 5 million from elsewhere) live on this area of only 45,000 sq km. It contains a metropolis of more than 2 million people, a large city with 1 million people, and 13 mid-sized and small cities with 100,000 to 500,000 people. It also embraces 250 towns at various levels. (And Hong Kong and Macao are not even included in these numbers.) The delta also is one of China's most economically developed areas. In 1991, total social output was 268.4 billion *yuan* RMB, national revenue created was 89.8 billion *yuan*, gross value of agricultural and industrial output (GVAIO) was 205.1 billion *yuan*, and the GVAIO annual rate of increase is 20 percent (Table 4.1).

Table 4.1

Key Indicators of National Economic Development in the Pearl River Delta (1980–1991)

Item	Unit	1980	1985	1990	1991
Total population	1,000	17,593.9	18,973.9	20,745.8	21,184.0
Non-agricultural population	1,000	4813.5	6263.0	7635.1	7976.9
GVAIO	1 billion yuan	19.588	42.497	113.823	205.102
Gross agricultural output	1 billion yuan	4.160	5.770	8.074	23.733
Village level and below GVIO	1 billion yuan	1.243	4.075	13.344	21.318
Average yearly wages of all employees	yuan	858	1,575	3,394	3,925
Net per capita farmer (*nongmin*) income	yuan	238	676	1,288	1,491

Source: *Guangdong Provincial Statistical Yearbook (1992).*

The successes of this area have become a focus of study for many Chinese and international scholars. On the question of urbanization alone, discussions have included Xu Xueqiang,[1] R. Yin-Wang Kwok,[2] Guldin,[3] and Victor F. S. Sit.[4] Since 1986, the authors of this article have accompanied Guldin in investigating and studying the area, concentrating on the non-economic factors in the delta's development such as culture and education, population movement and the media.[5] These investigations form the basis for the following study.

Our group carried out its first round of investigation from September to

December, 1992. We went to six places in the eastern part of the delta: Shekou in Shenzhen, Humen in Dongguan, Nangang in Huangpu, Luoyuan and Qingtang in Sihui, and Xinqiao in Gaoyao, and visited the management districts and villages under these townships. The reasons for our selections were: (1) they were on the line between Hong Kong and Guangzhou and could provide us with an idea of the cultural radiation effects of central cities; (2) their geographic locations and the formation of their communities had special characteristics; (3) their migration patterns varied; and (4) their economic structures each had special characteristics.

This chapter exploring the processes and modes of rural urbanization in the Pearl River Delta is mainly based on the data we obtained in the above round of investigations. Follow-up visits to some of these areas, however, continued over the next two years.

Based on geographic location, administrative level and other factors, the two authors have divided the Pearl River Delta's rural urbanization into different types, as described in detail below.

Rural Urbanization of the City Periphery

"City Periphery Village Communities" are a type of community widely found in the Chinese urbanization process, a product of China's special policies on land requisition and household registration. Such communities are situated in places where cities and rural areas have become integrated and possess elements of the way of life of both. They are different from city outskirts or villages in the ordinary sense. Their features include, for instance, high population-density with strong heterogeneity; preservation of some farming, though it is no longer the chief economic mode; all or part of the cultivated land has been requisitioned, but the individual retains land for housing or a small plot for self-cultivation; part of the community have become urban dwellers (have an urban *hukou*) [*Hukou,* or Household Registration System, is the key structural factor separating rural and urban residents.—Ed.] and part remain villagers; and diversified ways of making a living co-exist. The overall characteristic of such communities is that they are both urban and rural in nature. City suburbs today, especially those of large cities, include an extensive amount of territory, and that is why we are making a distinction by calling these "city periphery areas." Although "city periphery areas" are the earliest to begin the process of urbanization, they are the hardest to completely urbanize. Their most appropriate description would be "villages within cities." We cite below the example of Nanji village.

1. Village Overwhelmed by Development Zone.

Nanji belongs to Nangang township in the Huangpu District of Guangzhou. It is located in an integrated urban-rural area. The Guangzhou-Shenzhen highway runs nearby to the north, the Guangzhou Economic and Technical Development Zone lies to its east, Huangpu's Xingang Harbor to its south and the Huangpu Power Plant to its west. Nanji people say of themselves: "We are villagers registered as city residents, but we are not quite city residents either." This dual urban-rural character is the basic feature of this community.

Nanji has 10 economic cooperatives embracing 4,080 people of 1,700 families. They live in three natural villages divided by streams: Nanwan hamlet in the north where the Nanji Village Committee is located, covering 7 economic cooperatives (still habitually called production teams) with 2,500 people; Xiji hamlet with 1,000 people comprising the 8th and 9th production teams; and Dongji hamlet with 500 people facing Xiji across a stream. Beginning in the 1970s and up until 1988, *danwei* (work units) in the vicinity requisitioned large tracts of Nanji's land and many of the farming population became nonfarming. In 1978, 250 changed status; in 1984, another 800 changed status. By 1988, all had basically changed to urban resident status. On the one hand, people here acquired urban *hukou*; on the other, they came into sudden wealth at the cost of losing the land that had fed them.

Urbanization in Nanji was sudden. Faced with this sudden cultural change, both individuals and the community had an adjustment problem.

The Nanji Village Committee dealt with it as follows:

a. It came up with a reasonable way of distributing the land requisition fee [paid to compensate for the loss of their land.—Ed.] to avoid all of it being parceled out and squandered. Individuals were given relocation and seedling fees. Part of the funds were controlled by the team, part by the Village Committee.

b. Stipulations were made in regard to the use of the funds to avoid waste. They were divided into two parts: One part was put in the bank as collective savings (individuals get the interest) and the other used for investment.

c. A part of the land was preserved for local development, not to be requisitioned.

d. Interest from investments were used toward social benefits and other public causes.

Nanji has its own social security system:

a. It has set up one kindergarten each in the three natural villages and two elementary schools.
b. It has a bonus system for teachers. Teachers whose classes average above eighty in the unified national exams are given bonuses. Students who pass relevant exams and are accepted into senior middle schools and colleges are also given bonuses. Nine years of schooling are required.
c. In conjunction with the Guangzhou Worker's Hospital, it runs a hospital for the villagers.
d. It built the Nanwan Park, the biggest rural park in the Guangzhou Municipal District.
e. It has a recreational home for senior citizens.
f. It used to give everyone a stipend of 200–300 *yuan* every month (based on workpoints, the highest number of workpoints being 10).

Because of its abundant funds, social benefits are pretty good. Even people who do not work can live well enough. However, the system also restricts people in that they are afraid of losing the benefits. (People with regular jobs cannot enjoy them.) A shareholders' system is now in force and incomes are based on number of shares. This system is slightly different from the workpoint system and shares are distributed according to age: The older a person the more shares he or she gets (the most number of shares given is 8. People between fifty and sixty get 8 shares; people older than sixty get 7 shares.) The younger generation is very critical of this system.

Concentrating part of the requisition payments, Nanji built an industrial zone by the Guangzhou-Shenzhen highway. It invested 30 million *yuan* in the zone to build standard factory buildings and storage houses. 14 enterprises have settled here, all of them either *sanlai yibu* [enterprises that process, assemble, or manufacture customized goods from material supplied by foreign clients, or engage in compensation trade—Ed.] or *sanzi qiye* [joint, cooperative, or foreign ventures—Ed.]. Rent from the factories and storage buildings and management fees constitute the Village Committee's chief source of income, which it uses solely as collective welfare benefits. Committee cadre themselves are frugal and have no luxury cars or offices.

Adjustment policies differ in the three natural villages due to varying natural conditions. In Dongji hamlet, most villagers were originally *shuishangren* (boat people) [Also known in the West by the pejorative label, "Tanka" people.—Ed.] and settled on land only in the 1950s. Per-capita cultivated land averaged only 1 *mu*. They used to farm in the busy season and fish in the off season. Every family owned a boat and supplemented its farming income by fishing. Because of increasingly serious pollution, fish became scarce in the Pearl River and people fished less and less. In 1988, all of the hamlet's arable land except for 45 *mu* were requisitioned by the Guangzhou Economic and Technical Development Zone at 40,000 *yuan* per *mu* in addition to relocation and transitional living expenses.

Each production team's finances are separate from that of Nanji village, so that each possesses its own income. Chief sources of team income are as follows:

    a. Interest. Part of the requisition and relocation fees were put in the bank as fixed deposits. Interest is divided among individuals.

    b. Renting out land. Some land has been rented out to a company at 30 *yuan* per sq m, at a progressive increase of 5 percent every three years.

    c. Investing in more warehouses to lease out. (Previous storage space had been requisitioned.)

From these revenues, each individual in the production team can receive 2,000 to 2,500 *yuan* per year. Another part of the revenue goes into public undertakings such as kindergartens and elementary schools. Of the 400 villagers, 300 are of working age and the work they do is, mainly,

    a. As temporary workers at the Development Zone. Even though the zone gives priority in hiring to people from Nanji, most of them, mainly young women, do not want to become permanent workers because they would then have to give up relocation subsidies;

    b. Piecework—bringing back parts and components from the zone to assemble at home and earning wages per the piece. These are chiefly housewives;

    c. Conveying passengers on motorcycles. The village owns some fifty motorcycles, most of which are used to carry passengers in the zone. A day's average earnings amount to 20 or 30 *yuan*. This is a job for young men;

    d. Open small businesses, such as running stores and snack shops;

    e. Grow vegetables. Elderly people use the part of the land already requisitioned by the zone but not yet occupied to plant vegetables; and

    f. Raise pigs. Twenty families (out of 150) raise pigs, some up to a hundred pigs. Leftovers from the mess halls and restaurants of the zone are carted back as fodder.

Xiji's situation is similar to Dongji's. Before 1978, its chief occupation was farming supplemented by fishing. After the establishment of the development zone, all the cultivated land was requisitioned and villagers were granted urban hukou. This hamlet comprises the eighth and ninth production teams and has a population double the size of Dongji's. The hamlet's collective income comes from:

a. Two factory buildings with 4,000 sq m of floorspace financed by the hamlet. Rent from each sq m is 7 *yuan* per month.
b. One million *yuan*'s investment in a dredger (60 percent owned by the collective), which brings in over 1 million *yuan* of income a year.
c. Interest on fixed deposits.

Besides similar occupations as those engaged in by Dongji people, many Xiji people bought trucks (imported automatic dumping trucks, at a price of 100,000 *yuan* each), large freight vans (300,000 *yuan* each) as well as dredgers (1.3 million *yuan* each).

Nanwan village has seven economic cooperatives (production teams 1 to 7) with two thousand people. Another five hundred live in the hamlet although they are registered in the city. Still another twenty-six hundred are laborers from other places. The hamlet is thickly populated, but little of its land was requisitioned and it thus possesses less funds from land requisition. The collective has less money to distribute. In production team No. 2, for instance, the 1991 per-capita dividend was around 2,000 *yuan*. However, it has land resources including 400 *mu* of arable land and large tracts of slopes, and this is where Nanji selected the site of its industrial zone. Nanwan itself has also built an industrial zone where it erected factory buildings. Eleven companies, mostly from Hong Kong, have moved there. Villagers own 50 cars and trucks. Twenty percent of the families own motorcycles. Every family has built its own house.

Comparing the three natural villages, although Dongji has the best conditions being in the hinterland of the development zone and possessing a lot of start-up capital, its development has not been as swift as Nanwan, whose conditions are not as good.

Big changes have taken place in the life of the people of Nanji village. Besides every family owning a house, TV, refrigerator and other electrical appliances, the use of telephones, and gas for cooking is also spreading. The younger people are the first to change. Motorcycles, designer clothes, bars, dance halls, and karaoke are already part of their lives. Upon getting married, all furniture is bought at a shopping mall, while old-fashioned homemade furniture is discarded. Traditional customs have been preserved, however. On the first and fifteenth of each month and on holidays, incense is still burned to honor the spirits, and on holidays the gods are worshipped. Well-furnished living rooms all have altars for worship.

Nanwan is host to twenty-six hundred workers from other areas, mainly Hunan, Jiangxi, Sichuan, and Guangxi, 80 percent of them women. Some people from elsewhere in the province have also gone there, such as the Chaozhou people from the Shantou (Swatow) region. A Chaozhou-run factory mainly hires Shantou workers, the reason being that they speak the same language and so work better together. The large number of outside workers poses a security risk. Workers from Sichuan and Hunan, though having a language problem at first, have gradually learned the local dialect and get along well with local residents, especially their landlords.

Nanwan is mindful of its appearance and has built roads, installed sewage pipes, and other public facilities. It has also built a kindergarten and elementary school, as well as a park.

Nanji villagers, as far as clothing, food, housing, and transportation go, have reached a fairly good standard of living. They have no desire for crowded and noisy city life. They like their home environment, where they have lots of friends and own their own houses in quiet, comfortable surroundings. With money in their hands and transportation convenient, they can go into town anytime they want. All daily necessities are locally available. In 1988, when the agricultural population turned nonagricultural, the majority of the villagers refused to change their registration status and only did so upon the condition that their share of collective income would not be affected. This caused a reaction from people who had already changed status before 1988, who now wanted to give up their jobs and return to the village. For the above reasons, despite the fact that the majority in Nanji had become urban residents, they still lived under the jurisdiction of the old rural administrative organization. There is another reason it would be hard for Nanji to become completely urbanized. Although the entire Dongxi and Xiji populations had acquired urban resident status in 1988, after 1988 up to a hundred rurally registered people once again appeared, most of them having moved here after marriage or were newborn children (of mothers with rural *hukou*).

Adjustment strategies differ in different age groups. Middle-aged and elderly people are quite content with their present life and want security. They want to invest their money in the bank or rely on the rent they get from land and factory buildings. Younger people want to take risks and go into business. Conservatives are in the majority, however, and new investment programs are hard to pass. The generation gap is quite obvious and mutual complaints are common. The younger generation call the older generation misers and complain that the distribution policy favors them, while the latter complain that the young people have too easy a life and want nothing more than eating, drinking and making merry, and that they disdain small tasks but cannot perform big tasks.

People who've moved to the area from elsewhere are distinguishable by their dress. As for locals, middle-aged and elderly people are generally dressed like peasants, the older among them (especially women) still retaining the dress of the boat people. Young people are much more modern. The young men wear dungarees and sneakers and women have permed hair and use makeup.

2. "Extended urbanization process"—Lujiang village

Lujiang village belongs to Guangzhou City's Haizhu District and is now a true "village encircled by the city." It is located a mere 200 meters from the overpass where two major city roads, Xingang Lu and Guangzhou Avenue intersect. Since the 1940s, scholars have investigated and studied this village, probably because of the proximity of Zhongshan University (and of Lingnan University before 1952). In the 1980s, the Sociology Department of Zhongshan University did further tracking studies. All this brought Lujiang into world prominence and left a rare store of data completely recording its half-a-century-long urbanization process.[6] After entering Zhongshan University in 1978, one of the authors of this chapter, Zhou Daming, had also taken frequent walks in the village and visited its stores, thus eyewitnessing its changes. All these sources give us an account of the village's long road to urbanization.

a. Pastoral landscape—Lujiang village of the 1940s

Although the 1940s Lujiang as described by Mr. Yang Qingkun and others had already been affected by urban economic and cultural influences, it still retained the pastoral landscape of a rural village. In 1948, the village, 8 km from Guangzhou, was administratively under Panyu County. It had 1,100 inhabitants and cultivated 1,200 *mu* of land, averaging 1.08 *mu* per person. Population density was 1,158 per sq km. Villagers mainly engaged in farming; 75 percent of the families worked the fields while supplementing their incomes with side lines such as embroidery, work in the cities, and vending. Transportation was inconvenient. The only land route to Guangzhou was a 1.5–meter-wide mud path. A water route meant a detour of 5 to 6 kilometers.

The village had a self-contained economy relying on the land. Socially, kinship played an extremely important part. The major form of kinship was the clan organization and the Che and Mu families dominated the village socially and economically. A person's name decided his or her economic and social status and peer group. The family was the site of economic, religious, educational and recreational activity as well as the basic unit of production and consumption.

Lujiang had obvious features of the rural community in the 1940s, but because of its proximity to Guangzhou, was affected by the radiation of urban culture. Villagers could read Guangzhou dailies the same day. They could work in the city, peddle goods for sale, or sell vegetables in exchange for consumer goods. The power of the clan gradually waned and that of the government rose.

b. The city encircling the village—Lujiang in the 1950s to 1970s

Continuing throughout the 1950s, backward transportation between Lujiang and Guangzhou impeded its urbanization. Beginning in the 1960s, transportation improved. An 18–meter-wide highway passed through the village (Xingang Road). Bus service arrived, and people began to ride bicycles to the city. Different enterprises and undertakings relocated there. Urbanization speeded up.

Despite strict control of the urban population, Guangzhou's population still grew at a rapid pace after Liberation. To relieve the high population density, a part of the city's enterprises and undertakings were dispersed to the surrounding suburbs. Beginning in the 1960s, many moved into the Lujiang area, thus gradually encircling the village (work units only used cultivated land or slope land and left residential sites alone). Although these *danwei* were administratively and in terms of the *hukou* system separate from the village and the village was relatively independent and closed-in, the move did affect the village's former way of life.

First, the population structure changed. Land requisition was facilitated by hiring villagers as workers and changing their household registration status. As a result, part of Lujiang's population became state employees and urban residents, although they continued to live in the village. Second, the industrial structure changed. The proportion in agriculture dropped and that in industry and commerce rose. The agricultural structure itself changed. Acreage planted to paddy rice was reduced and replaced by vegetable-growing and livestock and poultry-raising. Third, the change in industrial structure brought a corresponding change in village occupation structure. The labor force gradually turned to the secondary and tertiary sectors. Fourth, living standards improved by a large margin. Large sums of land requisition payments and income from industry and subsidiary occupations brought radical changes in way of life, housing conditions, medical treatment and education.

c. Is it a city or a countryside village?

Beginning in the 1980s, transportation further developed. Xingang Road was widened to 38 meters. The 45–meter-wide Guangzhou Avenue was built. More work units moved in. Little cultivable land was left. In 1985, adjustments in the Guangzhou administrative region made Lujiang part of Zhuhai district, becoming an urban community.

Big changes took place. Because of a rise in land-requisition fees and cessation of employment by the state-owned enterprises, both the collective and individuals now had more startup funds. Large numbers of collectively and individually owned enterprises sprang up. People began to amass more income, while collective benefits and individual housing both improved. Many families owned more than one house, renting out those they did not need. The village started enterprises in embroidery, garments, iron-casting, plastics, knitwear, auto maintenance and repair, and steel windows manufacture. Taking advantage of its favorable geographic location, it also set up many department stores, food and beverage stores, and repair shops by the highways.

The population structure changed drastically. Besides those who changed to urban status because of the requisition of their land, an urban *hukou* could also be bought. This greatly increased the urban population. The village management setup also changed. A villagers' committee and a residents' committee were formed to separately manage those with rural or urban *hukou* status. People's thinking changed and educational level went up.

In short, Lujiang now has all the basic characteristics of urbanization: (1) a large population of high density; twenty-two hundred people now live in the village, making the density 1,300 per sq km; (2) a high degree of heterogeneity. Besides the original inhabitants, urban residents and outsiders (*wailai renkou*) (those who do not have a local *hukou*) have moved in. The latter came from all parts of the country, turning Lujiang into a pluralistic community; (3) a relatively high degree of occupational differentiation; and (4) universal spread of mass media.

So why do we persist in asking the question: "Is it a city or is it a countryside village?" A part of the people in Lujiang still have rural household registration status and more people with rural status will come in by marrying locals. Second, original inhabitants of the village have a strong sense of mutual identification. They have a subculture of their own as compared to the culture of Guangzhou. Third, building in the village was unplanned, making the rural environment hard to change completely in a short time.

3. Village within a village—migrant residential areas amid rural communities on the city periphery

The *Guangzhou Daily* had carried a report entitled "An Outsiders' City Is Rising North of the City," describing outsiders who have settled down in northern Guangzhou's integrated urban-rural area. Actually, this is a common phenomenon in rural communities on the city periphery. The author (Zhou Daming) has led some students in making a survey of one such migrant community and interviewed nearly a hundred people, which we will briefly describe below and again in Chapter 9 (detailed description has been published separately).[7]

This village is situated by the Xiaogang River and belongs to Lianxing village. Transportation is extremely convenient. After the Haiyin bridge opened to traffic, Dongshan district became immediately accessible. Docks and warehouses for building materials line the banks of the Xiaogang River and large numbers of temporary workers are hired. As early as a dozen years ago, many migrant laborers worked here and more arrived with the expansion of dock and warehouse facilities. According to villagers and outsiders living in the community, five thousand migrant laborers live here. We were a little skeptical of this figure, but this was the figure consistently given us. After visiting the crowded accommodations of the outsiders, the figure became more believable.

This village within a village is called Sichuan village—the majority of the dwellers originating from Sichuan. They are called the "mud guys" (*nishui lao*)—working in construction and repairs and transporting construction materials (actually they do whatever the bosses tell them to do). In the daytime, they await hiring on the streets, docks and warehouses. They bring their own lunchboxes, and return after dark. They live in temporary housing built along the river levees. Rooms are like small cages, each covering no more than 10 sq m of space with less than 1 sq m unoccupied. Each "cage" has three levels; each level has six cubicles about as big as train berths but not as high. Twelve to sixteen people share one room, leaving two cubicles for their belongings. The "cages" are built of brick. People crawl in at one end to sleep and cover the holes with a piece of cloth, which makes mosquito nets unnecessary. There is only one small window in the room, so the suffocation can be imagined. Each person pays 20 *yuan* a month for this. Migrants from other places in Guangdong live somewhat better, usually three to four a room.

Finding work in the daytime is not easy. A laborer earns money only when he is lucky and returns empty-handed when he is not. It is not easy to find a fixed spot to await hiring either. Negotiations are necessary and fights frequently break out over territories. Good relations have to be maintained with city officials. In some places, police extract monthly fees of at least 5 *yuan* from each worker. When fees are not paid, the laborer is either driven out or beaten up and sent to the "blind migrants" (*mangliu*) [Migrants are often referred to by the derogatory term *mangliu,* implying that they are "blindly" wandering around without rhyme or reason.—Ed.] repatriation center. The repatriation center demands a fine of 300 *yuan.* Those who cannot pay are beaten up before repatriation. Third, laborers are subject to the extortion of gangs. Gang members come daily or monthly to collect dues of varying amounts. Disaster overtakes those who cannot pay. In this community, a laborer has to pay rent, temporary *hukou* registration fees, and "protection" money to security personnel. Most of the latter are said to be not locals but from other areas of Guangdong. They do not touch local people, only *waishengren* ("out-of-province" people, i.e., non-Guangdongese).

Village outsiders also engage in other occupations, such as work in collective enterprises or for entrepreneurs, do blackmarket sales, go into business on their own, or set up as bosses on the piers, while others rent out rooms. These latter rent housing from the Linxiang villagers and live much better. Sometimes one family rents a house, sometimes several families rent one together.

Villagers are sympathetic to migrants and know well their hard life. Local employers emphasize that they are good to outsiders, paying them piecework wages and taking care of their medical insurance and housing. Outsiders are also good to the locals because, they say, they have to, since even "a strong dragon can not overcome a snake in its old haunts." Among outsiders, however, conflicts often break out between people from different provinces or regions. We witnessed a bloody fight between different factions of Sichuanese using knives and bricks. Sichuanese often fight with Hunanese, too, over business and territory.

The village has many factories built by locals and nonnatives. Most are civilian houses and provide a poor working environment. Rooms are crowded. Workers are mostly women. One garment factory had several dozen machines in one room beside cutting boards and masses of cloth and products, making passage nearly impossible. Fifty women worked in the room, which had only a few small windows. All of the land by the riverfront has been leased out to build warehouses. The bosses have built quite a lot of housing in this open space, and that which they do not use themselves, they rent out. The latter include the laborers' "housing" mentioned above. Apart from these, there are also many tenants whose origins are unknown.

The Urbanizing Extension of Market Towns

Market towns are also called "small towns," "country towns," or, officially, "designated townships" (*jianzhi zhen*). The population size is between that of a small city and that of a village. In the early 1980s, Mr. Fei Xiaotong had set off a wave of study of market towns.[8] Although people differ regarding the status and role of market towns, most agree that they are the points of integration of urban and rural communities and play an important part at the present stage. Development of towns in the Pearl River Delta, like market towns throughout the country, has been affected by central policy. In the twenty-six years between 1957 and 1983, the Delta had around thirty urban areas (including cities and designated townships). In 1984, the central government revised the administrative definition of townships and experimented with abolishing the *xiang* (district) [The *xiang* was the key subdivision of the *xian* (county) during noncommune times. When people's communes were established, the new commune was based on the old *xiang*.—Ed.] in favor of a system whereby townships exercised administrative jurisdiction over villages. This, plus the objective needs of economic development in the Delta, resulted in the rapid increase of towns. At the end of 1986, the Delta had 252 designated townships.

Below, we will observe town development with Humen Township as a case in point.

1. Humen—market town, or city?

Humen township, covering 175 sq km, belongs to Dongguan municipality (Dongguanshi). It has a population of eighty-four thousand (not including the "outsiders") and governs twenty-five *guanli qu* (management districts) and three residents' management districts. People conversant with contemporary history will have heard of Humen. When the authors visited Humen in 1979 (then called Taiping Town), it had only a few narrow, deserted and broken-down streets, being no different from other small towns. Today, its appearance has totally changed. The prosperity of its streets and stores is comparable to Guangzhou's. The city proper has expanded from 1 to 3.5 sq km (built up area) and the urban population is now ninety thousand (including provincial and municipal work units, troops, and migrant workers). The growth of the economy has been amazing.

Humen's history dates back to antiquity. During the Spring and Autumn Period, it belonged to Nanhai Prefecture and during the Western Jin, Dongguan Prefecture. In the Tang dynasty (A.D. 757), Dongguan became a county and Humen came under its jurisdiction. In the early Ming, it was under the Quekou subdistrict. After the mid-Ming, it became a military communications point, while by the end of the Ming, the naval command moved from Jiumenzhai to Humenzhai converting Taiping into a military and commercial strongpoint. During the Qing dynasty, Humen came under the jurisdiction of Quekou and in the 19th year of the reign of Daoguang, Lin Zexu (Lin Tse-hsu) set fire to opium here, an event that shook the world. Weiyuan and Jinyuan forts were added later. Guan Tianpei guarded Humen for six years and fought seven big battles with the British, finally dying in action. After the Opium Wars, Humen's Taiping became a transit point between Guangzhou and Hong Kong. Gambling, prostitution, drugs and smuggling became rampant and business and the services sector developed. People called it "Little Hong Kong." After the establishment of the Republic of China, it belonged to Dongguan's eighth and third districts, and in 1925, was designated Humen City. After 1949, it was a district under Dongguan County. But because of frequent changes in administrative division, it changed its name frequently, and in 1955, when the numerical designations were changed back to names, it was called Humen district. In 1957, when districts were abolished and *xiang* set up, the system was for big *xiang* to administer smaller *xiang*. Humen became two big xiang. In 1958, the *xiang* system was abolished and the Humen People's Commune established. In summer and autumn 1959, Taiping and Chang'an Communes split off from Humen Commune. In 1984, the commune system was abolished and the place was renamed the Humen District Office, Taiping Township. In 1985, the district was abolished and township expanded. Humen district combined with Taiping township to become today's Humen township.

Humen's socioeconomic development has been extremely rapid. In 1978, its GVAIO was 37.11 million *yuan*, but by 1990, had surged to 352.05 million *yuan* (in 1980 constant prices). The tax revenue in 1978 (the portion that Humen contracted to pay to the higher authorities) was 2.55 million *yuan*, and by 1990, had grown to 30 million. *Sanlai yibu* enterprises processing materials for foreign clients started from scratch and were making 100 million HK$ by 1990. The foreign currency generated was 5.21 million US$ in 1978 and increased to 37.11 million US$ in 1990. Total sales by state-owned businesses was 20.83 million *yuan* in 1978, and by 1989, reached 348 million *yuan*. The urban and rural savings balance of the masses in 1978 was 4.78 million and 310 million by 1989, with per-capita savings at 3,690 *yuan*. The township, besides state-owned and collective businesses, has a total of four thousand entrepreneurs in business, averaging one entrepreneur for every twenty-one people.

Humen's development can first of all be attributed to the improvement of its investment environment, which allowed a rural market town to become a multifunctional city.

a. Rapid construction of the urban infrastructure enabled the town to develop all sorts of ventures in harmonious coordination. As much as 150 million *yuan* were put into reconstruction of the old urban core, which grew from 1.2 to 4.8 sq km. The original four or five small streets totaling 2 kilometers now have been expanded to nine concrete roads totaling 9 kilometers. More throughways have been built from Humen to other places. Its section of the Guangzhou-Shenzhen trunk line has been widened to 45 meters, and a 620–meter-long and 12.5–meter-wide Weiyuan bridge was built that connects the highway with the car ferry.

b. Humen's Taiping Harbor has been rebuilt. Formerly, it had only half a dozen berths for boats of under a hundred tons; now it has thirty docks providing forty berths. A dock handling containers of a thousand to three thousand tons has been completed.

c. Energy and communications have improved. The township now has six thousand digitally controlled telephone lines and is now part of a network that enables it to hook up directly with 154 countries and regions in the world. The Taiping water works has a daily capacity of 140,000 cubic meters. Humen not only has the two biggest power plants (Shaojiao A and B plants) in the province, but also a transformer station of 110,000 volts.

d. Rural road construction has also been speeded up. There are now 60 kilometers of concrete roads in the rural areas with widths ranging from 7 to 12 meters capable of bearing fifty-ton trucks. In the township as a whole, all urban and rural roads are now built of concrete. All investments were financed by the township, management districts, collectives and individuals. Investments were repaid with interest. Financing for power generation alone reached 56.34 million *yuan*.

In the wake of its improved investment environment, Humen's industry has grown swiftly on the strength of its proximity to Hong Kong and Macao, the fact that it is the home of many overseas Chinese, and its well developed transportation facilities. The old Humen only had enterprises relying on manual labor such as iron forging, tailoring, shoe-making, bamboo and wood-working, boatbuilding, machine-building, and printing. Beginning in 1979, this completely changed. With *sanlai yibu* and joint, cooperative and foreign ventures opening the way, industry has had comprehensive development. By 1990, the township had attracted 420 million H.K. dollars of investment and brought in 32,000 sets of advanced equipment, built new factories with 700,000 sq m of floorspace, set up 435 *sanlai yibu* enterprises and 75 *sanzi qiye* (joint, cooperative, or foreign ventures), and established 14 industrial zones. It had established ten major industries including food, garment, arts and crafts, building materials, leather, furniture, hardware, communications, woolen knitwear, and electronics and electric appliances. Its products are now exported to Hong Kong, West Europe, the Americas, Southeast Asia and the Middle East. Starting with *sanlai yibu* low-grade processing, Humen enterprises have upgraded from labor-intensive to investment- and technology-intensive. Since 1990, they have set up such externally oriented key enterprises as the Dongguan CDC cable plant, the

Nanfang glass fiber plant, the Humen canning factory, and the Humen cement plant. The fast growth of externally-oriented industries has not only brought in more capital and the latest equipment, but also management expertise. This has provided training for a large number of specialized personnel in economic and enterprise management as well as large numbers of technical and skilled workers. GVAIO increased on average 30.2 percent annually between 1979 and 1990.

Industrial development has absorbed surplus rural labor power as well as stimulated agricultural development. Humen's agriculture started out by changing "grain as the key link" into diversified development of farming, forestry, livestock-raising, sidelines, and fishing. By 1989, the ratio of grain and cash crops had changed from 1979's 77:23 to 57:43. The ratio between planting, forestry, livestock-raising, sidelines and fishing was 38:3:15: 20:24. Adjustment of the agricultural structure has effectively improved results. Second, commodity production bases have been established. Humen has set up 122 export bases in recent years to earn foreign currency. They include 27 fruit farms with 20,000 *mu* of orchards for high-quality fruits, 16 aquatic farms that raise pigs, ducks, geese, chickens, and quails, 26 vegetable farms totaling 4,500 *mu* supplying 2.5 tons of vegetables yearly, 3 farm products processing bases, and production bases for superior and rare produce. Third, Humen has organically integrated agricultural development, suitably expanded scale of operation, and intensified production to develop a foreign-currency-earning commercial agriculture. The township now has 250 farming households (20 percent of the total number of farm households) which have suitably expanded the scale of their operation. The acreage under their management is 34,500 *mu,* or 54 percent of total farmland. Fourth, funds have been raised by every means to develop agriculture to make foreign currency. At present, all the different economic sectors— state-owned, collective, foreign-owned, joint ventures and individuals—are pitching in to develop agriculture to earn foreign currency. From 1979–89, 90 million *yuan* was invested to build irrigation projects, reclaim land, plant crops and develop aquatic products for this purpose. Another 11 million HK$ were brought in from outside and 5.1 million *yuan* was invested by every sort of *lianheqiye* (multifamily enterprises) to build export bases. Fifth, as agriculture is now oriented toward the global market, improving quality is a priority so that more foreign currency can be earned.

A major function of a town is the provision of comprehensive services. Humen has developed its tertiary sector along with the primary and secondary sectors. All levels—state-owned, collective and individual—have joined in this effort to develop all types of services at all levels. In 1990, state-owned commercial departments handled sales of 300 million *yuan*'s worth of commodities. They remain dominant on the market. The town's first level of collective commerce has developed quickly. The town now has nine big commercial corporations with several dozen subsidiaries. Humen has a unique mode of development—here "industry promotes trade, trade stimulates industry, and industry and trade grow together." In 1990, the nine big corporations generated a gross industrial output of 180.3 million *yuan*. Total commercial sales were 400 million *yuan*. They are not only the mainstay of Humen's tertiary industry but also an important part of Humen's economy. The township also has over 3,000 *getihu* businesses employing nearly 10,000 people. Eight new *getihu* business shopping centers and comprehensive farmer's markets have been opened covering 32,000 sq m of space. Some of them are open at night. Facilities for tourism, services and transportation have improved. The township has close to five hundred guest houses, restaurants, and shops. It has twenty-three inns with twenty-four hundred beds, twelve of these hostelries being hotels. Today, more than twenty thousand people pass through Humen daily. Daily departures number three hundred for passenger trains, fifty-seven hundred times for automotive vehicles, and three hundred times for boat or ship. There is also direct passenger and freight shipping to Hong Kong.

Recently, a news item reported: "Four years ago, the business office of the post office located on Taiping Zhixin Road was not at all crowded. There were no lines to send or receive money orders. Today, the new Humen Postal and Telecommunications Building at the mouth of Taiping Central Road, despite a huge service area several times bigger than before, is crowded to overflowing. On factory off-days, in particular, the place is more crowded than Guangzhou buses during rush hours. Sweating people with nonlocal accents each hold a little piece of paper printed with green grids—remittance cards. In Dongguan, there are 4,000 *sanlai yibu* enterprises that have attracted 700,000 to 800,000 migrant workers. Humen alone has 50,000 of them. In many villages, migrant workers outnumber locals.

Humen township has invested a lot of money in cultural facilities. It has four movie theaters, four cultural centers, seventeen libraries, sixty-eight basketball courts, thirty-eight badminton courts, a swimming center, and two soccer fields. The employees' spare-time school has a five-story teaching building offering courses in accounting, foreign languages, computer, enterprise management, and Chinese. The school provides fifty-six classes in twenty-seven specialties. There are also different kinds of training classes that have trained a total of twenty-one thousand students, or 52 percent of the township population. The cultural center covers 2,000 sq m of land and comprises Buildings A and B. It is complete with all kinds of recreational facilities and houses associations with four hundred members in literature, photography, music, local Chinese operas, calligraphy, and art. The Literary Association publishes the journal Huxiao (The Tiger's Roar) with a circulation of thirty-five thousand copies, making it the most widely circulated town-run paper in the whole country.

People in Humen are serious about education. The township now has thirty kindergartens, forty-four elementary schools, three junior middle schools, one regular senior middle school, one vocational senior middle school, one spare-time employees' secondary school, and one spare-time athletic school for youngsters. It also has branches of a TV university and an agricultural correspondence university. Teaching staff number 1,000. Elementary and secondary school students number 15,300. A multilevel educational structure has been built.

The township has put a lot of funds into education. From 1985 to the end of 1989, investment in capital construction in education has exceeded 12 million *yuan*. Twenty-six schools have been newly built, expanded or renovated involving 40,000 sq m, making up 56 percent of total school floor space. From 1989 to 1990 alone, the township government had appropriated 11.6 million *yuan* to education. In 1991, it further allocated 8 million *yuan* to build the township central elementary school, 3.5 million *yuan* to build an athletic field in the Weiyuan junior middle school, 2 million *yuan* to build classrooms at Humen junior middle school and 1.35 million to buy additional instruments and equipment for Humen junior middle school's science building. Rural management districts also finance many educational projects. The Longyan, Jinzhou, Nanzha, and Dongfeng management districts have each raised several million *yuan* to build schools. The township also stepped up overall planning of educational development, including adjustment of school distribution, trying out establishing schools at different levels and improving teachers' salaries and benefits. A bonus system is being promoted that encourages both teachers and students to perform well. As much as 1.1 million *yuan* has been raised as educational funds and appropriations have been made to build teachers' dormitories.

While improving basic education, the township also emphasizes the training of technical personnel. First of all, it "grasps three tasks" (*sange zhua*) to improve the population's quality:

a. It grasps spare-time training. Since 1986, Humen's vocational school, adult education training center and agricultural correspondence university have run a total of 392 classes with 25,000 students in 40 specialized technical training courses and seminars including those on electrician certification, electronics, industrial processes, enterprise management, accounting, planting and English. Relevant training courses and seminars were also provided at the management district level.

b. It grasps directed training. This has been done in recent years by the selection of two hundred cadres and workers to go to higher education institutions. The township TV university also provides college-level courses in Chinese, accounting, and business management.

c. It grasps vocational education. The secondary vocational school trains specialized practitioners.

In addition, the township has brought in large numbers of outside talent. Before 1988, Humen's industrial and commercial enterprises had only 24 people with an education at or above the secondary specialized level. In recent years, it has brought in talent through many channels and by 1991, already possessed 1,203 people with an education at or above the secondary specialized level. These people are playing increasingly crucial roles. For instance, the Humen Comprehensive Development Company hired two aquatic experts in 1989 to take care of the technical side of the aquatic farms. In two years, they were able to build up a very large breeding base whose 1990 output was 2.2 million *yuan* with a net income of 320,000 *yuan*. In 1991, the output reached 6 million.

Summarizing Humen's developmental trajectory, then, we can see the importance of a few key factors:

a. Its geographic location is important and transportation well developed. Humen faces the Pearl River estuary and is situated in the geometric center of Guangdong Province, Hong Kong and Macao, at the juncture of the eastern and western corridors of the Pearl River Delta (the juncture of the Guangzhou-Shenzhen-Zhujiang freeways). By land, it is in the middle section of the Guangzhou-Shenzhen highway; by water, it has the Taiping Harbor (designated as an open port by the State Council in 1983) that connects with the sea and handles an annual volume of 1 million tons. It is an area that the Humen-Nansha car ferry passes through. The Humen bridge linking the eastern and western banks of the Pearl River Delta is under construction. The outer Humen harbor (Weiyuan Harbor) is also being planned with a designed berth capacity of 3– to 5–ton cargo ships. These transportation facilities are unique in the province and provide a great motive force for its development.

b. It has a long history and rich tourist resources. Humen is known to the world as the place where Lin Zexu burned opium and many historical landmarks from that era have been preserved. They include the Shajiao Battery, the Weiyuan Battery, the "Gold Lock" and "Brass Pass" as well as the Opium War Museum. Besides human cultural resources, it is known for its oceanfront and other tourist attractions and draws 1 million Chinese and foreign tourists annually.

c. Humen is the native place of many overseas Chinese and is attractive to many compatriots from Hong Kong, Macao and other places. With patriotic fervor and local attachments, the latter have actively supported Humen's modernization.

The township plans to build itself into a port city mainly engaged in externally oriented industry but also developing business, trade and tourism. By the year 2010, the population is expected to grow to 200,000 to 500,000. The city will be divided into three large districts—Taiping Harbor, and the Southern and Northern Weiyuan districts. It will run 7.4 kilometers from east to west and 7.5 kilometers from north to south and will be linked by 6 bridges over the Taiping River. Besides the city proper, development is also planned for three satellite residential areas; Baisha in the north, Baizha in the east (including Longyan and Daning), and Nanzha in the south. When completed, it will be a city flanked by three townships.

2. Nangang township in Huangpu district

Nangang is situated at the eastern edge of the Huangpu district. It connects with Luogang township of the Baiyun district in the north, faces the Pearl River in the south, borders on Zengcheng County in the east, and links with Dasha township in the west, where the Guangzhou Economic and Technical Development Zone is located. The township has jurisdiction over 7 administrative villages and 108 natural villages and covers a total area of 57 sq km. It has a population of over 50,000 (of which 20,000–plus are agricultural population) and more than 1,000 Overseas Chinese and Hong Kong and Macao compatriots. It is an integrated urban-rural area that has, besides township population, people working in forty enterprises or undertakings belonging to the central, provincial, or municipal authorities, with more than 10,000 permanent residents. The township has 19,470 *mu* of cultivated land, and 10,417 *mu* of fruit trees. There are 7,118 agricultural households and 6,045 urban *hukou* households. In 1991, its GVIAO was 330 million *yuan*, of which 80 million came from agriculture and 250 million from industry. Per-capita distribution was 4,000 *yuan*, while the area holds 200 to 300 millions' worth of fixed assets.

Nangang has a long history. It was originally under the jurisdiction of Panyu, but came under Guangzhou City in 1951. In 1973 when Huangpu became a district, Nangang commune was set up by taking over seven production brigades of the suburban Luogang commune. In 1984, the commune was changed to a district and, in 1987, became a township. The region has some famous cultural sites—the Temple to the God of Nanhai and the Pavilion Where Fuxu Bathed the Sun built in the 14th year of the Kaibao reign under the Emperor Wenti of the Sui dynasty (A.D. 594). The Nanhai God Temple is located at the eastern estuary of the Pearl River. The area is a natural port and had been an important center of foreign trade since ancient times—it is the beginning of the "Silk Road of the Sea." The temple is located in Fuxu township, a thriving trading town. During the Song and Yuan dynasties, it was already quite prosperous, but after the Ming, the township declined and became a small village, the current Miaotou village. The Bathed the Sun pavilion was built in the Tang dynasty and enjoyed great fame in the Song. At the time, it looked out on the wide expanse of the sea. It is now about one *li* from the Pearl River.

Before Liberation, Nangang was a gambling, prostitution and opium town. Ordinary townspeople had an extremely hard life. After Liberation, development of agriculture, especially grain, was the priority, and the town developed slowly. Since 1978, however, changes have been rapid. Whereas before, 80 percent of the people engaged in farming, now 80 percent are in nonagricultural occupations in industry and commerce. Living standards have risen; families now own high-grade stereo equipment, TVs, telephones, modern furniture, and air-conditioning. In 1978, the township had only ten telephone sets of the hand-cranked type. Now a thousand modern telephone receivers have been installed and another two thousand-line switchboard is being installed, of which a hundred lines are available for international (IDD) calling. From the 1950s to 1987, people used to ride bicycles. After 1988, motorcycles replaced bicycles. There are now five thousand motorcycles of name brands and a lot more of lesser known brands. Six hundred cars are privately owned.

In 1986, Nangang took off economically. Industrial output rose 80 percent annually from 1986 to 1989; agricultural output rose 22 percent. Industry boomed at all levels. The township, village and cooperative (natural villages) all built industrial zones of various sizes and individual and multifamily enterprises sprang up. The GVIAO of the Shabu, Xiayuan, and Nanji villages have all surpassed the 10 million *yuan* mark.

In the view of the authors, the fundamental reason for Nangang's swift development can be attributed to the Guangzhou Economic and Technical Development Zone. First, the zone's favorable terms expanded to Nangang, making it attractive for foreign investment. Second, development of the zone's transportation, energy, and communications objectively provided Nangang with the conditions for development. Third, land requisition fees paid by the zone provided Nangang and especially its surrounding villages with startup capital. Fourth, development of the zone brought up land prices in and around Nangang, stimulating real estate development and bringing up rents on housing. That is why Nangang took off in 1986, the year after the zone was built.

As Nangang is a new town, it had no market town center from the past. Relatively speaking, every village is economically strong. The township is planning to build a center near its administrative building and blueprints have already been approved. Restaurants, hotels, schools and transportation depots have already been built. Residential and industrial areas are separate and many enterprises have already moved into the latter. Nangang is on the Guangzhou-Shenzhen highway, a place all traffic to Zengcheng, Dongguan, and Shenzhen must pass through. On its north is the new "Yunpu Economic and Technical Development Zone." Transportation is convenient, and this, along with the impetus provided by the development zone, will soon turn Nangang's blueprints into reality.

3. Xinqiao township in Gaoyao County

Xinqiao township lies on hilly land where the Pearl River Delta plains turn into the mountainous districts of western Guangdong. It is a peripheral area of the "extended delta." It covers 34.52 sq km and has 18,000 *mu* of mountainous land, 15,226 *mu* of cultivated land, 3,303 mu of aquatic breeding grounds and 13,000 *mu* of paddy rice fields. The township has 11 management districts and 1 residents' committee with 60 natural villages. Total population is 32,165, of which about 18,000 are in the labor force, and agricultural population is over 28,000. From 1978 to 1991, 3,516 people moved from the rural areas into neighborhoods in the township, under the *zili kouliang* policy [wherein these new town dwellers continue to be responsible for their own grain supply.—Ed.] making up almost half of the 8,000 people living in the town proper.

In the past, this place had devoted itself mainly to agriculture, especially rice planting. Industrially, it had only traditional bamboo crafts.

Since 1978, five major industries have sprung up. The first is auto repair. Eighteen such repair shops have been established by the township, districts and natural villages as well as multifamily enterprises with an annual output of 15 million *yuan*. The second is chemicals, including a fire-retardant materials factory and an indigo blue pigment plant. The third is construction, including the Gaoyao County No. 3 Construction Company with 3,200 workers which owns 3 million *yuan* of fixed assets and an annual income of 18 million *yuan*. The fourth is the light industry of textiles production, including the making of handbags and knitwear with an annual output of 32 million *yuan*. The last is bambooware making. The township, districts, and natural villages have set up some twenty-five factories with a thousand workers devoted to this craft. Products are sold to forty countries and regions of the world. Output amounts to more than 17 million *yuan* a year.

In 1991, the township's aggregate social output [that is, the production of all five sectors of the economy.—Ed.] was 110 million *yuan*, of which industrial-agricultural output was 78.91 million with agriculture occupying 45 percent or 35.6 million *yuan* of GVIAO and industry 55 percent or 43.31

million *yuan*. The same year, per-capita rural income was 1,081 *yuan* and aggregate savings of township residents amounted to 59.42 million *yuan*.

Material conditions improved along with economic development. Cultural and recreational facilities expanded. The township as a whole has a total of sixteen schools, of which thirteen are elementary schools, two are junior middle schools, and one is a six-year comprehensive middle school. Beginning in 1989, nine-year education was implemented.

Among the families, 80 percent now have TV sets, 30 percent of which are colored sets. Among urban residents, 80 percent of the homes own color TVs. The township has a movie theater which is open nightly. More than half the films shown are made in Hong Kong or Taiwan. There is also a theater where Cantonese Opera troupes frequently perform. There is one karaoke hall, five video viewing halls, seven video games arcades, and seven rural cultural activities rooms. On holidays and weekends, many sports events, cultural shows, and karaoke competitions are staged. The township supports seven sports teams.

Although in a relatively remote location, the township is strongly influenced by Hong Kong culture. This is because, first, it is host to several thousand Hong Kong and Macao compatriots (as well as those from Taiwan and other foreign places)—a total of 6,385 who have returned to invest in facilities, ranging from hospitals and schools, to indoor tapwater. Second, reciprocal visits have changed not only the local way of life, but also ideology. For instance, locals are said to be emulating Hong Kong people when they work hard to earn money. Third, locals are learning from the public media, mainly the movies, videos and TV. Half of the movies and videos are made in Hong Kong.

Xinqiao's labor structure has also changed. GVIO has begun to exceed GVAO. The nonagricultural population is increasing. Besides working in local enterprises, many people have left the area to work or do business. Workers who left to do construction work outside total more than three thousand. Migrant labor has also come into Xinqiao, including about three hundred from Sichuan, Guangxi, and elsewhere. Another two hundred outsiders have settled in the township.

Rural (Village and Management District) Urbanization

The village or management district is the current rural grass-roots organizational unit. Urbanization of the Pearl River Delta has spread to every village. Rapid rural urbanization is closely linked with the characteristics of the delta's economic development. The economic success of the delta is built on township enterprises, and the key to the success of township enterprises is pluralistic development—the "five wheels" turning together, that is, county, township, village, multifamily, and individual enterprises. Also, the delta's externally oriented agriculture guided by the market also encouraged rural urbanization, as witnessed by the following examples.

1. "Nobody wants an urban *hukou* anymore"—Daning Management District, Dongguan

The Daning management district belongs to Humen township in the Dongguan Municipality. It covers 5 sq km and has 4,500 mu of arable land, mainly semi-sandy fields. The population is only 1,970, making the land more than the population can handle. For a long time, the area carried out the policy of putting grain crops first. In industry, it had one farm tools service station. The district was not even self-sufficient in vegetables. In 1979, total GVIAO was a mere 950,000 *yuan*, per-capita distribution coming to 223 *yuan*. With the era of reforms and the externally-oriented policies, Daning made use of its geographic proximity to Hong Kong and its *sanlai yibu* enterprises spurred overall industrial development. In 1991, it had thirty-odd *sanlai yibu* and *sanzi qiye*. GVIAO climbed to 30.528 million *yuan*. Revenue from *sanlai yibu* processing paid to the state was 17.18 million HK$; per-capita distribution was 1,800 *yuan*.

The locally registered population of the district has not increased in twenty years. This zero population growth can be attributed to the fact that, besides good family planning, many people had moved to Hong Kong, Humen Town, or other Dongguan townships. The labor force, therefore, has always been inadequate. Currently, the district has a labor force of fewer than nine hundred. They are working in many different occupations: About two hundred to three hundred as managerial personnel in enterprises, more than three hundred in transportation (there are more than two hundred cars here and a hundred drivers), and the rest, more than a hundred, in business or industry.

To make up for its labor shortage, Daning has absorbed large numbers of migrant labor. The district has from eight thousand to ten thousand seasonal migrant workers distributed in the following fields:

a. Around 90 percent work in the *sanlai yibu* and *sanzi* enterprises.
b. Some work on construction sites, digging or filling land or doing other handy jobs. These people generally have brought their families and live in shanties, forming shanty villages.
c. Planting subcontracted land, mainly bananas, sugarcane, and vegetables. Most of these are Hakka people (from Meixian county).
d. Subcontracting fish ponds for fish-breeding and duck-raising. There are about 200 duck raisers from Zhejiang Province who raise the ducks around the fish ponds and use duck manure as fish feed. The

management district is willing to appropriate funds to build sheds to house the ducks, the duck-raisers and their families. Several hundred thousand ducks are in their flocks.

Most of the migrant labor, around 70 percent, are women. This is because the *sanlai yibu* and *sanzi* enterprises are mainly engaged in labor-intensive work and employers like female workers, who are considered (a) obedient, (b) good at detail work, and (c) unlikely to get into fights. Males mainly work in occupations requiring more physical strength. Average worker wages come to 350 *yuan*; the highest is 2,000 to 3,000 *yuan*. Probationary workers get 250. Lodging is free and 24 *yuan* a month is paid for meals (the factories subsidize each worker from 50 to 60 *yuan*). The factories also take care of *hukou* status management fees, labor management fees, and labor insurance. The Management District takes relatively good care of the organization and life of migrant laborers, holding periodic karaoke parties for them and annual employees' sports meets. These are held at night after work and last for several hours, enabling "peasant workers" (*mingong*) to participate also. Each factory has a Youth League branch and smaller groups, which carry on normal organizational life. They also take Youth Leaguers to visit Shenzhen and Guangzhou. [These are part of the Communist Youth League system.—Ed.]

The district is divided into three natural villages and has three industrial zones. The first industrial zone is sited right next to the seat of the district; later zones were built along the Guangzhou-Shenzhen highway. The first one is the largest. The site used to be a stretch of desolate mountain land where people did not dare cross alone. Now it has become a vibrant center of activity with more than twelve thousand people. A business street has sprung up in front of the dormitories and crowds are thick at lunchtime hanging out or shopping. Stores are chiefly clothing, food, and department stores, plus barbershops and hairdressers, and photography studios. Stores were built by the district and leased out to owners, who include Chaozhou people, local residents and some *waishengren*. The last are mostly people who worked here before and saved enough money to open stores. The outlay is not small: Each storefront leases for 900 *yuan* a month besides paying a security deposit of 20,000 *yuan* to the district. Leases are for 5 years and penalties are exacted from the deposit if violations occur. The place is even busier at night with movie theaters and video arcades open for business and street vendors plying their trade. Hawkers sell mostly low-grade stuff, although they sometimes give good value for the money. Clothing, for instance, includes:

a. out-dated or out-of-season stuff;
b. imitation designer wear; and

c. synthetic clothing, the majority being imitation designer.

Vendors of other wares say their business is less profitable. Hair stylists and photo studios are doing well, probably because wanting to look good is human nature.

The Daning management district concentrates on building factories and basic facilities to attract outside investment. It pays little attention to developing its own industries. Services are at low levels, so most villagers, outside business people and other visitors go to Taiping township for their consumer needs. The district's major income derives from renting out factory buildings, revenue paid by industrial enterprises, and different management fees. Some of this revenue is used for investment and some for public welfare. Senior citizens over sixty, for instance, get 30–50 *yuan* a month as subsidies; all expenses are paid for the *wubaohu* (guarantees for the aged, infirm, elderly widows and widowers, and orphans) households. Education is free from elementary to senior middle school. Students in secondary specialized schools and colleges are each subsidized 500 *yuan* per year. One million *yuan* was used to build a new elementary school, subsidize teachers' wages, and buy buses to take secondary school students back and forth from school. Inside the district, every farmer is subsidized 100 *yuan* a year in addition to being provided with free or low-cost water, power, seeds, farm implements, and plastic crop covers. Tap water pipes, lighted ball courts, cultural and recreation centers, and cement roads linking with trunk highways have been built. With the reinforcing of the collective economy, more welfare benefits have been provided. Individual incomes have also risen.

In the past, people wanted to live in the urban areas and longed for urban registration status. The situation has now reversed. Many who have moved to the urban areas want to move back. Some urban *hukou* were given to the district in exchange for land requisitioned. Nobody wanted them and the district had to mobilize people to take them. Even though people in Daning know that their area is not yet a city, they feel it's quickly going to become one. Their road of industrialization has certainly been swift; new industrial zones are rising and new restaurants and parks are being built.

Daning's way of life has changed radically. An economic structure dominated by industry and supplemented by agriculture has replaced the former monolithic farming economy; agricultural output is now only a third that of industrial output. Very few Daning families are still working on the farms. The majority are in industry and the tertiary sector. The modern way of life has come into every home. Home appliances, furniture sets, multi-storied buildings, motorcycles and cars have now become widespread. Young people dress fashionably in designer clothes and use only brand-name items.

Daning has been greatly influenced by Hong Kong. First, it has thirteen hundred relatives and townspeople from Hong Kong and Macao. Seventy percent of Daning families have relatives outside the country and keep in close touch with them. Many Hong Kong relatives return for visits, and many Daning people go to Hong Kong to do business, study its ways, or tour. Second, most of the investors in *sanlai yibu* and *sanzi* categories are Hong Kong people, as are their major executives and technical personnel. Management practice follows "Hong Kong style." Third, there is the colony's media influence. Hong Kong TV and radio programs and cassettes and videos are very popular. People who have visited Hong Kong come back full of praise for Hong Kong management styles, efficiency, and sanitation conditions. Some bad things are also said to derive from Hong Kong such as venereal disease, gambling, and prostitution.

Economically Daning is not the strongest among Humen's twenty-five management districts. Longyan, Nanzha, and Beizha are all stronger. In the past, Daning was not on any major transportation line and Humen township had designated it a part of Beizha satellite town, but since the district built a highway passing by its industrial zone which links up with the Guangzhou-Shenzhen highway, transportation is now very convenient. The district has also devised a comprehensive land use plan to reasonably distribute the industrial and business zones and residential areas. Daning can therefore be called a model for rural urbanization.

2. Daoyue Management District, Gaoyao County

This management district belongs to Xinqiao township, Gaoyao County, and is 30 *li* from the city of Zhaoqing. It is on the periphery of the developed "Little Pearl River Delta." It has three natural villages, 11 production cooperatives, 736 households and 2,577 people. It has 1,500 *mu* of cultivated land of which 680 are rice paddies. This was formerly an impoverished area where per-capita income was only 150 *yuan* in 1978. By 1991, this had risen to 1,184 *yuan*. Unlike the instances described above, Daoyue's road to prosperity depended mainly on labor export and side lines. In 1991, its GVIAO was 6.2 million *yuan*, of which agriculture made up only 12 percent. There are three key economic sectors:

    a. Construction industry: It sends 500 construction workers to subcontract projects in Guangzhou, Zhaoqing, and other places in the Pearl River Delta;

    b. A handicrafts industry. Bambooware uses local resources; and

    c. Trade, business, and industry. An additional two hundred people have gone out from the district to work in fields other than construction.

Daoyue's industry is not well developed. It has only three small enterprises making 20,000 *yuan* of profit. It has, however, found its road to wealth by taking advantage of local assets and now ranks among the 10 wealthiest districts in Zhaoqing. Traditional hand-made bambooware has found a niche in modern society. With incomes rising, people no longer want to live in the old, one-story dwellings of the past; they have built new, multistory brick houses. From 1978 to 1992, 780 houses were newly built in the district as a whole and per-capita living space is now 15 sq m. The district's rural households now own 550 TV sets (of which about 30 percent are color TVs). Ninety percent have cassette recorders; 10–15 percent have VCRs. People also own 30–odd motorcycles and 5 cars.

Collective revenue is primarily put into public undertakings. An investment of 165,000 *yuan* was used to repair and build cement roads to encircle the district; 130,000 was invested to bring in piped water, building ball courts in elementary schools and expand cultural facilities.

Revenue is also used for welfare:

a. All people over sixteen who have local *hukou* are provided with life insurance;

b. A system of scholarships has been set up to encourage students to further their education and bonuses for successful teachers are also offered;

c. Retirement pensions are provided for cadre of the Management District and cooperatives, and

d. Collective funds are used to cover taxes and miscellaneous expenses that local rural households are obliged to pay.

Daoyue, too, is very much under Hong Kong's influence. First, because of frequent communication with Hong Kong relatives and friends, not only are local people affected by its life-style but also its thinking. Second, Hong Kong and Macao investment in the district in public undertakings such as schools, hospitals, and waterworks has also had widespread influence. Third, the influence of mass communication, chiefly movies, TV and videos from Hong Kong, is strong. The district is also strongly influenced by Guangzhou, with such influence felt in even more ways.

Big changes have taken place in local people's thinking and behavior in the wake of economic development and under the influence of Hong Kong, Guangzhou, and other big cities. This is especially true in attitude toward women. In the past, men in this area were looked upon more favorably than women, and women suffered discrimination, not even being allowed to work outside the home. Today, many young women leave the district to work and when they return, not only has their appearance changed but they have also become stronger in character, are no longer afraid of going out in public, and are more poised and independent. They have a relatively stronger sense of business and affairs.

3. Xiabu Management District, Sihui County

Xiabu has made a name for itself as one of the 10 wealthiest districts in

Zhaoqing. The district's Party Secretary is a deputy to the 14th Congress of the Communist Party. The district belongs to Qingtang township under Sihui County and is located 20–odd *li* from the county town. It is on hilly land and borders a range of mountains to its northwest. Transportation and geographic conditions are not very good; neither is it close to Hong Kong or Macao or is it a native place of overseas Chinese. Its development, therefore, is very significant.

In 1989, the place had a population of 3,621 in 875 households, among which 1,059 made up the labor force. Total GVIAO was 9.756 million *yuan*, of which industrial output was 5,853,600 *yuan*. Per-capita income was 1,112 *yuan*. In 1991, industrial output doubled and per-capita income rose to 1,800 *yuan*.

Xiabu's development is characterized by the following:

a. It had an early start. Beginning in 1978, it diversified vigorously and set up a number of enterprises. GVIAO that year shot up to 2.776 million *yuan*, of which 52.7 percent or 1,464,200 *yuan* was from industry, thus surpassing agricultural output. This compares favorably with Humen of Dongguan, where industrial output outstripped farm output only by 1984.

b. It uses local resources to develop industry. Potter's clay is plentiful in this hilly area and ceramics is a traditional cottage industry. Many potters had left to work in Shiwan in Foshan in the past. The district got some of them to return and start ceramics enterprises. In 1978, twenty-seven workshops were started (of which eleven belonged to the village and sixteen to the district), and this increased to forty in 1989. Although the increase is not large numerically, the size of the workshops expanded rapidly. The district has now set up an industrial zone with some large-scale enterprises. The industrial ceramics enterprise alone produces more than 10 million *yuan*'s worth a year.

c. It not only develops industry, but also forestry and fishery. Large tracts of mountain land have been planted with fruit trees, mainly mandarin oranges, which are excellent in quality and sell for good prices. Fisheries are another major occupation. They are one reason Xiabu's agricultural output is so high.

d. Transportation is well developed to meet the needs of raw material supply and product sales. In 1989, the district had eighty-nine tractors and thirteen trucks devoted to this purpose (output is hard to calculate because they were privately owned).

e. District officials think and act boldly to lead Xiabu forward. They also have a good work style. The district office has seven cadres. Except for one minding the office, all are out at the grassroots every day.

From Table 4.2, we can see that Xiabu's policy in agriculture is to raise

Table 4.2

Agriculture in Xiabu Management District

Item	1978	1989	Comparison
Paddy rice (*mu*)	4,516	3,300	-1,216
Rice output (kg)	2,421,050	2,380,000	-41,050
Per-*mu* yield (kg)	538	720	+182
Oranges (*mu*)	1,045	1,710	+665
Total output (kg)	*	450,000	+450,000
Fish ponds (*mu*)	615	1,325	+710
Total output (kg)	46,125	165,625	+119,500
Peanuts (*mu*)	326	547	+221
Total output (kg)	35,860	92,990	+57,130
Sugarcane (*mu*)	425	—	-425
Total output (kg)	1,700	—	-1,700

*Fruit trees start to produce three to four years after planting.

unit yields and reduce planting in low-value items. It has completely eliminated sugarcane which sells only for a few cents a kilogram and cannot
even cover costs. It has also reduced paddy rice acreage by 27 percent,
although output decreased only by 2 percent. The extra land was used to
breed fish. Thus revenue per unit area increased but manpower used was
decreased. Peanuts, which earn more, have also been expanded.

Like other areas, Xiabu began planned development after the economy
improved. The Management District built elementary and secondary
schools with 1978's floor space tripling by 1989. Basketball courts with
night lighting and cultural recreation centers were built. Roads were re-
paved with cement to link different villages. An industrial zone has been
established and social security improved.

A rise in personal income has brought improved living standards. Eighty
percent of the families have built new homes. Ninety percent have TV sets.
Bicycles (the major means of transportation) average 1 per 1.8 persons; this
also implies the rise in nonagricultural population, who need to bike to
different types of work. Xiabu people are proud of the fact that they were
able to blaze their own trail without outside help. With its 6,000 *mu* of
forests, revenue promises to shoot up once the timber is ready for harvest.
The trees have also improved the environment.

Industrial Zones and Urbanization

Many different types of industrial zones have sprung up in the municipalities, townships and even villages of the Pearl River Delta. Although the aim was to develop industry, the objective result was to simultaneously promote urbanization in the districts themselves as well as their vicinities. Development of Nangang township and the villages under its jurisdiction as described above, for instance, is related to the rise of the Guangzhou Economic and Technical Development Zone. The Guangzhou Zone itself has shaped up into a community of more than ten thousand people that not only has industry but also banks, communications, financial services, restaurants, and other services. These in turn affect surrounding rural areas. The village industrial zone of Daning management district has also resulted in the rise of a commercial and services area because of the influx of migrant workers. Below, we will examine the example of the Shekou Industrial Zone, "Both a community and an enterprise."

This zone is located in the Shenzhen Special Economic Zone (SEZ) at the eastern bank of the Pearl River estuary by the Shenzhen Gulf and faces Hong Kong's New Territories district across a narrow band of water. Formerly, it was a stretch of desolate land uninhabited except by a few fishermen and their families. The industrial zone started construction in July 1979 and completed the first phase in 1982. Currently, the zone's total area is 9.3 sq km and its population has reached over fifty thousand. It has a harbor with annual freight capacity of 9 million tons, 288 *sanzi* enterprises, and 80 zone-owned enterprises. GVIO in 1991 was 3.35 billion *yuan*. In both rate of growth and per-capita output value, it is top-notch.

The Shekou Industrial Zone's development model is unique, and an important characteristic is that it is "both a community and an enterprise." The zone's management committee is also the enterprise's management as well as the administrative management agency of this community. Cadres assume a dual role, being both enterprise managers and community managers. The zone has not set up neighborhood organizations; it is itself a company belonging to the Hong Kong Mercantile Investment Corporation and its full name is "Mercantile Investment Corporation of Shekou Industrial Zone." Thus, even though it is located inside Shenzhen, it does not belong to the latter and has few ties with it. It is a "special zone" within a Special Zone. With the rapid growth of Shenzhen, however, Shekou is starting to feel left behind.

Shekou Industrial Special Zone has the following characteristics:
  a. Geographic environment. It is situated at the tip of a peninsula, a hub
     of water transport but relatively inconvenient by land. It is twenty

nautical miles away from central Hong Kong and offers fourteen daily roundtrips to Hong Kong in addition to daily runs to Macao, Zhuhai, and Guangzhou. It has extremely close ties with Hong Kong, including, besides trade, the influence of the latter's media. Apart from TV programs, Hong Kong newspapers are sold in Shekou on the same day. With its relatively independent geographical location, it is not very much affected by the political mood in the rest of the nation. This is perhaps why the reformers selected Shekou to become China's first special zone.

ı. Population structure. Shekou's population structure has the typical features of immigrant communities:

   i.   Swift population growth. At the end of 1979, it had a population of only 144. This grew to 5,203 in 1983, 45,000 in 1990, and surpassed 50,000 in 1992.

   ii.   In age structure, the zone is mainly populated by young people. One sees only young people on the streets—described by some as "somewhat like a street scene after a major disaster in a sci-fi film." According to statistics, average age was twenty-seven in 1992; 85 percent were under thirty-five.

   iii.   Concentrated occupational distribution. Employees in industry make up 85 percent.

   iv.   Gender. Females greatly exceed males. Of people under thirty, 79 percent are women.

   v.   Education. The level is high. Eleven percent are college graduates; 40 percent graduates of secondary and specialized schools and 40 percent junior middle school graduates.

c. Characteristics of economic structure.

   i.   Industry is predominant while the proportion in the tertiary sector is not large.

   ii.   In industry, electronics and electric appliances, clothing and textile enterprises predominate, making up 60 percent.

   iii.   Labor-intensive industrial enterprises still occupy a high proportion; examples are textiles and electronics enterprises.

   iv.   Foreign-oriented enterprises are predominant. Exports make up 70 percent of total industrial output.

d. Multiculturism. Shekou is an immigrant community with people from all regions including Guangdong's Chaozhou and Hakka districts and many people from Jiangsu, Zhejiang, Sichuan, and Beijing. Each brought their own local cultures, making Shekou a multicultural community. In language, for instance, Putonghua (Mandarin) is the lingua franca, which makes it unique in the Pearl River Delta. Food customs are also varied and include the Sichuan, Chaozhou, Guangdong, Hunan, and Beijing cuisines. Holidays and celebrations are diverse, as are different styles of life.

As an immigrant community, there is great population mobility. Whether a person stays on depends to a large extent on the person's education level and ability to adjust. As a special zone, household registration and border checks are strict. It is not easy to get a local zone *hukou*. All those with a Shekou *hukou* can enjoy a package of benefits including allocation of housing, home purchase on favorable terms, schooling, free medical treatment, and retirement pensions. There's a *hukou* quota, generally accorded management and technical personnel and senior workers. These people call themselves "white-collar" workers and others "blue-collar" workers. The "blue-collar" workers can be divided into contract workers and temporary workers. The latter are seasonal workers or "rotation workers" from the interior (this is a unique Shekou employee practice, in which local enterprises sign contracts with inland enterprises in the same lines or with their parent companies in the interior for the latter to supply skilled workers for a rotation of one to two years). Contract workers are [technical] personnel recruited through various channels such as invitation, examination, and screening; they have the possibility of obtaining a local *hukou*, a status that workers in general can hardly have access to. The wide gap between white- and blue-collar workers in Shekou is seldom found elsewhere. According to our survey, the white-collar stratum feel very good and consider themselves to be true "Shekou people," while the blue-collar stratum are discontented with their work and try hard to improve their position.

Shekou was the dream of the older generation of Chinese leaders, who hoped to make the country strong through industry. Industrial enterprises are therefore predominant in Shekou and services are not a priority. As an industrial zone, Shekou is not much different from other industrial zones in the interior in that the enterprises run society. The difference is in management methods and hiring practices. For the enterprise to run society was a necessity in the early days of Shekou, and it also proved effective. However, with the expansion of the zone, the burdens increased and became impediments to its development. This is particularly obvious in the way the traditional registration system is used to divide the population into "Shekou people" (*Shekouren*) and "non-Shekou people" (*feiShekouren*), a polarization reinforced by a package of benefits. The resultant stratum polarization will also affect its development.

Abutting on the Industrial Zone lies Shekou Town, which has also boomed on the strength of the zone's development. The two areas run into each other and most people no longer make any distinction between the two. The township is actually in the center of the zone. Though only 1.5 sq km, the township has five thousand permanent inhabitants and ten thousand temporary inhabitants. The place used to be a small fishing village. Most residents had dual registration status (Hong Kong/Macao ID and mainland *hukou*) and fishing was the chief occupation. Up until 1984, the township GVIAO was 2.6 million *yuan*. By 1992, industrial output had jumped to 500 million. Economic growth rate and rise in living standards both surpassed the Industrial Zone's. The township's development can be attributed to industrial zone development. First, the zone caused township land to appreciate. Second, since outsiders make no distinction between the zone and the township, investors have spilled over to the township. Third, because of land shortage in the zone, strict restrictions were imposed on development of labor-intensive enterprises inside the zone after 1985, and the township became the natural site for such enterprises. Fourth, the township's service industry, including commerce, real estate and farmer's markets, boomed to make up for the lack in the zone. These are the reasons that, even with a late start, the township developed so swiftly.

There was no planning in township development. The town simply took advantage of its proximity to the zone to make fewer investments in transportation and communications. It also did not have to take care of benefits such as employee housing. Though a boom town, most permanent inhabitants remain with farming or fishing *hukou* status. They are unwilling to change to urban status because peasants are allotted land to build housing while urban residents have to buy land for the same purpose. As land appreciated and rents mounted, nobody wanted a worthless urban *hukou*. This shows that reform of the *hukou* system which separates urban from rural residents is indispensable.

Discussion

In the above, we have described four types of rural urbanization in the Pearl River Delta. Below, we will discuss two pertinent problems.

1. Administrative confusion.

According to statistics provided by public security departments of Beijing, Wuhan, and Guangzhou, the crime rates in integrated urban-rural areas are far higher than that in cities and rural areas. That is why the authors consider integrated urban-rural areas (or rural communities on the fringe of cities) key areas for comprehensive urban administration. Why? First, because these rural communities are under no one's control. Within a village, there are several to dozens of state-owned enterprises and units which belong to different "strips" of command. They have little interaction; some have a lot of conflicts. Local governments are powerless over them. In addition, some village inhabitants are registered in the cities and some in the villages. Some families have switched to urban *hukou* and some have not. One village has both villagers' committees and residents' committees. Without a unified management agency to oversee the different systems, nobody is in control. Management of locals is thus poor, not to speak of managing a migrant population.

Second, in such communities, the inhabitants have considerable living space. Some own two to three multistory houses, some as many as five. Extra space is rented out. Rural communities should theoretically be short of land, but they actually have a lot of unoccupied land on the edges of villages, between the buildings of different organizations, or land already requisitioned but not put to use. These become places where migrants set up their own communities. In addition, there are plots allotted for peasants' self-use which have been left uncultivated. They either remain unused or are subcontracted by migrants, whose whole families live on it in temporary shacks. That is why such communities can absorb such large numbers of outsiders, who come from complex family backgrounds, are extremely mobile, and are very hard to manage. Most migrants live with relatives or *tongxiang* [people from their home county—Ed.] and their communities become "villages within villages" (or villages within urban areas), which add to the problem.

Third, lifestyles are changing rapidly in such communities and people have problems in adapting. On the one hand, many people have lost their land and have to give up farming ways. This is a sudden change not everyone can adjust to. On the other hand, many people suddenly get rich from large land requisition payments. Some use them to invest; some squander them. Some communities have been successful in employing these funds to leverage more prosperity and to build for the public good. However, because people no longer have to work, idlers have appeared, resulting in confusion in community life as well as a rise in gambling, drugs, prostitution, and burglaries.

2. Overly drawn-out urbanization process.

A common characteristic of these communities is the length of their urbanization process. This process started very early in Nanji and Lujiang villages, but neither has completed it to date. An overly long process of urbanization is neither favorable to comprehensive urban planning nor to comprehensive improvement of urban transportation, environment, and security. There are three major factors impeding the advance of urbanization: The first is the household registration system. In China, this system is the major urban-rural divider. Urban registration has been strictly controlled to limit urban population growth. Before 1980, it was most difficult to get an urban *hukou* and thus become consumers of commodity grain. In the early 1980s, fissures appeared in this wall and urban *hukou* status became available to people who provided their own food grain or who bought commodity housing, or who purchased *hukous* outright. Dongji and Xiji, Nanji village's two hamlets, both obtained urban registration status because their land was entirely requisitioned in 1988. A few years later, more rural *hukou* households appeared because by regulation registration status followed the mother and young men in the villages mostly married girls with rural *hukou* from other places or provinces, which meant that their offspring had rural *hukou* status as well. Moreover, Nanji village was still implementing a rural management system, which made increases in rural *hukou* easy. From the perspective of registration status, therefore, the coexistence of urban and rural status will continue.

The second reason is the question of land management. In China, urban land is state-owned while rural land is collectively owned. This policy affects the urbanization process of rural communities on city peripheries. Before 1985, compensation for requisitioned land was not high and villagers still wanted to switch to an urban *hukou*. As land prices rose, community and individual assets also grew and living standards improved. Villagers were no longer willing to switch status because, as members of the rural collective, they were eligible to be allotted land. Another major reason was that urban residents were given no land for dwellings while rural inhabitants were. This was a sizable source of wealth especially for people with several houses as real estate developed and land appreciated in the 1990s. Moreover, by that time urban registration status no longer came with rationed grain and edible oil supply and were no longer much use to rural inhabitants. Some families which had switched to urban status or who had become urban workers now quit their jobs and returned to the villages or spent money to buy back a rural *hukou*. This phenomenon of switching from spending money to buy urban *hukou* to spending money to buy rural *hukou* is deeply thought-provoking. What indeed is the future of the registration system?

The third factor impeding urbanization is the density of building in rural communities, which makes it hard to be incorporated by cities. Most such communities grew without planning and housing densities generally exceed that in cities. Buildings vary from two to five stories. No companies or *danwei* could afford to requisition their land and would not do so even if they could afford it. When the Guangzhou Economic and Technical Development Zone was buying land, it was unable to relocate Xiji and Dongji hamlets. An increasing number of rural communities on city outskirts thus became "villages within cities" and any effort to renovate would have to come from the hamlets themselves. This of course affects overall urban development.

The urban-rural conflict will thus remain for a long time. As more and more rural communities become "villages within cities," increasingly sharper conflicts will occur between villagers and surrounding enterprises and undertakings. The living environment deteriorates and pollution worsens. Rural collectives frequently exact monies beyond land compensation or make other requests. Most *danwei* are forced to accede to their wishes. After a time, this becomes the rule. If units do not come through, villagers stage demonstrations or dig up roads and cut off water and power supply. "Lifting" things from *danwei* in the vicinity (building materials, coal or iron) is even more common. To some villagers, this is their major source of income. Quarrels and fights, even gang fights, often break out. Estrangement and tension results, affecting normal community work and life.

To bring about all-around community improvement, a unified management agency must be set up in place of the former pluralistic management. Current neighborhood administrative organizations are at too low a level and not very effective. The residents' committees set up by large enterprises or *danwei* are merely nominal. There must also be coordination among urban and rural grass-roots organizations and units. Housing rentals must be put under more stringent control. Surplus space should be taxed, or a pertinent system established. Management of unused land should be reinforced and illegally built shacks taken down. Moral and ethical education should be strengthened and new "civilized villages" built. Investments and consumption should be guided in the right direction, so that people who have lost their land can quickly adapt to their new life.

To speed up urbanization of integrated urban-rural areas, urban planning regulations must first be enforced so that growth complies with overall planning. Second, development zones should accomplish land and *hukou* adjustments in status all at once. Third, a dual system of land ownership does not fit current conditions and should undergo reform. Fourth, rural planning should be quickly implemented; and can be planned just as if they were small urban districts. Fifth, construction of private housing should be strictly controlled. Owners of buildings exceeding size regulations should be fined and the buildings torn down. Sixth, ad hoc street-side free markets should be abolished and market control unified.

The Delta's Transformation

Rural urbanization, simply put, is the process of changing from a rural to urban way of life. It has five key dimensions:

a. Change in population structure; increase in nonagricultural population;

b. Change in production mode with relative increases in the proportion of the secondary and tertiary sectors; agricultural management changes from the traditional to the externally oriented mode, farm products becoming commodities, and agriculture modernizes;

c. Life-style elements such as clothing, food, housing, and transportation all undergo the changes wrought by urbanization.

d. Spread of mass media to rural society in the wake of rising living standards, becoming a motivating force of social change;

e. Change in thinking, turning from conservative, backward and old-fashioned thinking to open, modern and enterprising thinking; rise in educational and cultural level and human quality.

These five changes have all taken place in the townships and villages of the Pearl River Delta to varying degrees (Table 4.3).

a. Change in population structure. Table 4.1 showed that nonagricultural population in the Pearl River Delta rose from 4.8135 million in 1980 (27.3 percent of total) to 7.9769 million (37.6 percent of total) in 1991. Apart from the natural increase in the urban population and the relocation of urban dwellers from elsewhere, the major reason for this upturn is the switch from agricultural to nonagricultural status among the local population. Another segment of the locals who relocated to urban areas are called "three self-supporting" people (they take care of their own food grain, employment and housing). They make up a sizable proportion of the market towns and are confusing to tabulate. In Xinqiao township's periphery, for instance, they make up nearly half the population. The proportion may be even higher in *jizhen* in developed areas (referring to the population of towns which have become districts).

In regard to the change in the structure of the labor force, beginning in 1985, there was already more nonagricultural as compared to agricultural labor power in the Pearl River Delta. By 1990, 90 percent of the labor power in developed villages in the lesser Pearl River Delta were nonagriculture (in the local population alone). Accurate figures are difficult to arrive at because many people work in agriculture during the farming seasons while working in industry or other occupations at other times. In many townships, "farming-season holidays" are given. This is a unique feature of township enterprises.

Despite having left agricultural production, this 90 percent of the population actually "left the land but not the rural districts," that is, they still live in the villages while they work in the townships. A couple of years ago, during the morning rush hour, people on bicycles streamed into the urban

Table 4.3

Comparison of Six Villages' or Management Districts' Key Indicators (1991)

	Daning	Longyan	Nanshan	Xiabu[a]	Nanji	Daoyue
Total population	1,970	1,850	3,400	3,621	4,080	2,577
Nonagricultural labor force[b] (%)	90	90	95	66	97	80
GVIAO[c] (10,000 y.)	3,052.8	3,679	4,337	975.6	4,000	620
GVIO[c] (10,000 y.)	2,320	3,377	3,339	585	3,800[d]	545.6
% of indus. output in total output	76	91.7	77	60	95	88
Per capita income (y.)	1,800	1,720	2,200	1,112	4,200	1,182
Revenue paid by industry (10,000 H.K.$)	3,200	1,718	3,700	—	600	—

[a]1989 data.
[b]As percentage of total labor force.
[c]GVIAO = Gross Value Industrial and Agricultural Output; GVIO = Gross Value Industrial Output.
[d]Calculated as total of interest payments and rents received.

areas and, at day's end, streamed back. Now most people ride motorcycles. This phenomenon is no different from that in modern cities in the West; only the commuter vehicles differ.

   b. Change in production mode. This change is demonstrated in the Pearl River Delta by the following:

      i.   Greater industrial than agricultural output. If that of the tertiary sector is included, the proportion of agriculture is even smaller. In many developed areas, agricultural output is less than 5 percent of total social output.

ii. Adjustment of productive structure. In the 1980s, the emphasis was rural industry, and rural areas competed in raising industrial output. In the 1990s, the tertiary sector became the focus, and it served the primary and secondary sectors while promoting their development. The proportion of the service sector's output reaches as high as 40 percent of the total output in some areas and 20–30 percent in most areas.

iii. Updating and upgrading of rural industry. Rural industry started with labor-intensive products requiring low technical skill and minimal cost. Some were cottage industries. After a period of capital accumulation, rural areas began to invest in capital-intensive and technology-intensive enterprises. Original enterprises have also been renovated and updated. The *sanlai yibu* enterprises, which formed the largest number, have now changed into joint, cooperative, or foreign ventures (the *sanzi* enterprises) or put under local management.

iv. Changes in the way enterprises are managed. In the past, the township governments were directly in charge of these enterprises. Now they are under the charge of specialized departments and have more independence. In more developed townships, different types of company groups have formed linking all enterprises in the same system or of the same type, thus making large-scale management possible. The past situation of "small boats can easier shift direction" has changed to "large ships do not fear wind and waves."

Agricultural management has also changed radically. First, diversification took place. High-cost, high-quality products were chosen. Within agriculture, a big structural change is the large-acreage reduction of grain crops and sugar cane and corresponding increase in cash crops and fish-breeding. Fruit, vegetables, flowers, pond fish, and poultry have expanded swiftly to supply the world market through neighboring Hong Kong and Macao. The delta's agriculture is externally oriented and output increases rapidly. Before 1988, people thought that money could buy all the grain needed and grain acreage was sharply curtailed. In 1988, a severe grain shortage resulted and grain prices skyrocketed. Neighboring provinces refused to supply grain, and Guangdong was forced to import it from other countries with precious foreign currency. Under the circumstances, the new slogan was "without industry, no wealth and without agriculture, no security," and guidelines were set for minimum permissible output of rice, and so per-unit yield went up by a large margin. Second, the management mode of agriculture changed. With the rise of externally-oriented agriculture, a host of "consolidated trading-industrial-agricultural companies" (at the village and township levels) were set up after 1986. The "trade" here referred to foreign trade, "industry" to industrial processing, and "agriculture" to farm production. Such production systems promoted industry and agriculture for foreign trade needs. Since entering the 1990s, a new form of organization was born out of necessity, called "company plus farming household." The agricultural trading company organizes the processing and sales of farm products produced by peasants. The company signs contracts with peasants and the two share the risks. These companies thus link thousands of peasant households, forming production bases of some scale. The former is responsible for supplying fine strains of seeds, fertilizers and other necessary production items and providing technical personnel for periodic instruction. Peasant households fulfill the contracts and sell produce to the companies. Such companies organizing fruit, vegetable, fish, poultry, and flower production are burgeoning. In the authors' view, under the conditions of the output contracting system and dispersed farming, such an organizational form is quite appropriate.

c. Change in life-style. In the Pearl River Delta, the rural life-style is now scarcely different from its urban counterpart. In developed townships, living standards and incomes are in fact higher than those in large and mid-sized cities. Younger people dress like Hong Kong residents in designer jeans and designer sneakers. Makeup and permed hair are common among the women. People over 50, however, still dress casually. People clad in loose farm-style clothes and sandals and carrying fat checkbooks while strolling into local restaurants is one sight you will find only in Guangdong. As for entrepreneurs (of rural township enterprises), *getihu,* and rural officials, they wear designer shirts and Western suits.

Villagers now live a lot better than urban dwellers. Most own multistory houses (those symbols of cities!) decorated in ever fancier styles. The interior design also shows rising western influence. Houses have multiple bathrooms and living rooms fitted with cocktail bars. Some bedrooms are flanked by wide balconies and greenhouses where flowers are grown. The latter beautify the environment and the sale of the flowers possibly add to household income. Whereas people used to make their own furniture, now they buy the latest styles of furniture from the stores.

Villagers in the delta have always been health conscious. This plus the fact that housing is built only in planned areas has given residential areas a garden-like appearance. Some villages now have paved roads, sidewalks shaded by trees and night lighting on the streets, making them no different from the cities. Per-capita living space averages 15 sq m and more. Every house has power and more are installing tap water. Peasants now eat better than urban people. They no longer raise their own vegetables on their own plots but buy fresh vegetables, rice, and edible oil from street fairs. Bigger villages have street markets, daily, while townships have farmer's markets. Some villagers eat breakfasts in *dim sum*-style teahouses or buy snacks for breakfast. Styles of food are diversifying, including traditional Cantonese food, Western style bread and pastries, and northern Chinese dumplings (*jiaozi*) and fried fritters (*you tiao*). Some families have refrigerators to store food.

In transportation, bicycles were formerly the major means of conveyance and everyone in the family (except children and the elderly) owned one. They were generally used within a radius of 10 *li*. Motorcycles have now also become widespread and are found in large numbers on township streets. Young people are especially fond of them and use them not only to get around but to make money as a taxi service. Some individuals own mid-sized buses, and they cooperate by each running a section of major roads, linking up with others to create long-distance passenger transportation. The authors had the experience of changing buses three times to go from Guangzhou to Zhuhai. Passengers were "sold" from one bus to the other, locally called "selling piglets" (*mai jujai*). This method has actually become popular among private bus owners throughout the country. Large buses are owned by the state, the collective, or individuals, but because of subcontracting, they are all run by *getihu*. Furthermore, some townships also have train and boat transport. Because of the many means of transportation available, most of which work around the clock, travelling is very convenient. Traffic jams are a problem throughout the delta. For instance, when we went to Humen, which was only ninety kilometers away, it took from 1 in the afternoon until 7 in the evening. Of course, a new highway has now been completed and an expressway is under construction, and traffic conditions should improve. One can no longer find any villagers who have never visited Guangzhou or some medium-sized city or other. Entrepreneurs, marketing and sales people and individual business people travel throughout the country. Judging from food, clothing, living conditions and transportation, there is no longer any apparent distinction between urban and rural areas in the Pearl River Delta.

d. Spread of mass media. In our view, along with rural development and the progress of rural urbanization, the networks formed by kinship, common dwelling place, and social strata no longer meet the people's need for an overarching framework which integrates culture with society. They have been replaced by the mass media. The expanded role of the media is, therefore, a major feature of rural urbanization. In fact, the media is a major channel through which urban influences reach the rural areas. Media influence has been especially strong in the Pearl River Delta because of media infrastructure construction and the expansion of information channels.

In Guangdong Province as a whole, a media network has been formed with the central city Guangzhou as the primary source and mid-sized cities as the secondary source of radiation to the smaller cities and townships. In 1990, the province had 87 radio stations and 39 television stations, 89 A-class cable channels (which could air their own shows) and 176 B-class cable channels. Hotels for foreign visitors provided 227 closed circuit channels and shared 3,041 antennas. In 1990, the province published a total of 2,248 book titles in 280.69 million copies, 91 newspapers of which 4 had circulations over 600,000, and 5 periodicals with circulations of over 700,000 copies each. Ninety percent of the facilities are concentrated in large or mid-sized cities.

Because of proximity to Hong Kong, this region is also affected by the Hong Kong media. Hong Kong has state-of-the-art telecommunication networks and mass media facilities as well as 100 international news agencies, presses and radio stations. It is a center of global information. Two TV networks in Hong Kong air four full schedules daily (two in English and two in Cantonese). A satellite station set up in 1991 broadcasts round-the-clock in Mandarin to Southeast Asia and the major part of the Chinese mainland. Hong Kong has, in addition, twelve radio broadcast stations. These TV and radio networks are all accessible in the Pearl River Delta. Hong Kong publishing is even more developed. Its publications exceed Guangdong's in number. Macao's media also reaches the western parts of the delta near that Portuguese colony.

The delta has adequate receptors for media information. According to a random sampling conducted by the Statistical Bureau in 1990, every hundred urban households owned 74.53 color TV sets, 33.33 black-and-white TV sets, and 77.33 cassette recorders. In our survey of rural Pearl River Delta homes, we found 83.2 percent of the families owned TV sets (both color and black and white), 10 percent owned VCRs, and a higher rate of cassette recorders as compared to cities.

Television is a major media tool. TV sets and the *TV Weekly* (*Dianshe Zhoubao*) have spread very fast in the delta, with 100 percent of the families in developed areas and over 70 percent of the families in peripheral areas owning sets and subscriptions.

According to our research, the Hong Kong media is more influential than Guangdong's. Seventy-three percent and 53 percent of the delta's inhabitants respectively receive Hong Kong TV and radio. Guangdong and other local programs are second in popularity. Very few people watch or listen to the Central station. [The key Chinese TV outlet for "official" Beijing news and views; broadcast of course in Putonghua.—Ed.]

The Guangdong and Hong Kong mass media are playing a major role in promoting economic development and cultural integration in the Pearl River Delta. Aside from providing business information they also help delta people form new economic concepts and learn new ways in production, distribution, management and trade. Culturally, they broaden and homogenize the delta's culture. In language, for instance, delta dialects are losing ground to Guangzhou and Hong Kong standards as speakers of the local patois get fewer and fewer.

The mass media not only helps people in the delta learn about the world but also helps develop local connections beyond their previous horizons. Such ties are more subtle and effective than administrative ties and have a more direct bearing on changes in rural ways of life and thinking. Today, the thinking of people in the delta is extremely liberated and strongly commercial, and people have a lot of enterprising spirit.

e. Changes in thinking. The thinking of the people in the Pearl River Delta has evolved from the traditional to the modern. We conducted a survey entitled "Culture, Education, and Modernity" with a set of indices of modernity including motivation concepts of family, achievement, old-fashioned habits, and concepts of authority. We compared the Pearl River Delta to other places in terms of these four dimensions and discovered that the former had higher marks in modernity, especially in motive for achievement, reflecting a willingness to invest and an enterprising spirit. The authors are of the opinion that the change in the thinking of the delta people is the single most important factor and the crux of its success in economic development.

Paths of Development

The trigger mechanism of rural urbanization in the delta is multifaceted. Humen is a traditional market town with a long history, some periods of which were prosperous. Decline set in after the Anti-Japanese War. Its reinvigoration can be attributed to processing for foreign clients (*sanlai yibu*). Superficially, the injection of Hong Kong capital, or what is commonly referred to as the advantage of being close to Hong Kong and Macao, was what set it off. Upon deeper thought, however, a question arises. Why was it that Humen and nearby Shunde County were the earliest to begin outside processing, and not Baoan (Shenzhen had not yet become a city) and Zhuhai, which were closest to Hong Kong and Macao? The answer is in the liberated thinking of Humen and Shunde and their alacrity in accepting new ideas and things. Dongguan municipality set up an office in charge of foreign processing which took care of registration of enterprises in this industry. Applicants could be registered in half a day if all documents were ready. In 1978 when reform and the open policy was first implemented, capitalism was still regarded as a monster, and this idea was not easy to overcome. That was the reason that *sanlai yibu* first began in Dongguan and Shunde, then Nanhai and Zhongshan. These four regions later became the "four dragons" of the Pearl River Delta (the "four dragons" later also took different roads of development). Humen accumulated funds and experience through processing and later built its own industry and services. Its services started relatively early, and this was the reason for the township's rapid development and reform. The secret of Humen's rapid accumulation of funds was large-scale hiring of cheaper migrant labor, while local labor was put into tertiary industries such as transportation, food and beverages, and commerce. Migrant labor, besides working in the factories, also worked on specialized farms. Humen was thus able to increase farm output simultaneously with development of the secondary and tertiary sectors. As agriculture here is externally oriented and products are of high quality and sell for good prices mainly in Hong Kong and Macao, it still retains a relatively significant proportion of total output. The division of labor here is such that migrant labor is in the frontlines of production and Humen's local labor force is mainly devoted to goods distribution and sales and management.

Daoyue management district under Xinqiao township in Gaoyao County is situated in Guangdong's hinterland and relatively far from Hong Kong and Guangzhou. In 1978, it was a poor area with per-capita annual income reaching only 145 *yuan*. Its road of development was unique in that it utilized local human and material resources. It drew on its traditional craft of bambooware. It also had many native sons and daughters dispersed in Hong Kong, Macao and other places, through whom it set up networks of foreign sales. Such handicrafts needed little investment and had few risks. They could be made at home. By linking the families, relevant companies were able to utilize large amounts of dispersed labor for relatively large-scale production. Though similar in form to traditional cottage industry, this type of industry has now linked up with the global market. Daoyue's second major industry is construction, another industry requiring little investment but intensive labor. The delta has been building on a large scale and has a great need for construction. This industry, too, gets big returns from little investment. Xinqiao's auto repair industry is also a local mainstay. It has a geographic advantage there because of the Zhaoqing-Yungfu and Xinxing county highways passing through.

Many market towns in the peripheral areas of the Pearl River Delta have similar experiences as that of Xinqiao's—that of making the best of local assets and starting with businesses that require little investment but make big profits and absorb a lot of labor, such as construction teams, building materials factories (brick, cement, timber) or labor export. Labor exported to more developed areas not only brings income but also technology and experience. After accumulating funds, returning migrants then start their own industries. This was also the road taken by Xiabu in Qingtang township of Sihui, which utilized its pottery clay resources to expand its traditional ceramics industry. Before 1978, local potters had all left to work in Foshan's Shihwan. After 1978, they were invited to come back to set up ceramics factories. Starting with hand crafting and backward tools, these factories now have automatic production lines and are growing in size. Xiabu also emphasizes agriculture, especially orange-growing and fish-breeding, and is thus able to maintain agricultural growth.

Nanji's economic startup took yet another path. It acquired large sums of money abruptly because of land requisition by the state. At first, the investment strategy was conservative — that of depositing money in the bank for interest. With the depreciation of the RMB, this became unprofitable and it began to look for other uses for its funds. Again, it utilized local assets, in this case, expansion of storage facilities to lease to enterprises in the development zone. Then it bought fleets of cars and excavators to fill land for the development zone and Huangpu Harbor. Finally it built its own industrial zone and set up joint, cooperative and foreign ventures (*sanzi* enterprises) as well as industrial processing for foreign clients. Because Nanji started out with the most funds, it was the one most afraid of taking risks and losing money as a result of careless investment. It therefore adopted the safest investment methods (each major project had to be approved at coop members' meetings). Gradually, however, it did set up its own enterprises. The village is now planning to build malls and commercial buildings and develop real estate, so that its money can earn a better return. The official in charge of planning, however, told us with some misgiving that "this may be hard to pass at the members' meeting, because older people are so conservative."

Despite diverse take-off modes, industry and services developed in all these townships. The townships, while growing self-reliantly, made increasingly large financial contributions to the country. Larger collective income also provided local people with better social services through construction of such facilities as roads, drainage, communications and power.

Townships and villages also followed set plans when establishing industrial and residential areas. They all followed a similar process wherein their industries were at first dispersed, then became more concentrated. The earliest enterprises were either located on the original sites of commune or brigade enterprises, empty houses belonging to the collective, or civilian houses. Some remain so to this day. Later enterprises were concentrated in planned zones. Total concentration is not something that can be done over the short term, because enterprises are owned by individuals, groups of families, or the collective. Local populations have already put issues of environment, sanitation and pollution on their agendas. The final resolution will depend on them. Environmental conditions are comparatively better in townships and villages which are economically viable, since they understand the importance of optimizing the investment environment.

Despite the problems that remain in market town development in the Pearl River Delta, generally speaking, transportation, communications, housing, energy and benefits in *jizhen* (including seats of counties which have changed into municipalities) are better than existing cities, especially large cities. Actually, large and mid-sized cities often take advantage of counties under their jurisdiction to expand their own urban area, they pass from "cities administering counties" to "cities plundering counties"; that is one reason counties and townships greatly resent the system whereby cities have jurisdiction over counties. Many counties request to be changed into cities in order to gain relative autonomy. In national policy, counties and cities are accorded different treatment, the latter getting more autonomy than the former and legally allowed to retain a part of their revenues for city construction. After counties become cities, however, there are new problems. They have to start their own service systems. Furthermore, municipalities to which they formerly belonged (municipalities at the local level), such as Jiangmen and Foshan, are deprived of a hinterland, becoming isolated isles. The outcome of rural urbanization should be better coordination between cities and rural areas and among cities, not opposition between new and old cities.

Judging from the Pearl River Delta, the basis of market town development is the village or management district. Even though villages within the same township experience uneven development, there will always be a few that form the mainstay. Many scholars feel that township enterprises should be concentrated in the towns so that village populations shift toward them; the concentration of industry will also give it the scale necessary for best results. This may be an ideal outcome and may take some time to realize. As described above, even the relative concentration of rural industry took many years. In the past, the hope was that cities would stimulate the rural areas. This was tried for 30 years without much result. Counties were put under city jurisdiction precisely for this reason, but it did not work, and cities, on the contrary, exploited the counties. That was why counties had to be given "independence" and change into cities themselves. Similarly, county towns could not stimulate townships. Townships developed on their own power. One experience that was successful in the Pearl River Delta was the township's way of letting "all five wheels turn together" (the county, township, village, multifamily enterprises, and *getihu*) so that every stratum was motivated. This was the way that these townships left poverty behind and accumulated funds.

In Taiwan's experience of industrialization, industry also went to the rural areas in the 1960s and numerous individual village industrial enterprises were formed. As modern large industry developed on the basis of capital accumulation, however, product costs dropped and quality improved. Rural industry could in no way compete with it because of higher wages and inferior product quality. Rural industry gradually disappeared. With the decline in rural industry, the population began to concentrate in cities and towns, turning all Taiwan into a highly urbanized region. In the authors' opinion, it was precisely because of its period of rural industrialization that Taiwan's urbanization did not have the huge unemployment problem other developing countries did. Taiwan's experience can perhaps be helpful to the Pearl River Delta in demonstrating that, savage as competition is, by the time individual or multifamily enterprises are forced to shut down, they may have already accumulated enough capital to turn to something else. Administrative control and designation of "priorities" will only backfire.

From Table 4.3, we can see that industrial output at the village level of the localities cited have all surpassed agricultural output and that nonagricultural labor has become predominant. These have become "stars" on the local horizon, making the townships that have jurisdiction over them "stars" as well. They show that only when all levels of industry are developed do market town prosperity and rural urbanization transpire.

Conclusion

The above case studies and analyses show that the Pearl River Delta is a successful model of rural urbanization. Some people consider "rural urbanization" one factor contributing to the success of the "Pearl River model." They maintain that two manifestations of the delta's rural urbanization are: First, taking the quickest road to rural urbanization by swiftly developing township enterprises and forming a network of small towns. Second, improvement of public utilities and facilities including energy, transportation and communications; swift development of education, science, culture, health, sports and tourism, and establishment of a social welfare system.

Simultaneous with rural urbanization, some cities have also made big strides forward. The reclassification of counties into cities is a direct result of rural urbanization. In the delta in 1978, only Guangzhou, Foshan, Jiangmen, Zhuhai, Zhaoqing, Huizhou, Hong Kong, and Macao were cities. In 1979, Shenzhen was added. In 1982, Zhongshan and Dongguan counties were made into cities (with isometric borders). In 1985, the system of giving cities jurisdiction over counties was implemented and Qingyuan County was made a city (exercising jurisdiction over six counties). In the 1990s, many other counties became cities, including Shunde, Nanhai, Taishan, Xinhui, Kaiping, Sanshui, Panyu, Huaxian, and Zengcheng (areas unchanged), while Baoan and Doumen were put under Shenzhen and Zhuhai. Thus, of the 21 counties included in the Pearl River Delta Economic Development Zone in 1987, only ten designated counties were left, several of which are also applying to change to city status. Some counties with economic strength and relatively large populations can hope to become small cities soon. The Pearl River Delta now embraces 22 cities (including Hong Kong and Macao), along with 273 designated townships at an average distance of ten kilometers from each other. A large metropolitan area is thus rising.

This metropolis stands on the legs of a tripod: the first leg is that of Hong Kong and Shenzhen with 8 million people; the second, Guangzhou and Foshan with 10 million people; and, the third, Macao and Zhuhai with 1 million people. Total population exceeds 30 million, making this one of the largest metropolises of the world. After Hong Kong and Macao's sovereignty reverts to China, these two cities will increasingly integrate with the Pearl River Delta. The "Guangzhou-Hong Kong-Macao" metropolis will actually shape up before the year 2000.

Currently, there are two central cities in this region: Guangzhou, the political and cultural center, and Hong Kong, the economic and information center. With "the economy in command" today, the tie between the Pearl River Delta and Hong Kong promises to become ever closer. In transportation, Guangzhou used to be the hub, but more and more counties and cities are bypassing it to connect directly with Hong Kong. All cities, counties and townships that own ports have established direct water routes to Hong Kong so as to avoid Guangzhou and Shenzhen. The car ferry from Nansha to Humen provides a fast route to Hong Kong from the western parts of the delta. After it opened, it quickly reached saturation capacity; a matter of five thousand cars are ferried across daily. To supplement this, Humen is building a bridge across the Pearl River near the ferry. Huizhou is also building a railroad and a high-speed highway to Hong Kong. Some people have suggested a super-long bridge spanning the Pearl River linking Zhuhai with Hong Kong. Although this conflicts with the building of Gaolan Harbor in west Zhuhai, it does reflect the delta's reliance on Hong Kong.

In fact, Hong Kong has turned the Pearl River Delta into its hinterland. Besides directly investing in ten thousand processing companies there, it has also financed a host of other projects (including joint ventures) in energy, transportation, real estate development, tourism, and hotels and restaurants. On the other hand, counties and cities in the delta have also invested a huge but unspecified amount of capital in Hong Kong. All county or municipal governments, large companies and large designated townships have set up companies in Hong Kong which engaged in entrepot trade in earlier years but now devote themselves purely to investment. The brisk exchange between Hong Kong and the delta derives mainly from economic activity.

In the authors' view, the Pearl River Delta's economic reliance on Hong Kong is expected to decrease in the future. The major reasons are as follows:

1. With the growth of capital accumulation, the delta will increasingly invest in its own industries. The proportion of its industry given over to processing will diminish.
2. With improvement of transportation and communications, more business experience and further policy liberalization, the delta will directly enter into the global economic system, thereby obviating Hong Kong's entrepot function.
3. With development, people will demand a higher quality of life and a better environment. Labor-intensive processing industries will shift to other regions (where economic and wage levels are lower).
4. Aside from investing overseas, the area will invest in China's interior to build up its own hinterland. Decreasing reliance, however, does not mean reduced ties with Hong Kong.

In the Pearl River Delta, the rural society itself fostered its urban growth. Hence urban and rural areas are highly integrated. The new cities that have arisen all show greater viability and coordination than older ones marked by dualistic separation. The Pearl River Delta's mode of rural urbanization not only provides a model for China, but perhaps also for other developing countries of the third world.

Notes

1. Xu Xueqiang, Liu Chi, and Zeng Xiangzhang, *Development of the Pearl River Delta and Urbanization* (Guangzhou: Zhongshan University Press, 1988).

2. R. Yin-Wang Kwok et al., eds., *Chinese Urban Reform—What Model Now?* (Armonk, N.Y.: M.E. Sharpe, 1990).

3. G.E. Guldin, ed., *Urbanizing China* (Greenwood Press, 1992); G. E. Guldin and Aidan Southall, eds., *Urban Anthropology in China* (Leiden, The Netherlands: E. J. Brill, 1993).

4. Victor F.S. Sit, ed., *Chinese Cities: The Growth of the Metropolis since 1949* (Hong Kong: Oxford University Press, 1985).

5. Zhou Daming, "Mass Media and Mass Culture in the Pearl River Delta," *Shehuixue yanjiu* (Sociological studies) (1990); "Population Shift in the Pearl River Delta," *Shehui kexue zhanxian* (Social Science Frontlines), 2 (1990); "Study of the Pearl River Delta's Rural Culture and Education and Modernity," *Shehuixue yanjiu* (Sociological studies) (1990); "Distributional Characteristics and Classification of Outside Labor Force in the Pearl River Delta," *Collection of Theses on "Review of Economic Development in the Pearl River Delta and Future Prospects"* (Guangzhou: Zhongshan University Press, 1992); *Economic Development, Culture, and Education in the Pearl River Delta*, vol. 1 (Zhongshan University Press, 1993).

6. C.K. Yang, *A Chinese Village in Early Communist Transition* (Boston: Massachusetts Institute of Technology Press, 1959).

7. Zhou Daming, "Investigation and Analysis of 'Dispersed Outside Labor' in Guangzhou," *Shehuixue yanjiu* (Sociological studies) (1994).

"Workers Wanted to Till Land: 20 Yuan per Mu." Daning GLQ, Dongguan City, Guangdong. *(Photo by Gregory Guldin)*

Loss of Cropland to New Construction. Dazuo Village, Congwu Township, Fujian. *(Photo by Gregory Guldin)*

Residential Reconstruction. Anhai City, Fujian. *(Photo by Gregory Guldin)*

New Road. Yi Village, Eshan County, Yunnan. *(Photo by Gregory Guldin)*

Shuangjiang Town, Eshan County, Yunnan. *(Photo by Gregory Guldin)*

Caitang Industrial Zone, Xiamen SEZ, Fujian. *(Photo by Shi Yilong)*

Naiqiong Town and Duilongdeqing County-run Roadside Inn; Tibet.
(Photo by Li Tao and Gelek)

New Houses/Storefronts Being Built by Blue Hukou-holders in Yangshufang, Liaoning. *(Photo by Lisa Hoffman)*

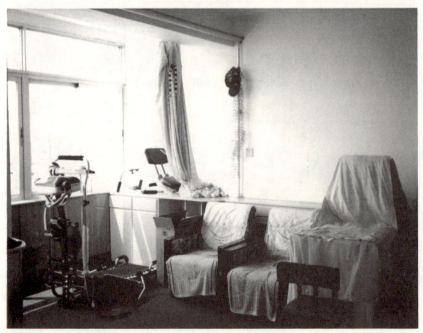

Prosperous Household. Beile Town, Liaoning. *(Photo by Lisa Hoffman)*

New Residential Area. Caitang, Xiamen SEZ, Fujian. *(Photo by Shi Yilong)*

Interior Design. Caitang Village,
Xiamen SEZ, Fujian.
(Photo by Shi Yilong)

Nomads and Farmers exchange goods. Naiqiong Zhen, Tibet.
(Photo by Li Tao and Gelek)

New Television Set. Naiqiong Town, Tibet. *(Photo by Li Tao and Gelek)*

Duilongdeqing Primary School. *(Photo by Li Tao and Gelek)*

Tractor-transport of the Qinke Harvest. Duilongdeqing, Tibet.
(Photo by Li Tao and Gelek)

Migrant Laborers Congregate Near Guangzhou Train Station.
(Photo by Zhou Daming)

Migrant Laborers' Dorm. Xinqiao Town Factory, Gaoyao County, Guangdong.
(Photo by Gregory Guldin)

Gregory Guldin (L) and Shi Yilong (R) Receive Dazuo Village Hospitality. Fujian. *(Photo by Zhou Daming)*

Gregory Guldin (2nd on left), and Zhou Daming (inhaling) Share Fruits of Yi Village Tobacco Harvest. Eshan County, Yunnan. *(Photo by Ma Laoshi)*

Prof. Liu Zhongquan (L, Center) and Jinzhou Official at Beile Town Market.
(Photo by Lisa Hoffman)

The Market in Beile, Liaoning. *(Photo by Lisa Hoffman)*

Beile Town Manager Chi (L) with Lisa Hoffman (R) in Garment Workshop.
(Photo by Liu Zhongquan)

Young Women Working in Garment Factory; Beile Town, Liaoning.
(Photo by Lisa Hoffman)

Zhou Daming (L), Lan Daju (C), and Zhang Yingqiang (R). Xiamen City, Fujian. *(Photo by Gregory Guldin)*

Gelek. Potala Palace, Lhasa, Tibet. *(Photo by Li Tao and Gelek)*

5

One Model of Chinese Urbanization

The Urbanization Process in Xiamen City's Caitang Village

Shi Yilong

This chapter explores the road of Chinese urbanization through on-site investigation of a rural village on the outskirts of a city. To attain this goal, we must first have a clear theoretical understanding of the definition of urbanization. With this foundation, we can then investigate the forms that urbanization in China has taken.

I. The Concept of Urbanization

In China, when discussing the definition of *"chengshihua"* or *"dushihua,"* most people feel it means the concentration of population in cities and towns. (Although both are usually translated to mean "urbanization," *dushihua* has more of a flavor of "metropolitanization."—Ed.) The *Demography Dictionary,* for instance, defines urbanization as the process of the proportional increase of people living in cities and towns. More accurately, it refers to the process of the agricultural population becoming a nonagricultural population as it concentrates in the cities.[1] The *Dictionary of Cultural Studies* says that urbanization refers to the movement of rural population flow into cities and the growth of cities.[2] The *Concise Demography Dictio-*

The fieldwork for this study received support from the United Board for Christian Higher Education in Asia, to whom we tender our sincere thanks.

nary writes: Urbanization is the "urbanization of population" and is also called "*chengzhenhua*" ("town-ification"). This is the process whereby rural population gradually turns into urban population.[3] The *Urban Economics Dictionary* describes urbanization as the coming together of three sociohistorical processes: the process of change caused by natural urban population increase and shift; the process of the formation of new cities; and the process of adjustment and merging of urban and rural geographic demarcations.[4] The *Outline of Urban Studies* says: "Urbanization is a process, not an outcome. It is the process whereby population and social productive forces shift toward and concentrate in the cities."[5] Further, *New Modern Terminology* says that urbanization refers to the ongoing process whereby population and socioproductive forces gradually shift to and concentrate in the cities. The major characteristic of urbanization is the relative concentration of the labor force and its shift to such secondary and tertiary industries as manufacturing and services, and to education, science and technology, and information.[6] This was, in fact, also the view of this author before really delving into the study of urban anthropology. For the definition of "urbanization" in the *Concise Cultural Anthropological Dictionary,* I had written: "urbanization," also called "population urbanization" and "townification," refers to the process whereby the agricultural population (individually or in groups) becomes nonagricultural population and concentrates in the cities. However, as I began to go deeper into urban anthropology and the study of Chinese urbanization, I discovered that that concept was one-sided and did not conform to Chinese realities.

First, although the phenomenon of population shift to and concentration in the cities does exist in China, it does not represent urbanization in its entirety. The concept has another part, and that is the urbanization of rural areas. The definition of urbanization as population concentration in the cities and towns can lead only to the expansion of existing cities, not the urbanization of rural regions. A logical deduction from the above would be that the outflow of rural population can only shrink or reduce the rural area. Although some people, in making this definition, elaborate that the urbanization process involves three parallel developments—natural urban population increase, influx of rural population into the cities, and rural industrialization, so that the rural way of life becomes increasingly closer to the urban way of life[7]—as we have analyzed above, logically, the definition as it stands can lead only to the former two developments, not the third. With the rural population concentrating in the cities, the population remaining in the rural areas must necessarily shrink, which makes industrialization and the change into the urban way of life difficult. The latter can come only with other variables, such as rural economic development, urban influences, etc. The above definition has not conveyed this level of meaning; its fatal flaw is that it reflects only one part, not the whole or essence, of urbanization. It is a reflection of a one-sided understanding of the urbanization concept.

Second, in Chinese practice, a social environment for natural population concentration in the cities and towns does not exist. In other words, in the modernization process in China today, the phenomenon of population shift or concentration in the cities is controlled and restricted by the social system and various policies and hence is unnatural. That is to say, the "pull" of cities—relatively more employment opportunities—and the "push" from the rural areas—the existence of a large labor surplus, advocacy for certain areas to get rich first, and the opening and development of the coastal areas ahead of other places—are factors that should naturally cause the rural population to move toward the cities. But the Chinese social system stipulates a strict household registration system; at the same time, though promoting a socialist market economy, China still emphasizes planned urban development. Thus, intentionally or not, some systems and policies restrict the natural concentration of surplus agricultural population in the cities. During the three years of natural disasters from 1959 to 1962, for instance, the country had implemented a policy of adjustment and mobilized a portion of the urban employees to return to the rural areas. A few years ago, the portion of labor from out of town in excess of urban needs was called *mangliu* ("blind flow"), and administrative measures were taken to mobilize or send them back home. In the past two years, temporary residence permits and labor permits became requisite in the effort to organize the inflowing labor force better. These are clear examples. Because of these concrete circumstances, China's urbanization process has to take diverse forms. The definition of urbanization as the concentration of population in the cities and towns cannot explain these multiple phenomena or the essence of urbanization, or summarize the realities in China.

Third, because of the above-mentioned systemic restrictions, some scholars studying Chinese modernization and urbanization advocate the development of small cities and towns, attempting to concentrate surplus agricultural population there. They claim that this is the special characteristic of Chinese urbanization and the only road it can take, since the capacity of existing Chinese cities to absorb surplus agricultural population is extremely limited and there are many real problems with the formation of new cities.[8] The building of small cities and towns is certainly one way of urbanization, and the process may well spread to surrounding rural areas. It is not, however, the only way. Under China's present conditions, the amount of surplus rural population small cities and towns can absorb is also limited; the latter will be unable to absorb all of the former. For instance, small cities and towns are relatively well developed in Jiangsu Province. According to analysis by some comrades, up to 1990 only some 3 million-plus of the province's 10 million surplus rural manpower had been absorbed by its small cities and towns, leaving out over 60 percent.[9] That demonstrates both the big potential of small cities and towns and the limited nature of their capacity. Furthermore, the populations of small cities and towns are not stationary; the slightest event can trigger large fluctuations. Some people have pointed out, for example, that in 1990 when the market was soft, the number of employees in township enterprises decreased by about 10 million, compared with 1989.[10] This shows not only the limited capacity of small cities and towns, but their susceptibility to a host of influences. Their capacity to concentrate or absorb surplus rural manpower is both limited and unstable.

Thus, to define urbanization as the concentration of rural population in the cities is both one-sided and fails to grasp the essence of the process. It is incapable, in practice, of helping to guide urbanization in China or resolving its problems. Actually, some sociologists have already detected this flaw. They consider that definition to be the view of demographers, not sociologists. The *Sociology Dictionary,* for instance, defines it thus: Urbanization is a form of social change. Under the entry for the primary sense of the term, it explains: "The process by which the rural population continually concentrates in the cities and new industrial areas, thus enlarging the scale of cities and increasing their numbers. A clear-cut characteristic is the yearly rise of the urban population and drop in rural population in total national population." However, "this is the concept expounded by demographers." Sociologists, on the other hand, regard it as "a process by which, as cities rapidly develop, they spread and disseminate their unique lifestyles, ideologies and concepts, and cultural modes to the rural areas, thus gradually narrowing the cultural gap between cities and rural areas. This is the view held by most sociologists."[11] Obviously, this definition already perceives the one-sidedness of the definition of urbanization as the concentration of rural population in the cities. Nevertheless, it has not grasped the essence of urbanization. It still emphasizes the influence of urban development on rural areas. Although it sees the outcome as the narrowing of the cultural gap, it fails to specify how this could be accomplished. This definition is still explaining only one part of the significance of urbanization, the unidirectional influence of cities on rural areas, not the significance of rural urbanization. It is still one-sided and lacks workable significance.

It seems that an applicable and workable definition of urbanization is the key. What, then, should it be? In this author's view, urbanization should be defined as the acquisition of the urban way of life; the urbanization process should be defined as the process of acquiring the urban lifestyle. Although this is a simple definition, it is reasonable and reveals the essence of the phenomenon.

First, when we examine the practice of modernization at home and abroad, we see that the phenomenon of a large section of the rural population shifting to and concentrating in the cities does exist because of the urban "pull" of employment opportunities and the rural "push" of excessive labor. This, however, is a superficial phenomenon, because the goal of rural people who concentrate in the cities is to find jobs and settle down, so that eventually they can become city dwellers. In other words, they go not as tourists, visitors, or for business, nor for any other temporary purpose, but to relocate and become part of the city population so that they can acquire the urban way of life. Thus, the concentration of people in the cities and towns is not the result; the result or essence is acquisition of the way of life and nothing else.

Second, judging from current conditions, every country has cities and villages. Urbanization really has to do with villages. In other words, urbanization is the question of how to transform or change rural villages so that they become more like cities and rural dwellers can live like city dwellers. For cities and city residents, there is no need to urbanize, only to modernize, or expand and swallow up surrounding rural areas. Thus, the view that urbanization has to do with urbanizing rural areas is correct. In view of present conditions, however, it is not realistic to seek to change all rural areas into cities. We can only say that, under the influence of modern transportation and communication and through the relationship between cities and rural areas, rural areas will, under urban influence, gradually adopt the urban way of life. This, of course, refers to the rural areas at large; we are not excluding the possibility that some villages will spontaneously develop into cities, although other variables are necessary for this to happen.

Third, since the effect or essence of urbanization is the acquisition of the urban way of life and urbanization is the urbanizing of rural areas, we cannot perceive urbanization as the simple process of population concentration in the cities. As we have emphasized earlier, this can only be part of the meaning of urbanization. What is important is that the rural population, even without leaving their villages, can attain urbanization. In the course of economic development, the rural areas will gradually acquire enough financial strength to enable them to enjoy the material life currently enjoyed by city dwellers. Moreover, the process of urbanization is not restricted to changes in location and jobs; more important, the process should change the social values of the rural population.

Fourth, those who believe that urbanization means urban population concentration actually also understand that this includes acquisition of the urban way of life. For instance, the *Demography Dictionary* describes the urbanization process as three parallel developments: the natural increase of the urban population; the influx of large numbers of the rural inhabitants into cities; and rural industrialization and increasing acceptance of urban lifestyles. In other words, apart from the first development, which cannot be considered a phenomenon of urbanization, they do see the phenomenon of acquisition of the urban lifestyles, although without realizing that this is the essence of urbanization. They see it only as one development, thus confusing epiphenomenon and basic essence. This is where they go wrong.

Fifth, defining urbanization as the acquisition of the urban way of life not only enables us to grasp the essence, but also gives us more flexibility in handling the process. In the past, because urbanization was defined as the urban concentration of population, our policies focused on the capacity and development of the cities in handling urbanization-related issues. And when Chinese realities put limits on natural development in these areas, people turned their eyes to the development of small cities and towns, hoping thus to resolve the unavoidable issue of urbanization. Practice in the past dozen years has shown that, though such guidance cannot be said to be entirely wrong, it does have problems. By confirming that the essence is the acquisition of the urban way of life, our policies and measures can be more flexible and realistic: not only can we suitably expand the scale of small, mid-sized, and large cities, as well as towns, to absorb more surplus rural labor into the secondary and tertiary industries, but we can also develop rural economies through diverse means, so that the social values of the rural population change gradually and it acquires the urban way of life, thus truly becoming urbanized. This is something unattainable by simply concentrating rural population in the cities. As a matter of fact, if we were to follow the old definition, we could easily fall into the problem of "over-urbanization" such as has happened in some third world countries.

In summary, in this author's view, defining urbanization as the acquisition of the urban way of life not only enables us to grasp the essence of the urbanization issue but also puts us in a more flexible position in handling urbanization-related issues and helps us understand and study urbanization as it relates to rural China. In other words, when we confirm the definition of urbanization as the acquisition of the urban way of life, we can then see that in China, the process is not confined to the single pattern of urban population concentration but can have many modes. Based on this understanding, we can then examine the urbanization process of one rural village.

II. Changes in Caitang's Overall Economic Structure

The Caitang Administrative Village is a rural area under change on Xiamen Island, in the city's nearby suburbs. Situated north of Yundingyan, it is only 5 km from the Xiamen train station, a 20–minute ride by bike. The village originally had three natural villages, Dashe, Xiaoshe, and Gudishi. In 1962, Xiaoshe hamlet was requisitioned as part of the site of a lakeside reservoir and its inhabitants moved to Dashe. The administrative village now embraces two hamlets, Caitang and Gudishi villages. On its eastern, western, and northern sides, Caitang borders on the reservoir lake while Gudishi borders the reservoir on its eastern side. To the south of Caitang is a road that links with the asphalt highway from Lianban to Hecuo, giving easy access to Xiamen city. During 1984–85, the administrative village had 205 households with 1,030 people. During May-July, 1993, it had 223 households with 1,196 people.

Caitang's economy has always been closely bound with that of Xiamen. Its main occupation in the past was to grow vegetables for Xiamen as one of the eleven vegetable suppliers of the Xiamen Municipal Vegetable Company. The company guided Caitang's vegetable growing by linking vegetables with grain and fertilizers. That is, it purchased the village's vegetables and sold back to it corresponding quantities of food grain and fertilizers. Administratively, Caitang did not belong to the company, but to the former Qianxian ("Frontlines") Commune and later Heshan *xiang*. In 1987, with State Council approval, Xiamen Municipality adjusted its administrative districting and set up the new Huli District. Caitang and other villages to the north of Xiamen came under Huli District's Heshan Township, thus becoming a village in the municipality. Along with Xiamen's economic development, Caitang's overall economic structure also underwent a tremendous change.

In the past, Caitang relied on vegetable production, and its specialty was betel nuts, which were large and soft. According to 1978 statistics, the village's aggregate income that year was some 375,000 *yuan,* of which 216,000 *yuan,* or 57.6 percent, was agricultural income. Of the latter, income from vegetables made up 181,000 *yuan,* or 83.66 percent of total agricultural income and 48.3 percent of aggregate income. Grain grown for village consumption yielded some 27,000 *yuan,* or 12.66 percent of total agricultural income and 7.2 percent of aggregate income. The chief oil crop was peanuts, yielding an income of 7,935 *yuan,* or 3.66 percent of agricultural income and 2.1 percent of aggregate income. Income from subsidiary sources was 76,319 *yuan,*[12] 20.4 percent of aggregate income. Of this, the chief product was greenhouse mushrooms, income from which was 57,149 *yuan,* or 74.9 percent of total subsidiary income and 15.3 percent of aggregate income. The rest of its income came from machine-made bricks manufactured by the production teams, which yielded 19,170 *yuan,* or 25.1 percent of subsidiary income and 5.1 percent of aggregate income. In addition, in 1978, Caitang owned a brigade enterprise which calculated its accounting independently. This enterprise had workshops for farm-tool repairs, zinc-plating, machine-sawing, and a machine-pressed-brick plant. Its income that year was 68,506 *yuan,* roughly 18.4 percent of aggregate income. This plus the industrial income from machine-pressed-brick plants in other production teams yielded a total of 87,676 *yuan,* or 23.5 percent of aggregate income. The village also received 8,347 *yuan* in income, or 2.1 percent of the aggregate, from keeping cattle, pigs, chickens, ducks, and fish, and 3,374 *yuan,* or 0.8 percent of the aggregate, from other sources, mainly retail stores. Adding up these figures, we can see that agricultural income (including farming, forestry, livestock, subsidiary occupations, and fish-breeding) was around 284,000 *yuan,* making up 75.7 percent of aggregate income, and industrial income was 88,000 *yuan,* or 23.5 percent of the aggregate. In 1978, therefore, Caitang's overall economic structure was predominantly agricultural with industry playing a supplementary role.

In October 1980, the State Council formally gave Xiamen approval to establish a special economic zone. In October 1981 when the zone began construction, it was located in the Huli village area at the northwestern part of the island with an area of 2.5 sq km. It was also called the Huli Industrial Zone. In March 1984, with the approval of the State Council, the scope of the Xiamen SEZ was expanded from Huli to the whole 131–sq km island and including Gulangyu and other islands. Its aim was to "build it up into a comprehensive, foreign-oriented SEZ dominated by industry but simultaneously developing tourism, commerce, and real estate" and gradually implement some policies of a free port. Construction burgeoned on the island and from 1981 to 1990, Xiamen's capital construction investment in industry alone was 1.916 billion *yuan,* making up 37.08 percent of its total capital construction investment of 5.167 billion *yuan* in the period. This was 5.76 times the 332 million *yuan* industrial investment of the 31 previous years combined.[13] This large-scale capital construction provided the background for Caitang's overall economic structural change. That is to say, Caitang and other villages like it effected their preliminary transformation from an agriculture-dominated to an industry-dominated economic structure in the process of the SEZ's extensive capital construction by developing their building materials and transportation industries. This gradual, initial process of change is illustrated in Table 5.1.

Table 5.1 shows the transformation from a reliance on agriculture to a

Table 5.1

Major Indexes of Economic Change in Caiting Village, 1978–1984

	Agriculture						Industry							Collective reserve funds	Per-capita income (yuan)	Per-household income (yuan)
	Total income	Total output value	Vegetables	Self-produced grain	Animal husbandry, fishing	Mushrooms	Total output value	Of production teams	Run by production brigades	Construction	Transportation	Trade, food, beverage	Payroll of commune-run enterprise			
1978	37.5	21.6	18.1	2.7	0.8	5.7	8.8	1.9	6.9			0.3		5.2	166	924
1979	50.8	20.7	15.4	3.9	0.8	7.4	21.8	6.5	15.3			0.2		4.3	182	1,011
1980	67	19.4	14.8	3.7	1.6	8.6	37	15.5	21.5			0.4		6.1	266.7	1,456
1981	75.9	19.2	13.4	3.2	1.1	2	55	33	22			0.5		5.1	310	1,662
1982	105	17.8	15.6	3.6	0.2	2	84	55.6	23.4	5		0.9	0.1	11.4	450	2,283
1983	112.5	28.4	24.1	4.3	9.6		72.7	72.7				0.6	1.2	10	600	3,096
1984	229.6	32.4	27.2	4.3	5.4		188.7	110.5		35.6	42.6	1.7	1.6	6	766.2	3,850

Source: Figures provided in Fujian Province agricultural economic statistical charts were sorted out and regrouped under our own headings. For example, industry was included in sideline occupations in the original statistics.

reliance on industry in Caitang's overall financial revenue to have begun in 1979. During that year, its total industrial revenue exceeded 50 percent of the total for the first time, and thereafter increased annually in step with Xiamen's large-scale capital construction. Caitang's Number Five production team was the first to set up a machine-pressed-brick plant. Subsequently, the production brigade and other production teams followed suit, and after 1980, with the expansion of capital construction in the SEZ, these plants also expanded. By 1984, besides the brigade's brick plant, and one plant in each of the five production teams, a few individuals had also raised funds to set up a joint venture of their own. At the same time Caitang also had two kiln-fired red-brick factories: one run cooperatively by people in Caitang and Changla villages and the other by Caitang people alone. In addition, there was a tile kiln, a square-brick kiln, a brick kiln, a limestone plant, and a stone quarry. Moreover, people went to neighboring Hongwen, Xilin, and Tujue villages as well as military barracks and a service team of a cloth dyeing and printing plant to subcontract pressed-brick plants. Caitang also set up a construction team relatively early. The team originally belonged to a construction company on the outskirts of Xiamen, but experienced some ups and downs and got on the right track only in 1982, after which it began to make money. In 1982, its revenue was 50,000 *yuan*, or 4.8 percent of Caitang's aggregate total. By 1984, its income had risen to 356,000 *yuan*, or 15.5 percent of the aggregate.

The rise of Caitang's transportation business was also an offshoot of SEZ capital construction. The brigade enterprise formerly owned only one car and two tractors and the different production teams owned around thirteen manually operated tractors. When agriculture was predominant, these vehicles were mainly used to send vegetables to the Xiamen Vegetable Company and bring back liquid fertilizer. After starting the brick plants, these vehicles began to be used for bringing in locally unavailable materials necessary in making the bricks, such as clay with high sand content, lime, coal cinder, and coal dust. This expanded Caitang's transportation business, and by 1984, it owned seven Liberation-brand cars, two two-and-a-half-ton Fujian-brand cars, one large tractor, and fifty-four manual tractors. By 1984, in addition to the brigade's farm tool repair workshop, zinc-plating workshop, and machine-sawing workshop, five individuals had started a Fuchang machinery factory to process iron implements. Other individuals had set up food processing factories. The number of restaurants and small shops selling daily articles also increased to eight.

By the end of 1984, therefore, after some years of effort, Caitang's aggregate industrial and agricultural income had reached 2.296 million *yuan*, of which 324,000 *yuan*, or 14.1 percent, was from agriculture. Among agricultural income, 43,000 *yuan* was from grain crops, 1.7 times the 27,000 *yuan* from grain crops in 1978. Its proportion in the aggregate income, however, was only 1.8 percent, being much lower than the 7.2 percent in 1978. Revenue from vegetables had also increased to 272,000 *yuan,* a 50 percent rise from 1978, but its proportion of the aggregate income, too, had dropped from 48.3 percent to 11.8 percent. At the same time, industrial revenue had been constantly rising. In 1978, its proportion in the aggregate was 23.5 percent. In 1980, it had risen to 55.2 percent. In 1984, industrial revenue reached 1.887 million *yuan,* or 82.2 percent of the aggregate, being 21 times that in 1978. Some former subsidiary lines like mushroom growing were completely closed off in 1983. Statistically, in 1984, transportation and construction were tracked as two separate businesses, the revenues being respectively 426,000 *yuan* and 356,000 *yuan,* or 22.6 percent and 18.9 percent of the total industrial revenue and 18.6 percent and 15.5 percent of aggregate income. Revenue from the factories came to 1.105 million *yuan,* or 48.1 percent of the aggregate. In addition, Caitang's commercial and food industry revenues in 1984 were 17,000 *yuan,* or 0.7 percent of the aggregate. The wages of workers in enterprises at the commune level totaled 16,000 *yuan,* another 0.7 percent of the aggregate. From the above, it can be seen that by 1984, industry had fully replaced agriculture in the dominant position of Caitang's income structure. This shows the initial change in Caitang's economic structure.

After 1984, Xiamen's economic construction maintained sustained growth and Caitang's economy continued to grow in its wake. Its economic structure continued to be dominated by industry. The number of its industrial enterprises continued to increase along with its industrial output value. After 1988, in particular, industry, commerce, and services grew at a steady pace, and by 1992, effected a big change. See Table 5.2 for this process.

As Table 5.2 shows, after 1988, the major part of Caitang's revenue continued to derive from industrial enterprises, including those in construction and transportation. Total industrial output rose annually, from 1.695 million *yuan* in 1988 to 11.95 million *yuan* in 1992, with its proportion in the aggregate income remaining around 70 percent. The number of industrial enterprises also increased annually. Although agricultural income, too, rose, its proportion of aggregate income fluctuated around the 15 percent mark.

In 1989, enterprises with foreign investment started up in villages on Xiamen's outskirts, including Caitang. On December 23, 1989, Caitang established its first exclusively foreign-owned company, the Xiamen Holiday Arts and Crafts Co. Ltd. It manufactured small labor-intensive arts-and-crafts and gift items made from metal, clay, resin, cloth, and wood as well

Table 5.2

Major Indexes of Economic Change in Caiting Village, 1988–1992 (yuan 10,000)

		Agriculture				Industrial enterprises				Tertiary sector					
	Total income	Total output value	Vegetables	Self-produced grain	Animal husbandry, fishery	Total output value	Industry	Construction	Transportation	Trade, food, beverage	Services	Financial income of the village	Per-capita income (yuan)	Per-household income (yuan)	Enterprises with foreign capital
1988	398	57.6	38.2	15.8	35.7	280.7	169.5	41.2	70	14	10	8.7	1,113	6,078	
1989	416.5	65.9	43.8	22.1	24.6	302	170	48	84	14	10	9.8	1,225	6,791	
1990	452.6	82.4	64.5	10.4	32.2	318	156	70	92	10	10	10.9	1,311	7,254	
1991	528.9	76.3	64.7	11.6	32.6	390	185	95	110	10	20	9.9	1,474	7,965	
1992	1,797.3	65.6	51.5	9.95	37.3	1,451	1,195	135	121	162	81.4	115.2	2,284	11,724	2,250

Source: Fujian Provincial Financial Statement, on Rural Economy, etc.

as musical electronic toys. Subsequently, more enterprises with foreign investment as well as joint ventures with domestic capital were started, forming into a small industrial zone on the section of highway from Lianban to Hecuo. Some individual and joint enterprises also went into business. By 1992, the village had over 30 enterprises in various forms: solely foreign-owned, village-owned, jointly owned by the village and other domestic localities (*neilian*), as well as individually owned and joint shareholding by individuals. Companies or outlets for trading, steel products, interior decoration, and real estate as well as gas stations were also started. Compared to the past, Caitang industry no longer depended on construction materials and transportation, but had diversified. This was the reason for the large breakthrough the village effected in its economy in 1992. In that year, its total output reached 17.973 million *yuan,* breaking the 10 million mark for the first time. Of this, 14.51 million *yuan,* or 80.73 percent, came from industry.

Second, although the proportion of income from construction and transportation had not risen by a large margin, its output value as compared to 1984 showed a huge rise. That of the construction industry rose from 356,000 *yuan* to 1.35 million *yuan,* a 2.7–fold increase. That from transportation rose from 426,000 *yuan* in 1984 to 1.21 million *yuan* in 1992, a 2.8–fold increase. By 1992, Caitang residents owned over 100 vehicles of various types. As compared with the past, the difference was in the larger number of small passenger cars owned. The village as a whole owned thirty passenger cars, fifteen 1.75–ton tool trucks, and twenty farm vehicles, in addition to a number of minivans. The increase in large freight vans was not large—there were eight of these in 1992.

Since the hiring of workers for enterprises with foreign investment was basically done in interior regions away from Xiamen, large numbers of migrant workers came to Caitang. By 1993, such migrant workers with temporary resident permits in Caitang numbered 1,200, which exceeded the number of native villagers. This has stimulated the rapid development of the village's food, housing, and service industries, including bathhouses and barbershops, which rose to more than thirty, or a three- to fourfold increase over that in 1984. Before 1991, revenue from the food industry remained around 100,000 *yuan.* By 1992, it had jumped to 1.62 million, a fifteenfold increase. Output from the service industries had also been around 100,000 *yuan* before; this doubled to 200,000 in 1991 and quadrupled again to 814,000 *yuan* by 1992. In comparison, agricultural income, though higher than that of 1984, had decreased slightly from the high tide of 1990. After rising to 824,000 in 1990, it dropped to 656,000 in 1991 and 1992; its proportion in the village's 17.973 million *yuan* product was an insignificant 3.6 percent. Even though we were unable to obtain 1993 statistics when we investigated Caitang that year, we could see from the trend starting in 1991 that the village's future economy will revolve heavily around secondary and tertiary industries. Agricultural output will rise year by year, but it will never again dominate Caitang's economic structure.

III. Changes in Caitang's Employment Structure

The change in Caitang's overall economic structure has also brought about a change in its employment structure. In 1978, the village had 912 people in 162 households; 412 were fully or semi-employed. Apart from 45 people in the brigade enterprise and some workers in production team brick plants, the majority of the labor force was engaged in pure farming, mainly vegetable growing. By 1984, the population grew to 1,030 in 205 households with 556 fully or semi-employed. In May that year, all land was subcontracted out to the families. Some members of each family worked the land under their responsibility while others worked in industry or subsidiary occupations. Some specialized households appeared. According to statistics, at least 132 of the 205 households specialized in industry or subsidiary occupations—64 percent of the total number of households. Some specialized in transportation. Others subcontracted the work of brick factories in their own or surrounding villages. Still others financed and ran their own small plants manufacturing machine-pressed or construction bricks. Some worked in commune or village factories or found work in the cities. Caitang's employment structure became oriented toward industry and subsidiary occupations. Not only that, the village absorbed some outside labor; in the smaller village enterprises, all but the management were such workers. For instance, of the 242 employees at the seven machine-pressed-brick factories, most were workers from Longhai County; at the machine-pressed-brick plant, apart from two management personnel, the rest of the forty-odd workers and management were all from Fuqing.

In specialized households, more women tended the fields while men worked in industry or subsidiary occupations, helping out on the farms only in the busy seasons. For instance, in Zeng Liangde's family of eight, apart from two granddaughters in elementary school, the elder son subcontracted a brigade vehicle which he used for transporting goods, the younger son was a manager in a food processing factory Zeng owned, the elder daughter-in-law and daughter ran a small grocery shop he also owned, while Zeng's wife took care of the home and raised pigs, chickens, and ducks. Zeng himself, besides owning the food processing factory and store, was the village's representative at the Xiamen Vegetable Company. Through his liaison with the company, he brought back information as to what vegetables were in demand. He also settled accounts with the company on behalf of the village and oversaw shipments of grain and fertilizers resold to it by the state, which were then distributed among the production teams. The farm work was taken care of by his wife, daughter-in-law, and daughter, among other work. In busy transplanting and harvesting seasons, the whole family helped out.

Second, compared with the past, by 1984 the intensity of farm work done by Caitang's womenfolk had also decreased. According to Mr. Zeng Qishan, our landlord, when he drove a freight truck for the brigade and his wife was growing vegetables some years back, despite the sprinkler system the village provided, his wife still had to get up at four or five o'clock each morning to water the vegetables, apply fertilizer, or cut fresh greens. Vegetables have a short growing cycle and need lots of water and fertilizer. To retain moisture in summer, the fields had to be watered four or five times a day and applied with diluted fertilizer twice daily. The work was backbreaking. Mr. Zeng himself drove the vegetables to the city every day and was able to sleep late, often rising at 7 or 8 A.M. By May 1984, when the land had been subcontracted to the families, all families had the right to decide what to grow. Under such circumstances his wife could sleep later, while he had to rise at four or five in the morning to load the trucks and make more runs and income because he was then subcontracting transport in partnership with some other people.

Third, because of the increase in the proportion of industry and subsidiary occupations, Caitang's labor force became inadequate to supply these two "battle lines" fully. Their solution was, on the one hand, to absorb some migrant workers into industry and subsidiary occupations and, on the other, to convert part of the vegetable cropland to paddy rice. Paddy rice needs comparatively less labor except at the transplanting and harvest seasons. They could thus save some manpower for industry and subsidiary occupations, which were more profitable than vegetables. Some families went still further. They gave up heavy farm work altogether and instead hired hands during the busy seasons while doing the lighter chores in managing the fields themselves. At the same time they also replaced manual weeding with herbicides, saving a lot of physical labor. A few families, where both husbands and wives worked in industry or subsidiary occupations, subcontracted their land to others. That was why by 1984, many families had completely broken away from farming and were devoted solely to industry or subsidiary occupations.

This situation was even more widespread in the 1990s. When we conducted our fieldwork in 1993, households chiefly devoted to vegetable growing numbered fewer than sixty, or 25.8 percent of the 233 households.

Even some households long renowned for their vegetable growing had changed or were considering changing to other lines. Mr. Wei Weixing, for instance, was a well-respected vegetable grower who was cited as a *xiang* model laborer in 1984. When we visited him in 1993, he was no longer growing vegetables but had turned all four *mu* of the farmland his family subcontracted over to paddy rice, sweet potatoes, and peanuts. He harvested 2,000 catties of rice, 400 catties of peanuts, and 1,000 catties of sweet potatoes in 1992. The only vegetables he grew were for the family's own consumption. He now also worked in a village heat-plating plant, of which he was a shareholder. He had also opened a bathhouse.

Another example was the brothers Gao Qi and Gao Jian, whose families specialized in vegetable growing in the early 1990s. From 1990 to 1992, according to other villagers, each family averaged 20,000 *yuan* net annually from vegetables alone, which was no less than incomes made in industry or subsidiary occupations or earned by factory workers. In 1993, however, they decided to change to other work because of the arduousness of vegetable growing and the long hours in which they were exposed to the elements.

Currently, males in the village work mainly in industry or subsidiary occupations while women work mainly in the fields. Some fields have also been subcontracted to outside workers. In 1993, we made a random sampling of fifty Caitang families. Tables 5.3 and 5.4, showing male and female employment distribution respectively, are based on the available data and our survey of 100 people.

These tables show that only 15 percent of the males relied solely on farming for income. Thirteen people, or 13 percent, did both farming and nonfarm work. Apart from two people who were supported by others, 70 percent of the males were engaged in nonfarm work. In addition, among those doing both farming and other work, farming was not their chief occupation; they usually helped out in the fields only during busy seasons. Most of these had changed from vegetable growing to grain growing, enabling them to devote more energy to nonfarm lines such as industry, business, transportation, or construction. Some who still did farming were retirees, who helped out because younger people were reluctant to work in the fields. When differentiated by age, younger people did less farm work than older people. Older people often complained that the younger generation nowadays did not even know how to hold a plowshare. Such complaints give a good indication of the future direction of Caitang's male labor force.

The above data also show that a relatively large number of women did farm work. If we include women solely engaged in farm work, plus those doing both housework and farming, as well as those who also raised poultry and livestock (directly related to farming), the number is thirty-four. Seven

Table 5.3

Distribution of Male Employment

Age	Industry only	Commerce only	Transportation	Construction	Food and beverage	Service	Medical	Village cadre	On welfare	Farming only	Industry and farming	Transportation and farming	Industry and nonagri-cultural occupation	More than two non-agricultural occupations	Other occupations and farming	Subtotal
Over 50	2	1					1		2	6	3		5	3	2	25
40–49	3		2					1		3						9
30–39	5	3	14	3		2		1		5		3	2	2	3	43
Under 29	6	2	8	3	1	2				1	1	1	1			23
Sub-total	16	6	24	3	1	4	1	2	2	15	4	4	8	5	5	100

Table 5.4

Distribution of Female Employment

Age	Industry only	Commerce only	Transportation	Food and beverage	Service	Medical	Farming only	Housewife	Farming and housewife	Farming, animal husbandry, and housewife	On welfare and housewife	Industry and housewife	Commerce and housewife	Farming, housewife, and other occupations	Industry and commerce	Food and beverage and house renting	Subtotal
Over 50						1		14	4	1				1			22
40–49								2	5	1	5			2			15
30–39	5		1	1				2	12	7	4	2	2	3		1	38
Under 29	12	2		1	2		2	2	2					1	1		25
Sub-total	17	2	1	2	2	1	2	20	23	9	9	2	2	7	1	1	100

women (Table 5.4) both farmed and worked in industry or subsidiary occupations. Those who did chiefly farm work along with those who did some farm work add up to forty-one. In other words, 41 percent had something to do with farming. The rest had nothing whatever to do with farming. Subtracting the number—twenty-one—who were homemakers and did no farming or other work (including one dependent on outside support), thirty-eight women were engaged in work apart from farming. Like the males, more of the younger women were in the secondary and tertiary sectors—industry, business, or services. Thus, in the village as a whole, about 70 percent of the males and 38 percent of the females were doing no farm work. This was a tremendous change from the situation in 1984, when only a few people did not work the land. This trend promises to continue until the employment structure turns completely nonagricultural.

These changes were also clearly reflected in the home. We have already mentioned Zeng Liangde's family. By 1993, Zeng was no longer working in vegetables but was helping the village run the heat-plating factory. He dropped in at the factory when necessary and remained home to play with his grandchildren and take care of his store the rest of the day. His wife was still mainly doing household chores. His sons had set up separate households. The elder one was still driving a freight truck, although he now owned rather than subcontracted it. The elder daughter-in-law, a capable woman, was managing a paper-carton factory that she had subcontracted. The older of the young couple's two daughters was studying at an intermediate-level specialized school in Quanzhou and the younger was in a local junior middle school (*chuzhong*).

Zeng's younger son was also doing well. The little grocery store and food processing factory were both in his name, and his and his wife's chief occupation was taking care of the store and the factory. They also owned a half-ton truck to transport goods as well as shares in the village heat-plating factory and terrazzo plant. They had two preschool daughters whose care they had entrusted to the grandparents. Zeng Liangde's daughter was single and lived at home. She worked at the Heshan Credit Cooperative and had her own income. In addition, Zeng had contracted eight *mu* of land in 1984, two of which were requisitioned by the village in the early 1990s, when it started to build industry. Besides growing some vegetables for self-consumption, he had planted the remaining six *mu* with rice. The womenfolk were completely in charge of the farm work; the men took no hand in it at all.

As for our former landlord Zeng Qishan, he was still driving a truck in 1993, although his wife no longer grew vegetables for the market. They had turned to planting grain. Zeng did some temporary work in the factories and worked in the fields only in the busy seasons. Their elder son, a second-grade elementary school student in 1984, was now seventeen. He did not go on to middle school but took a job. At the time of our survey, he was working at a refrigeration engineering company in the village and installing air conditioners. When this author again visited the village in February 1994, that son had taken a job selling motorcycles at a store in Lianban. He had never worked in the fields and knew nothing about farm work. His father told me they were sending him to a driving school and planning to buy a truck so that he could work in transportation in the future and make his own living. Zeng told me that, by doing so, he had discharged his obligation as a father.

To date, the distribution of Caitang's labor force shows that the major part are in industrial enterprises and the tertiary sector. With the further expansion of the Caitang industrial zone (in 1993, seventeen enterprises signed agreements with Caitang to set up factories there), farmland is going to shrink further. Moreover, with the arrival of more migrants, they may subcontract much of the remaining farmland, which will allow more of the local population to leave the land. As in other areas that are rapidly developing, however, the natives would rather become small business owners or use their land requisition fees to buy shares in factories or businesses and thus become small investors, than work in the factories themselves.

IV. Changes in Acquisition of Urban Lifestyles

Supported by capital construction in Xiamen, Caitang's industry and subsidiary occupations received a firm kick start. In the course of the SEZ's sustained and stable economic development, they further expanded. This has brought about a profound change in Caitang's economic structure and the distribution of its labor force, which resulted in rising net income year by year. (See Tables 5.5 and 5.6.)

The two tables show that in 1978, per capita net income was 166 *yuan;* multiplied by an average of 5.6 people per household brings the per-household net income to 930 *yuan.* By 1984, when Caitang's economy had been initially transformed and more people were working in industry and subsidiary occupations, the per capita income rose to 766.2 *yuan* and the per-household income to 3,850 *yuan,* a fourfold increase from that in 1978. By 1992, other occupations had developed with the influx of foreign and domestic capital, and per capita income rose still further, from 1,474 *yuan* in 1991 to 2,284 *yuan,* a 50 percent increase. If we multiply this by 1,196 people and divide it by 233 households, the per-household income was around 11,724 *yuan,* three times that of 1984 and 12.5 times that of 1978. In addition, compared to urban employees, Caitang residents paid no

Table 5.5

Changes in Per-Capita and Per-Household Net Incomes in Caitang, 1978-84

Year	No. of households	Population	Labor force	Per-capita income (*yuan*)	Per-household income (*yuan*)
1978	162	902	412	166	930
1979	164	911	378	203	1,128
1980	167	912	397	266.7	1,456
1981	175	938	415	310	1,662
1982	192	974	499	450	2,283
1983	194	1,001	497	600	3,096
1984	205	1,030	556	766.2	3,850

Source: Rural statistics compiled by Fujian Province.

Table 5.6

Changes in Per Capita and Per-Household Net Incomes in Caitang, 1988–92

Year	Number of households	Population	Total work force	Work force in family businesses	Work force for new economic ass'ns.	Work force for village-run e'prises.	Per capita income (*yuan*)	Per household income (*yuan*)
1988	204	1,114	679	466	115	98	1,113	6,078
1989	206	1,142	649	566	53	30	1,225	6,791
1990	210	1,162	694	492	138	64	1,311	7,254
1991	218	1,178	599	358	124	117	1,474	7,965
1992	233	1,196	655	203	260	192	2,284	11,724

Source: Rural statistics compiled by Fujian Province.

rent and water fees and supplied their own vegetables, poultry, and eggs; their daily cash expenses were thus somewhat smaller than those of urban residents. With incomes rising, the lifestyle of people in Caitang has undergone a significant change and is becoming increasingly urbanized.

In the past, Caitang houses were one-story structures of either three or five rooms—with one living room flanked by two or four bedrooms. In 1962 when the reservoir was built, villagers were relocated to simple one-story homes. Little new housing was built thereafter up to 1978. In the 1980s, when the village's economic structure was transformed and people's incomes rose, villagers rushed to build new houses. By 1984, 80 percent were building or already living in new homes. In architecture, they had retained the old three- or five-room style with a courtyard in the middle.

There were one or two rooms in the front and two bedrooms plus a living room at the back. However, the previous gable-shape tile roofs were mostly replaced by stone-made flat roofs covering houses of two stories.

Beginning in late 1984, one family broke tradition and started to build a modern "Western-style" house. Other families followed suit and Western-style houses proliferated. Two- or three-story homes soon appeared in exotic styles. In 1984, the first story of most houses was built of marble and the second story of painted red brick. In the 1990s, most new homes were built of concrete or concrete plus brick walls laid over with tiles. The village is now full of new houses, and a lot of construction is still going on. On my earlier survey in March 1993, only the first row of houses had been built; the rest had not even started. In a short eight months, a dozen new houses had sprung up in this small residential area. This also shows the urgency of people here to move into new homes. One of the houses belongs to Zeng Qishan. He told us that he was building the three-story structure for his son. He had spent 90,000 *yuan* on the foundation structure alone. Exterior and interior finishing was estimated at another 300,000 *yuan*, so he had to put it off until later when he earned more money. According to the owner, the finished house cost him 400,000 *yuan* (including finishing).

This shows the affluence of people in Caitang today. With all this new housing, the average per capita floor space is now 40 sq m, much higher than the space occupied by urban dwellers. Almost every family has one of these villa-type houses. New housing came complete with bathrooms, replacing outhouses that preserved manure for fertilizer. So-called city folks such as myself, living in apartment buildings, could only sigh in envy of their living conditions.

Whereas old housing had earthen floors, new houses are laid with cement or with glossy or glazed bricks sporting floral designs. Ceramic glazed bricks are liberally placed to cover the surface of the lower part of the walls, and living rooms are installed with ceiling fans and chandeliers. In the 1990s, some homes had terrazzo flooring and aluminum door and window casings. Many have carpets and air conditioning. Whereas in 1984, many families still had spirit platforms and "Eight Immortal Tables" in their living rooms, today these have been replaced with bars stocked with an array of fashionable wines and liquors. Changes have also taken place in people's acquisition of some high-priced consumer products. A survey made in 1983 (Table 5.7) contrasted the situation in 1983 and previously.

As the table shows, before 1978, the village had only a few television sets, but by 1983, 41 percent of the families had TV sets and 19.5 percent had cassette recorders. Before 1978, few families had motorcycles, automobiles, or tractors. By 1984, virtually every family had cassette recorders and

Table 5.7

High-Priced Consumer Products Owned by Caitang People

	Before 1959	Before 1978	1983
Television	—	3	81
Cassette recorder	—	—	38
Washing machine	—	—	2
Bicycle	2	120	270
Sewing machine	1	93	199
Electric fan	—	—	70
Wristwatch	—	200	551
Sofa	—	—	30
Motorcycle	—	—	2
Automobile	—	—	5
Tractor	—	8	15
Ox cart	—	15	5
Flat board pedicab	—	10	18
Pedicab	—	—	1

black-and-white TV sets. Imported color TVs first appeared in some wealthy families, and the number of sets is increasing. A few families own VCRs. Refrigerators also came into use. Imported motorcycles, including Yamahas, Sanyos, and Hondas, increased in number; Jialing-brand motorcycles, once fashionable, were no longer so. By 1993, living standards had further risen in Caitang. We visited fifty families at the time to get a rough idea of their current lifestyle. Let us take a look at a few families with different income levels.

1. *Number 34* is a family of five with four who work. The informant owns a small factory. His son subcontracts a construction team and has joint ownership in a refrigeration engineering company. His second daughter drives a car and does other work. The third daughter is at a specialized middle school out of town. His wife does housework and farm work. The annual family income is about 120,000 *yuan,* which is considered wealthy. They occupy 270 sq m of living space, averaging over 50 m per person. This house, built in the early 1980s, has been renovated and had modern bathrooms added. It is air-conditioned. High-grade consumer products owned include a Toyota Crown sedan, two window air-conditioner units, a 25" Sony color TV, a 170–liter Hitachi refrigerator, a Sony J27 VCR, a Ricoh instamatic camera, two motorcycles (Yamasaki 125 and Suzuki V 125), and a Gaobao washing machine. A couch set bought in 1984 has been replaced by a set of redwood armchairs, a telephone has been installed, and they own a cellular phone and several beepers. Liquefied gas is used for cooking. In 1992, the elder daughter got married and the family spent

between 60,000 and 70,000 *yuan* for the wedding. The family's 1992 household expenses came to 20,000–25,000 *yuan*.

2. *Number 35* is a family of five with four who work. The informant is a woman cadre, a widow. She works several jobs and has an annual income of 10,000 *yuan*. Her elder son and daughter-in-law subcontract a gas station and earn a joint yearly income of 40,000 *yuan*. Her younger son is taking a driving course and has no income. There is a grandson. The family's annual income is 50,000 *yuan* and is considered an upper-middle-income household. Living space totals 360 sq m, averaging over 70 sq m per person. The family owns one 19" and one 21" color TV (one in her own house and one in her eldest son's house), refrigerators, motorcycles, and bicycles, a set of stereo sound equipment, a cassette recorder, a washing machine, and a couch set. Liquefied gas is used for cooking. She is currently planning to buy a passenger car for the younger son to use for business.

3. *Number 36* is a family of six with five working. The informant does farm work and is a member of the joint security corps. His wife works at home and in the fields. His first and second daughters and first son work in village factories and the youngest daughter goes to school. The family's annual income is 20,000 *yuan*. It is considered a lower-middle-income family. The family occupies 200 sq m of space, averaging over 30 sq m per person. It owns one black-and-white TV, one refrigerator, three bicycles, and a couch set. Its 1992 household expenses were 6,000 *yuan*. The informant says 1993 income will be higher and plans to buy a color TV and a motorcycle at year's end, so that people would not look down on them.

4. *Number 27* is an elderly couple, who have sons living apart from them. The informant works in a factory and receives 4,000 *yuan* annual income. His wife takes care of their home. Their two sons give them a total of 2,400 *yuan* for support every year, making their yearly income 6,400 *yuan*. This is a relatively low-income family. Nevertheless, they own a color TV, a refrigerator, stereo sound equipment, a couch set, and a motorcycle. The elder son's family has five air-conditioning units, a large 33" color TV, a VCR, a stereo, a washing machine, a refrigerator, and a Suzuki 125 motorcycle. He owns a three-and-a-half-story house with a garage on the ground floor. Each story has a bathroom. The flooring is terrazzo, and window and door casings are made of aluminum. The family keeps a large wolfhound. The second son also owns a motorcycle, a color TV, and a washing machine. He works in the food industry and hence has a refrigerator and an icebox at home.

We would also like to mention the big changes in Zeng Qishan's home. Back in 1984, he already had a large liquor bar in his living room, a 21" color TV, and an Italian-style couch set. By 1993, he had updated the bar to a smaller and more modern version and had bought a 33" color TV. He also had a telephone, VCR, refrigerator, washing machine, and gas range. As mentioned earlier, at the end of 1993, the inside foundation structure of his new house had also been built.

Based on the above, and looking at the big picture, first we can see that by the end of 1993, the village as a whole had 280 two- to three-story new houses in various architectural styles, averaging 1.2 houses per family. The interiors of most were beautifully finished and furnished, including fully equipped bathrooms. As for electrical appliances, one hundred percent of the families had TVs, 80 percent of them had color sets. VCRs and stereos were also common. With labor power getting tight and tap water having been installed, refrigerators and washing machines had become common, despite the fact that people once believed hand washing to be much cleaner.

Third, in transportation, most bicycles have been replaced by motorcycles. With the latter's number increasing constantly, even Caitang people could not tell you the exact number. Some said that the village now had fifty to sixty vehicles of various types, including passenger cars, trucks, "little breads" (minivans), and farm vehicles. Some of these were used in business, but others were used solely to carry people to do their daily chores or even by family members exclusively as prestige symbols.

Fourth, in communications, the village now had seventy telephone lines, eight cellular phones, and 100 beepers, and the number was still increasing. The post office had received a spate of applications for more telephone lines because the demand was far from satisfied.

Fifth, in cooking, every family was now using coal processed by a village coal plant and many were using liquefied gas for its convenient, time-saving features and because it was clean. A small gas flame could do all the boiling, stir-frying, steaming, and deep-frying necessary without constantly having to add coal or stoke the fire, or clean up the coal residue.

Sixth, in other aspects of life, the village barber used to cut hair for five *fen* a head. In the 1980s, people thought his haircuts too "hick" and began to frequent the city barbershops instead. Popular urban hairstyles and perms began to appear. With the influx of migrant workers, service trades boomed and two hair salons opened in the village. The young people liked to dress their hair fashionably after the popular Hong Kong singer Liu Dehua. In the past, before the arrival of the Spring Festival, people used to ask the village tailor to come to their homes to make each person one or two new suits of clothes for the year. In the 1980s, they considered this too "provincial" and bought their clothes in the ready-made departments of clothing stores. Some doing business began to wear Western flannel suits and ties. This phenomenon has spread even wider today. It is no longer a rare sight to see villagers wearing designer clothes such as Jinlilai, Playboy, and Pierre Cardin. As for food, although the volume of vegetables and grain sold back to the villages has decreased, people are eating more meat, fish, and shrimp and fewer staple foods. In addition, with the conversion of vegetable to grain crops, people grew more than enough grain to fulfill their own needs, and even if they did not, they could always buy it on the market. Now, many people go to buy vegetables daily at the village market. According to the renowned vegetable grower Wei Weixing, his family now spends 100 *yuan* or more on vegetables a month and 200 *yuan* on meat and eggs. They supply their own grain and do not have to buy it. This phenomenon shows that the old image of the vegetable farmer growing his own vegetables has already changed greatly.

We see from the above that significant changes by the early 1990s had taken place in Caitang's economic structure, distribution of labor power, and way of life. Compared with registered residents of Xiamen city, the economic activities of the majority of Caitang's inhabitants were no different than those of city residents, the only difference being that most Caitang families still had land and a few worked the land to get rich. In the process of constantly raising their incomes, Caitang villagers' lifestyles had become increasingly similar to urban lifestyles. Essentially, they had every advantage enjoyed by ordinary city residents and in fact had surpassed the latter in income, living conditions, and transportation facilities. The quality of their life was steadily rising; in fact, they had become the envy of city dwellers. We have every reason to say that Caitang has gradually acquired an urban way of life through developing industry and subsidiary occupations and raising income, against the background of the economic construction of the Xiamen SEZ. This may be one model or road to urbanization in China.

V. Caitang Becoming Xiamen?

The above demonstrates that due to the efforts of Caitang's own population and on the basis of their economic take-off, urbanization has begun. If this continues, the entire urbanization process—that is, the urbanization of their way of life—promises to be completed in the not-too-distant future. We should also realize, however, that this mode of urbanization will not remain the only mode in Caitang because of the village's unique geographic location, which made it a part of the Xiamen municipality. Thus, on the one hand, through their own efforts, through developing their economy and raising incomes, through ties with the city, and under its influence and the influence of the media, the people of Caitang had initially acquired an urban way of life. When we asked what differences existed between Caitang and the cities, many inhabitants would tell us: "We live like city people; we can get everything." "There's no big difference; our village is almost a city." On the other hand, as a village under the jurisdiction of Xiamen city, as Xiamen expands, urbanized Caitang will be "swallowed" by Xiamen and become one of its constituent districts. This process is slowly evolving, and it is closely linked to the municipality's overall development plan.

Xiamen's comprehensive city planning began in the 1980s. Rapid change, however, necessitated constant revision and updating. In 1990, an "adjustment plan" was generated to project future developments. This adjustment plan was approved by the provincial government in June of that year.[14] As shown in the adjustment plan and map, the urban area was to cover 450 sq km. Building of the city proper would be concentrated on the west side of the Yingtan-Xiamen railroad; development of the east side of the tracks would be put off until a more appropriate date, while satellite towns such as Jimei, Xinlin, and Haicang would be developed. Thus, both sides of the tracks were included in the plan, which made it necessary for Caitang's development of residential and industrial land to integrate, not clash with, the overall Xiamen plan. Since the Luling Highway was planned to go by the southern limits of Caitang, the village's residential area could not go beyond the Luling Highway while its industrial zone had to be south of the highway. Restricted by the overall plan, Caitang had to make adjustments in its own city planning with the support of the city planning and land bureaus of Xiamen. Its overall plan was to divide the village into three areas: one residential, one industrial, and one agricultural. The entire village would be divided into squares by the 12–meter-wide Luling Highway, the main trunk line, along with several 7–meter-wide secondary roads. This would link the village with Xiamen (through Luling and the highway from Hecuo to Lianban). They also planned to improve or build elementary schools, kindergartens, medical and recreational centers, shopping centers, markets, service outlets, and parking lots and plant a lot of trees. When completed, Caitang would become a model district, or a so-called small satellite town.

After Deng Xiaoping's southern tour and the talks he gave, Xiamen readjusted its economic development plans and made still more progress. The 1990 adjustment plan was found to be inadequate in view of the new situation. The building of a "Greater Xiamen" was proposed and the overall city plan was further revised.

A new comprehensive planning[15] map drawn up in 1993 revealed that Xiamen's city proper would not be limited to the western part of the Yingtan-Xiamen railway but would include the eastern part. All suburban towns—not just Jimei, Xinlin, and Haicang—would become satellite towns. Xiamen municipality would be much larger than that in the 1990 plan. The 1993 plan clearly included Caitang in the municipality. At present, the eastern part of the tracks is already being opened up. Construction of the Luling Highway passing through Caitang has begun and is moving east. We believe, therefore, that the village will be linked to the municipality in the not-too-distant future and become a small district or "corner" in it. At that time, the people of Caitang who have already acquired the urban way of life, or who can be said to have been urbanized, will finally become city residents, not just urbanized people with rural registration.

Notes

1. *Renkouxue cidian* (Demography Dictionary). Ed. Liu Zheng et al. Beijing: People's Publishing House, 1986 ed., p. 367.

2. *Wenhuaxue cidian* (Dictionary of Cultural Studies). Ed. Tan Guangguang, Feng Li, Chen Pu et al. Beijing: Central Nationalities Institute Publishers, 1988 ed., p. 60.

3. *Jianming renkouxue cidian* (Concise Demography Dictionary). Ed. Han Mingxi, Li Deguang et al. Lanzhou: Gansu People's Publishing House, 1987 ed., p. 275.

4. *Chengshi jingji cidian* (Urban Economics Dictionary). Ed. Cui Xinhuan et al. Chongqing: Sichuan Scientific and Technological Publishing House, 1986 ed., p. 57.

5. *Chengshixue gailun* (Outline of Urban Studies). Ed. Huang Jizhong, Xia Renfan et al. Shenyang: Shenyang Publishing House, 1989 ed., p. 21.

6. *Dangdai xinshuyu* (New Modern Terminology). Ed. Jin Zhe, Yao Yongchuan, Chen Xiejun et al. Shanghai: Shanghai People's Publishing House, 1988 ed., p. 551.

7. *Renkouxue cidian* (Demography Dictionary). Ed. Liu Zheng et al. Beijing: People's Publishing House, 1986 ed., p. 367.

8. See Yang Zhongguang and Liao Kangyu, "The Road to Urbanization with Chinese Characteristics," *Jingji yanjiu* (Economic Research), 1984:8; also, Wu Dasheng et al., "Coordinated Development of Cities and Small Towns," *Shehuixue yanjiu* (Sociological Research), 1988:2.

9. Yang Shanmin, "Modernization: Strategic Choices in Urban Development," *Shandong shehui kexue* (Shandong Social Science), 1990:2.

10. Li Peilin, "Another Invisible Hand: Transformation of Social Structure," *Zhongguo shehui kexue* (Chinese Social Science), 1990:5.

11. *Shehuixue cidian* (Sociology Dictionary). Shanghai: Shanghai Dictionary Publishing House, 1992, p. 316.

12. Industry was then included in subsidiary occupations. This changed only after 1984, when industry, construction, and transportation began to be listed separately.

13. *Xiamen jingji tequ jianshe gailan* (Overview of Construction at the Xiamen SEZ). Beijing: China Statistical Publishers, 1991, p. 8.

14. "Overall City Plan of Xiamen in Brief," *Xiamen jingji jianshe gailan* (Overview of Economic Construction at the Xiamen SEZ). Beijing: China Statistical Publishers, 1990, pp. 199–200.

15. Quoted from *Zhongguo Xiamen Haicang touzi zhinan* (Guide to Investment in Haicang, Xiamen, China). Xiamen.

6

Rural Urbanization on the Liaodong Peninsula

A Village, a Town, and a *Nongmin Cheng*

Lisa Hoffman and Liu Zhongquan

When talking about the new tall buildings and other construction in his hometown, a sixty-eight-year-old man in Beile *zhen,* one of our three field sites, told us, "I never thought I would see this in my lifetime." He was referring to the fact that after living in a small family house and farming most of his life, he was now living in an apartment building with central

This research was done in 1996, in conjunction with Lisa Hoffman's dissertation fieldwork, which was generously funded by the Committee on Scholarly Communication with China, the Foreign Language and Area Studies Fellowship, and the Center for Studies in Higher Education at University of California at Berkeley. All of the investigations and discussions were done as cooperation between Liu Zhongquan, Professor of Sociology at Dalian University of Technology, and Lisa Hoffman, an anthropology doctoral candidate at U.C. Berkeley. After discussions of what should be included and the significance of each research site, the chapter was written in English by Ms. Hoffman. When necessary, Prof. Liu is credited with certain arguments and these are noted in the text.

Both authors are grateful to Mr. Tang Dongsheng (Director of the Second Department of the Rural Working Committee for Policy Research [*Dalian shi nong wei zheng yan erchu*] and Deputy Secretary General of Dalian's Suburbia Economic Research Association [*Dalian shi chengjiao jingji yanjiuhui*]) and Dalian Municipal Government in general, as well as to the local leaders in Beile, Yangjia, and Yangshufang. Without their cooperation and help this research would not have been possible. Lisa Hoffman would also like to thank Neil Diamant, Greg Guldin, Susan Hoffman, and Ren Hai for their careful readings and insightful comments on earlier versions.

heating and tap water while two of his three children were working outside of agriculture. Is this what is meant by rural urbanization? In this chapter we discuss the urbanization process on the Liaodong Peninsula in northeastern China and look at how local leaders are enacting reforms in the area to help their localities urbanize and develop. Our aim here is twofold. First, we begin to explore *what it means to urbanize;* and see how that process often is identified in terms of physical changes to the landscape and how people spend their days. Do they work in offices, factories, or on the land? Do they live in apartment buildings and buy all of their food in the market? Second, we work to understand *what has propelled some areas* near Dalian city to make so many changes in the past several years.

We argue here that local leadership, regional reforms, and the type of economic system on which the rural area's development is based are critical elements in the urbanization process. The series of policy changes, infrastructure investments, and reforms in the early nineties has provided room for the entrepreneurial talents of certain local leaders to flourish, influencing which localities would make moves to "urbanize" their rural area, as well as the way these urbanization processes are experienced by local residents. Regional reforms and developments, within the context of a general governmental concern with promoting the growth of small towns and township enterprises, also frame our discussion. And finally, the type of economic system is important in terms of Dalian's history of heavy industry and collective ownership. Below, we first address the economic issue, then review urbanization policy issues in the area, and then provide three examples of local leadership concerned with the details of rural urbanization.

The three sites—Beile, Yangjia, and Yangshufang—are all in the greater Dalian administrative area and are part of the growing "urban belt" in the Bohai Sea region (Liu, Ji, and Chang 1995; see Figure 6.1). Beile Town is an example of what we call "expressway urbanization" because of its location next to the road and the way local leaders have promoted development. The second site, Yangjia Village, is located between two larger, more urban areas, one being a special economic zone that relies heavily on foreign investment. Thus, Yangjia is an example of reliance on foreign investment for rural urbanization. Yangshufang, the home of Dayang Enterprise Group, on the other hand, represents farmer-initiated development in the form of a *nongmin cheng*—a farmer's town.

At each of the sites we met with local leaders and were accompanied by a Dalian Municipal Government official who was responsible for research on suburbs and rural areas.[1] Our opportunities to speak with local residents and workers were limited, and in some instances did not exist at all. Thus, the interpretations presented here should be read as official representations

Figure 6.1 **Dalian Administrative Area**

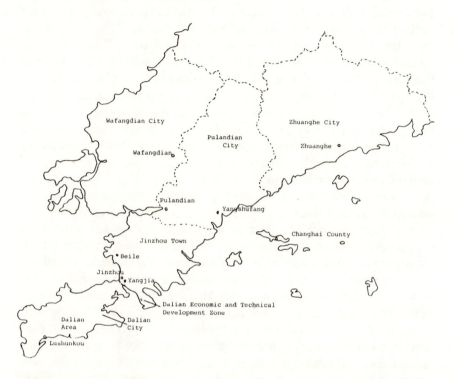

of local development. We did, however, return to Beile and Yangjia in September 1996 and spoke with several local residents, accompanied by local administrators only (local Women's Federation and Old Folks' Committee). Their comments are included below.

Regional Economic Particularities

When comparing rural urbanization research done in southern China (as reported by Zhou and others in this volume) to the research presented here, we do not want to argue that this geographic division is a major determining factor. Yet because of divergences in historical processes and experiences, there are some modest regional variations that should be noted and that may contribute to local forms of urbanization. Dalian, a major port city in northeast China located on the Liaodong Peninsula in Liaoning Province, is one of China's fourteen "Open Cities" and started building one of China's first Economic and Technical Development Zones (*jingji jishu kaifaqu*) in 1985 (hereafter, the Zone).

Neighboring Lushun (Port Arthur) was occupied by the British in 1858 and became a Chinese naval base in the 1880s, but Dalian itself was a small fishing village until 1898 when the Russians "forced China by gunboat diplomacy to accept a twenty-five-year Russian lease of Dalian and Port Arthur" (Clausen and Thogersen 1995: 24). Russia built the first wharf and railroads to Changchun during their occupation of Dalian, which ended in 1905 with the Russo-Japanese War. Japanese forces remained in northeast China from 1905 to 1945, setting up the Manchukuo puppet government in 1932, expanding Dalian City during the colonialization, and developing heavy industry across the northeast. Currently, many Japanese companies are returning to the Dalian area to invest in projects, reorienting their presence and influence in the region.

The northeast continues to be known for its large, state-run, heavy-industry enterprises that are concentrated in power, oil refineries, chemicals, machinery, and automobiles.[2] During the 1960s, village-run enterprises (*cunban qiye*), which later became township enterprises, grew up around the large state-owned factories in the Dalian area.[3] These small, collectively owned enterprises would get materials from the large state enterprises so as to make parts or process the materials according to the needs of the state factories or local rural area. For example, around the steel factories and shipbuilding factories in Dalian, small collective projects opened that used scrap metal to make agricultural tools or oil products from the oil refineries to make chemical fertilizers. The growth of these small manufacturers was reinforced by the fact that the state-run factories were willing to hire only these collectives (*jiti*) to do the work. A collective provided a "safer" feeling to the factory, as it was usually large enough to do the project and the state was more likely to trust a collective to do the job and to do it correctly.

This is a different experience from that of southern China, where light industry and household enterprise are more prominent and where villages have relied heavily on individual enterprises (*getihu*) for general economic development in the reform era (see also Johnson 1993). The examples we provide in this chapter, however, all rely on collective forms of economic investment and ownership (*jiti*) for basic rural industrialization and urbanization, although the process is never the same in each place. The cultural processes that make these economic systems different, such as the sexual division of labor, are important issues to understand as well, but unfortunately they are beyond the scope of this chapter.[4]

In addition, related to the emphasis on heavy industry, in Dalian there was a high concentration of technical experts (*jishu rencai*) in the state-run factories who retired and used their knowledge and technical skills to help build the growing township enterprises in the 1980s and 1990s. In fact,

Dalian historically had the highest concentration of "talent" (*rencai*) in the northeast (currently 360,000 skilled persons), as college-trained graduates were assigned to these heavy-industry units by the government. Their business experience and exposure to "modern" and outside ideas are other reasons the township enterprises in the northeast moved into the international economy and began exporting early, Liu Zhongquan argues. In other words, many of the township enterprise managers were *not* farmers who had moved into factory work, but instead were workers from state-run factories who had received a formal education and had been living in large urban areas.

Urbanization Policy Issues

Is There an Urbanization Standard?

Part of the problem when researching urbanization processes in China is working with official Chinese definitions of urban versus rural life. The definition of *urban* "has been affected by a uniquely Chinese perspective on the notion of 'urban,' based largely on a combination of where people live and whether the state or the commune is responsible for providing for their grain needs" (Goldstein 1990: 676–677). Not only grain, but the whole system of household registration institutionalized the urban-rural distinction (see Whyte and Parish 1984; Zhou 1996). Now that grain is available on the market, ration coupons are not needed to buy products in the cities; likewise, as the housing system is reformed, many of these distinctions are no longer pertinent. We ask if there are other urbanization standards researchers should be using.

The municipal government official accompanying us explained, in six points, what he understood to be markers of urban life and the urbanization process (*chengshihua biaozhun*). First is the type of work in which the residents engage. In the past, the people in these areas all worked the land, but then they became workers, doctors, and service workers, expanding economic opportunities. Second is housing. The small family homes have been torn down and replaced with apartment buildings (*loufang*) and villas (*bieshu*). Third are the improvements in plumbing (i.e., people have indoor bathrooms) and electricity. Fourth are advancements in communications and transportation, including residential phone service and paved roads. Fifth is the increase in cultural activities, ranging from the construction of schools to greater availability of home entertainment equipment and movie theaters. The final point is the development of the service industry, including hospitals, retail stores, barbers, and beauty parlors (cf. Guldin, chap. 3, this volume; Wang 1995).

Considering these factors, one can understand why some researchers feel there is a difference between the urban statistics and the way many people are actually living their lives (see also Chan 1994). Families may have agricultural household registrations, may be living in old one-story houses but working in factories, and often may be traveling to the city for business or leisure, moving along avenues that see frequent flows of "urban" people, goods, and information (Guldin 1992). Including such lifestyles in the calculation of what is urban avoids the tendency to associate "urban" with a particular place or administrative region and instead focuses on people's cultural practices. In fact, John Fincher concludes that "judged by *how* Chinese use their time, the population is almost certainly already predominantly urban. The population may soon also be urban by definitions of *where* they use most of their time" (1990: 51, emphasis in original).

It is also useful to refer to Arjun Appadurai's notion of ethnoscapes (1991),[5] which aims to incorporate people's imaginations (not spatially bound) in their cultural repertoire. Media images, labor practices, and even financial relationships that come from "elsewhere" (global scale and more local scales) are impacting the "possibilities" and imaginations in particular places. Appadurai argues that "more persons in more parts of the world consider a wider set of possible lives than they ever did before" (1991: 197), which easily can be argued for China's rural migrants today. As farmers watch television in a small village in Liaoning Province, family members begin to think about other options, economically and culturally. A recent article in the *China Daily* (3/5/96: 10) emphasizes the growing importance of mass media, particularly television, radio, and newspapers, in rural people's lives, which resonates with this notion of ethnoscapes and how the imagination can propel people to migrate and hence fuel the growth of small towns in rural areas. The author Yue Xin (1996) argues that "rural Chinese have begun turning their eyes to a more distant horizon and developing an interest in a world that they now see has become increasingly intertwined with their own." With economic reforms, village residents now spend less time with the "daily struggle for food and shelter" and more time learning about what is going on outside of their local communities. Incorporating this aspect of migration into our studies of urbanization and the flow of people and ideas is critical to expanding our understanding beyond rigidly territorialized notions of urban or rural life.

The Growth of Small Towns and Township Enterprises

In order to stem the flow of rural migrants to large urban centers, the central government is advocating the growth of small towns and the diversification of economic opportunities in "rural" areas. This includes pushing for industrial growth by establishing township enterprises (*xiangzhen qiye*); agricultural diversification (e.g., vegetables, fisheries, orchards); and service industries such as construction, transportation, and restaurants. Such options are meant to absorb surplus labor within rural areas, concentrate rural populations in small towns, and hence control the growth of large cities (see also Wang 1996).

The growth of these small towns is central to rural urbanization research, but the terminology referring to small towns and villages is quite confusing. Ma Rong explains that "in official statistical analyses 'town' (*zhen*) is a level of government in the administrative system of China that falls between 'city' (*shi*) or 'county' (*xian*) on the one hand and 'village committee' (*cunmin weiyuanhui*) on the other. In the Chinese administrative system, a 'designated town' (*jianzhi zhen*) is under either a city or a county.[6] A town is placed administratively at the same level as a *xiang* ('a subcounty district,' formerly a commune), but a town government has more cadres than a *xiang* and also has special funds for public construction in town" (1992: 119). But he also argues that through more detailed work, researchers must distinguish among county towns (*xian zhen*), designated towns (*jianzhi zhen*), and *xiang* towns (*xiang zhen*)—the previous rural commune system (1992: 121–127)—since relying on classifications alone does not explain the lifestyle or urbanization trends at a site.

In the Dalian City administrative area, there are seventy-seven designated towns. Most critical in determining which would be ratified as a designated town were their scale, the infrastructure and technological conditions, and their development potential. A designated town is really meant to be a center for surrounding areas and therefore must have the base to support further development. As Ma Rong has noted, the most critical difference for local leaders between a *xiang* (in the rural system) and a *zhen* (in the urban system) is that the *zhen* receives some state investment. For instance, the local state government offices of the Tax Bureau, Public Security Bureau, and banks should receive state funds when the town becomes a *jianzhi zhen*. Reclassification can provide "the power to levy certain taxes and to control funds for development made available by the state" (Goldstein 1990: 675).

Our concern here, however, is with *how* villages of 1,000 people are developing the local economy, building township enterprises, attracting surplus labor from other areas, building housing and other services for the growing population, and according to the policy, aiming eventually to become small cities (*xiao chengshi*) of 30,000 people. Our three field sites, Beile, Yangjia, and Yangshufang, are lower on the urban hierarchy than the desired ideal of the small city classification at this time, and therefore they provide good examples of different strategies for town building, economic diversification, and population concentration. The local leaders' strategies cannot be analyzed in a vacuum; rather, they must be evaluated in the context of government policies that encourage linking small towns and cities to larger urban centers, while also making them attractive places for rural migrants to stay (Hua 1995).

An important element of rural migration is the *hukou* system, which has been used to control the movement of populations. In China, every person must have a household registration, or *hukou,* which gives the individual the legal right to be a resident of a locality and grants access to housing, medical coverage, and ration coupons. *Hukou* are broadly separated into two categories: agricultural (*nongye*) and nonagricultural/urban (*fei-nong-ye*). In the early 1960s, the government "tightened and upgraded the household registration system," and since then most "citizens have been forbidden to change their officially registered residence without the authorization of the local government at both origin and destination" (Gui and Liu 1992: 533). Presently, however, there is an increasing "floating population" of primarily rural migrants who move to other areas without obtaining government consent to pursue work or join family members (see also Zhou 1993; Solinger 1985).[7]

Although there has been a general easing of the agricultural-nonagricultural (urban) *hukou* distinction recently, other parts of the system still seriously restrict a family's options, such as education. If a family has an urban registration and their child takes the entrance exam for a local technical school (*zhiye zhongxue* and *jishu xuexiao*), the child could be admitted with scores marginally lower than a child with an agricultural *hukou.* This policy aims to control the flow of agricultural *hukou* holders into urban areas by restricting their numbers in lower-level secondary education. In addition, sometimes technical schools do not admit agricultural registration holders at all if the local administration has determined there is no use for this particular specialty in the countryside, as the government wants agricultural *hukou* holders to go back after they graduate. Top universities, such as the key universities, are "*hukou* blind" for admittance, however.

The children of urban *hukou* holders also have more job options, as they can go to a township enterprise, state-run enterprise, or a collective enterprise, whereas those with agricultural registrations can go only to the township enterprises or to the foreign enterprises (e.g., in the Zone). At the same time, a *nongye hukou* has benefits, especially for those living in the suburban districts of Lushunkou, Ganjingzi, and Jinzhou around Dalian. Many of these residents have higher salaries (owing to the household responsibility system and profit increases in private and collective enterprises) than those in state-run factories in the cities. Moreover, there is more living space and they can build their own houses, perhaps renting them to others. *Hukou* distinctions do not, however, necessarily reflect lifestyle and economic activities.

The Dalian Area and Its Industrial Small Zones

Dalian has moved along with the national call for rural urbanization and the growth of township enterprises, but it also has devised policies to deal with problems that have emerged during this process. The most significant problem facing the expansion and growth of township enterprises is dispersion of enterprises in the area. Their lack of centralization means investment capital, labor, resources, and equipment are dispersed and less effective. The push for township enterprises has created weak infrastructures and infrastructure duplication, plus areas have difficulty attracting laborers if they cannot support the growing population. In addition, dispersed enterprises have led to environmental pollution that the government wants to control more closely.

To address these problems, the Municipal Government followed examples in the south and established fourteen "industrial small zones" (*gongye xiaoqu*), primarily along the Shenyang-Dalian Expressway, that were ratified by the province in 1992 (two have since been demoted because of lack of development, totaling twelve today). The areas are also known as Economic and Technical Development Small Zones (*jingji jishu kaifa xiaoqu*) because of the preferential economic policies granted, such as lower land prices, the ability to attract foreign investors, and special loans. In these areas, the scale of the enterprises can increase, the infrastructure problems can be solved by pooling resources, and pollution problems can be better controlled. This kind of development plan is called "coming together" (*lianpian kaifa*). The small towns are expected to rely on the big cities—that is, the small industrial areas are to link up with the city resources (see also Wang 1995).

The Dalian region includes both larger urban areas and many small towns. Currently, Dalian City government is administratively responsible for four city districts (Zhongshan, Xigang, Shahekou, and Ganjingzi) and two suburban areas (Jinzhou and Lushunkou) that cover a total of 12,574 sq km.[8] In addition, the general administrative area of the Municipal Government includes three county-level cities—Pulandian, Zhuanghe, Wafangdian—and Changhai County (a county made up of islands), as well as the new city area called the Economic and Technical Development Zone (see Figure 6.1). The inclusion of surrounding rural counties in "urban" boundaries, such as these cities, was done to control urban sprawl by implementing comprehensive development strategies. Such boundary changes and redefinitions of urban areas has resulted in a surge in urban population, but this should not be seen as an expression of real "urban" growth (Linge and Forbes 1990; Ma 1992). The administrative jurisdiction of Dalian was extended beyond the original city limits in the 1960s. Victor Sit refers to this process as the promotion of "a new concept of the city, that is, a self-sufficient city region" in which the surrounding agricultural areas are controlled more directly by the city government in order to ensure that there is a source of grain and nonstaple foods (1985: 31).[9] In the Dalian area, control of pollution and encouragement of urban and rural areas to help each other develop are important as well (see also Liu et al. 1994).

The examples of rural urbanization below are all in the greater Dalian administrative area and all include the following processes: agricultural registration holders move into nonagricultural work, agricultural land disappears, and there is investment in what many identify with urban infrastructure (e.g., apartment buildings, central supply of water and heat, grain and vegetable markets).[10] The first is Beile, a town in Jinzhou District that has based its growth and economic diversification on the Shenyang-Dalian Expressway built alongside the village in 1991.[11] Beile has emphasized business and trade, and has built a large, regional market to promote growth in the area. The second example is Yangjia, a very small village in between Jinzhou City (also in Jinzhou District) and Dalian's Economic and Technical Development Zone, which is known for its reliance on foreign capital for infrastructure and economic development. In 1992, it was certified as Dalian City Yangjia Economic Development Small Zone (*Dalian shi Yangjia jingji kaifa xiaoqu*), and it offers special policies similar to the Zone. The final example is Yangshufang, a "rural resident's" or "farmer's town," or *nongmin cheng,* developed by Li Guilian, a successful female entrepreneur in the fashion industry. Yangshufang is in Pulandian District, about forty minutes from Pulandian City.

The Three Field Sites: The Interplay of Policy and Leadership

Beile: Expressway Urbanization

When we exited the Shenyang-Dalian Expressway, we immediately came upon a small community with several buildings along the roadway, as well as many cars and motorbikes waiting for passengers. The driver took us through the large gate with traditional architectural touches, which bears the complex characters: *Bei Le.* The streets were busy as we passed a stretch of *getihu,* or individual enterprises, selling primarily sofas, chairs, and lamps. We then pulled into the parking lot of one of the tallest buildings (four stories) in Beile, which houses the offices of Mr. Chi Fusheng, who serves as village head (*cunzhang*) and doubles as general manager of the Beile General Company.

Manager Chi is recognized as an important reason Beile has urbanized and developed. An older man told us, "Nineteen eighty-four is when the village leader took power; we must recognize this is why the greatest change started then." It was at that time that there was a collective investment by local people in a textile factory, led by Manager Chi. During the 1980s and early 1990s, they continued investing in factories for industries as various as sewing machine needles,[12] textiles, dyeing, furniture making, chemicals, and food processing, including several joint-venture projects, but it was not until 1992 that Beile organized itself economically as a group (*jituan*) and set up the General Company.

Most significant, however, was the construction of the expressway that runs right next to the village. Manager Chi actively encouraged these new conditions, sent investigators out to the surrounding area to determine community needs, decided they would build a large commodities market, and then applied for a permit from the Dalian Municipal Government. In 1995, after the market was opened and the Dalian Government recognized the area's economic development and its ability to attract and support surplus labor from surrounding areas, Beile village became a small town. Previously Beile Village was part of Ershi Lipu *zhen,* but now it is called Beile *zhen.*

In addition, in 1995 Liaoning Province certified 100 satellite towns (*weixing cheng zhen*) in the province, including Beile, a satellite of Jinzhou City. This classification included 200,000 RMB for infrastructure development and a provincial ratification of the classification change from village (*cun*) to town (*zhen*). Beile also bought other villages' land and grasped the surrounding area in its administrative reach. This expanded area's population is around 10,000 residents, but the ideal goal is 30,000—the official size of a small city (*xiao chengshi*). Beile also is called an Economic and Technical Development Small Zone (*jingji jishu kaifa xiaoqu*). As we discuss below, the interplay of policy reform and entrepreneurial skills of the local leaders is affecting the type of rural urbanization and economic diversification a village experiences.[13]

The Market

The market has more than 2,000 booths, covers 46,000 sq m, and is the largest market in southern Liaoning Province. During our fall 1996 visit to

Beile, they were expanding the size slightly and sealing off several parts to better protect the booths from wind and rain. The site is well positioned along local roads, the expressway, and train routes, and is mainly meant as a place where people from surrounding towns can come to buy products they will sell in their home towns. It serves both as a wholesale market and as a retail market (at wholesale prices) for locals. Initial investment by the collective was more than 80 million RMB, which an older man confided was controversial. "Many people were opposed to building and investing so much money in the market. They wanted to grow fruit instead of building it, but they only saw the short-term benefits. Now we can see that it has brought a lot of development. And we have a township enterprise which makes apple juice. Still there are people who oppose this, but it is definitely the right way." Last year the total output value of the service industry in Beile was 300 million RMB, two-thirds of which is from business in the Market.

Products range from shoes and food products to used parts of homes resold to make green houses. It costs 2,500 RMB annually to rent 10 sq m of booth space in the market. Next door is a large store opened by the collective where individual entrepreneurs can rent space at a higher price if they do not want to be in the Market. One and a half meters of counter space in the store costs 2,000–3,000 RMB a year to rent. A man from Zhejiang Province, who was sent to this area originally to do decoration work, decided to stay on and rent a counter in the department store. He now is selling lights and other accessories for interior decoration. Also, some larger stores from Jinzhou City come here and rent space to sell their products.

Population, Welfare, and Migration

Owing to the strict separation of rural and urban populations in the *hukou* system, it is important to review how the numbers break down in these urbanizing areas. The population of Beile (immediate village area) totals 1,500 (as of April 1996), 500 of whom have nonagricultural household registrations and 1,000 of whom have agricultural registrations. But 90 percent of the population is engaged in industrial and other nonagricultural work (see Factories section below), while only 10 percent are doing agricultural work, which consists mostly of growing apples, vegetables, and some grain. There are 600–700 people from other areas living in Beile and they come from a number of different provinces. The difference between the local people and those from outside (*waidiren*) is that most nonlocal residents (in-migrants) do not receive local welfare packages (e.g., grain, oil, milk, gas) and their *hukou* are managed by the local Public Security Bureau branch rather than the town government because they have temporary registrations (*linshi hukou*). Yet there are several ways for outsiders to get local, permanent registrations and hence be eligible for benefits. To change their registration and remain in Beile, newcomers can buy a home, which requires around 50,000 RMB, or if they have a special or needed skill, then the town will provide housing and the *hukou* for them (as they do for technicians, or *jishu renyuan*). Also, if they invest a minimum of 8,000 RMB in the economy, they are allowed to stay.

Beile has printed a set of regulations concerning household registration, social welfare, old-age pension, medical insurance, and family planning that they distribute to newcomers and local residents. The *hukou* section, for instance, covers what you should do if you are an in-migrant or if a Beile resident marries an outsider. Although most in-migrants are from other small towns and villages, some city *hukou* holders and college graduates have moved to Beile. Currently there are over thirty technicians (mostly in the foodstuffs industry) with college degrees in Beile, whom the township enterprises hired through Dalian City's Talented Person's Labor Market (*rencai shichang*). There are a number of reasons such graduates are willing to work in township enterprises and live in smaller communities, Manager Chi explained. Higher salaries attract these city folk,[14] which average around 14,000 RMB a year and top out at 50–60,000 RMB a year in Beile.[15] This is compared to a salary of 7,000–8,000 RMB a year in a state-run enterprise in the city. In addition, the town provides spacious homes for technicians after they marry.

In general, Beile management is proud of the social welfare and benefits they can provide owing to their recent economic prosperity. "The collective takes care of everything now," Mr. Chi stated over lunch, "the collective car is used to take a mother and her newborn baby home from the hospital, as well as take the family to the funeral of a relative." To further emphasize the current social-welfare role of the collective,[16] Manager Chi gave the example of a criminal who had been released from prison and sent back to the village. Chi will work to reform him, find him a wife, give him a job, and provide housing so he will not be tempted to commit another crime.[17]

The benefits in Beile include grain, oil, meat, milk, liquefied gas, heating costs, medical guarantees, and old-age pensions.[18] For instance, if one has a village *hukou* and works in a village enterprise or agricultural organization, then the individual and his or her family receive these benefits, but if someone voluntarily leaves a job, resigns, or is discharged, benefits are canceled. If the individual would like to continue receiving benefits, however, he or she must start paying a fee upon leaving work. But if the individual resigns, is fired, or leaves again, then that person cannot pay for benefits again. For the in-migrants, if they open businesses and work at least five years in Beile, they can receive benefits, but if they register to do business in the market and do not do so for an entire year, they cannot receive benefits.

The in-migrants come from many different provinces, although the majority are, not surprisingly, from elsewhere in the northeast. One couple, both nonagricultural *hukou* holders, moved to Beile in 1992 from a town in Heilongjiang Province. They had a store selling primarily bedding and curtains in their hometown and planned on opening one where they settled. Originally they went to Dalian, but decided the prices were too high and that it was too difficult to start their kind of store. They were the first to open this kind of store in Beile (with a jewelry shop added), but now there are already seven such shops in town. The young husband explained that "business is good here, also the environment, the atmosphere, every aspect is good here." In addition to better business opportunities for small enterprises and cheap prices for vegetables and meats, Beile offers special policies to attract investors. "The welfare is very good here," the woman said, "they take care of their residents."

Factories

Visits to factories in Beile show that a significant portion of those who have agricultural registrations are living in small towns and are not doing agricultural work. In fact, walking into a factory in Beile, one would not immediately know if he or she was in this "village" or had stepped into a factory site in Shenzhen.

The first stop was a thread and weaving factory whose workers were almost all female. This factory started later than the others and just recently invested in three machines from Taiwan. The second factory was a dyeing operation with over 300 workers, primarily male, who used machines from Korea. Above the dyeing plant, clothes are made from the dyed materials and then exported according to the customers' requirements. Women were doing all of the sewing work and they were expected to work as long as necessary to complete the job. When we visited the workroom they were making children's undershirts for export to Japan.

The third factory was the large Pure Love Apple Juice Company which makes 100 percent apple juice, no sugar added. The factory covers 40,000 sq m and was a state-run company but is now a joint-venture with a partner from Hong Kong. There are only 100 workers here, including the managers, because the business relies on computers to run many of the machines. The factory now takes 20,000 tons of apples, but the Dalian area produces 900,000 tons of apples so the managers are interested in expanding and are adding a section that will make concentrated juice. Because the area produces so many apples, the Municipal Government was willing to give loans to set up this company to use the surplus fruit.

The Urbanizing Experience in Beile

When discussing an urban way of life, so much has to do with residents' own perceptions of their daily schedules and lifestyles. When the young couple that had migrated from Heilongjiang commented on the changes in Beile since they arrived, for example, both referred to the number of taxis around the market. "Also, there are roads, they have built apartment buildings, and the beautification is all really good in town." In another interview, an old man explained, "Our lifestyle is already at the same level as those in Dalian. We buy vegetables in the market and now our farmers are workers in the agricultural industry rather than peasants (*nongye gongren* versus *nongmin*) . . . very few people in Dalian live like us, we are lucky here." This man also attributed much of what he identified as Beile's success to Manager Chi. "He is very open-minded. If the leaders can do well and if they are flexible, then the village can get industry. Other places nearby are still farming."

"They have to find work for you here because we have no land to farm," he went on, "so we can work eight hours a day and then come home. Beile village is better off because of this. In fact, most of those who work in the fields are workers [*gongren*]." In his own family, his one son does temporary construction work, his younger daughter (thirty years old, one child) lives across the hall and works in the village administration looking after the market, but his oldest daughter (thirty-nine years old, two children) lives in a village nearby and works on the land.

Other changes that blur the urban-rural dichotomy include new consumption practices and leisure items in homes. For example, the young couple's home has a telephone, television, stereo, and video machine. During their leisure time they watch television, but in general do not have a lot of time for entertainment activities like dancing or traveling, although they did just return from a trip to Shanghai and scenic Huang Shan, where they spent over 10,000 RMB.

Mr. Chi was proud to tell us that there are three karaoke and dancing halls in the town. People have more leisure time now, he explained, because residents are not raising animals or growing their own vegetables when living in the big apartment buildings. So when they go home from work they have spare time to sing karaoke and watch television. He estimated that 60 percent of the residents have karaoke machines, 100 percent have TVs, and 80 percent have phones in their homes. Beile also offers a number of restaurants and hotels (half state-run and half collective-run). The post office and banks are all state-run and come with state recognition of their official township status, and transportation and warehouse services are 90 percent privately or individually owned and 10 percent are collective-run.

Another commonly used marker of urbanization and development by local administrators is the move from traditional family homes to apartment buildings. Beile is no exception. In 1987, Beile first invested in two buildings (forty-eight homes) to provide housing for married workers and now has a total of twenty-two buildings. These apartments all have bathrooms, Manager Chi boasted. Yet the housing problem has been solved for only half of the local population. Many are still in small houses, but when asked if everyone was willing to move to the big buildings, he responded emphatically, "Yes!" Why? Because these buildings have piped gas and water supply.

In 1993, one of our interviewees, his wife, and mother-in-law moved into a 78.7 sq m apartment and his daughter, her husband, and her child live across the hall in a 67.8 sq m apartment. "Before we had to go very far away for water; we had never heard of such a thing before [central water and heat]. . . . Life is much better now; we can see it" in the form of televisions, refrigerators, roads, street lamps, and so on. "Our life is good now," he went on. "In 1992 we bought a color television, and in 1991 we bought a refrigerator." When they first moved, however, they were not used to it, but now they would not go back to their old one-story home. "It was too dirty there," the daughter said, followed by her mother who claimed, "Of course, we wanted to move; that was an old broken-down house."

We also visited some surprisingly large apartments built for higher officials (*cunmin weiyuanhui*, or village committee) in 1993 after apartments for workers had been built. They were very well equipped with items also commonly seen in urban homes. The first stop was a two-story, seven-room, 120+ sq m home for four people (two parents and two children). Upstairs in the bedroom they had a smaller Sony TV and a Legend computer, and downstairs in the main living area there was a larger Toshiba TV, a Panasonic karaoke machine, and a Kenwood stereo system plus a Sony multi-disc player. The second home was in the bottom half of this building and also two floors, but was much more sparsely furnished than the first. It has six rooms for five people (the parents, two children, and the husband's mother). All of their electrical appliances were famous domestic brands that they bought in Dalian City. Such consumptive practices and such attitudes as "our lifestyle is already at the same level as those in Dalian" emphasize the lack of congruence between official classifications and residents' perceptions of their changing lives—for which Manager Chi is held in high esteem.

Yangjia: Reliance on Foreign Investment for Urbanization

Yangjia (about 30 km from Dalian City proper) is located between Dalian's Economic and Technical Development Zone and Jinzhou City and is representative of the kind of urbanization processes that can occur in the ambiguous boundary between large cities and their surrounding "countryside" (unofficially, *chengxiang jiehe bu* and *chengshi bianyuan qu*). Our research found that the way village leaders decide to use their geographic advantage and work to get favorable investment policies has had a significant impact on physical and lifestyle changes. As one resident told us, things really started changing in 1992, when the new local leader came to power: "He is willing to do things; he is courageous."

The time when Shen Lianglun became the village leader (*cunzhang*) was also the time of Deng Xiaoping's exhortative tour of southern China in 1992, which was used by local leaders to define a turning point in Yangjia's history. Shen was faced with four of the village's nine enterprises going bankrupt when he took office, and he decided to turn the village's collective economy into an enterprise, a *qiye*, in order to do business and sign contracts with foreign companies. From that time on, Mr. Shen, like Manager Chi of Beile, served as both the village head and the general manager of Dalian Jinyang Corporation, exhibiting how local leaders engage conditions that allow their entrepreneurial abilities to prosper. Political power and the enterprise previously had been separated, but after 1992 these could be put together so that a *cunzhang* (village head) could also be a *zong jingli* (general manager) of a corporation. An area that used to export workers because local opportunities were too few soon not only saw its own residents come back to their hometown to work but also became a labor importing area.

Yangjia had been a poor village with not very fertile land, but its proximity to the city of Jinzhou allowed it to rely on this prosperous neighbor.[19] In addition, Dalian's Economic and Technical Development Zone is on the other side of the village, with construction begun in 1984. The Zone relies primarily on foreign investment for its growth and expansion, which clearly has had a strong impact on Yangjia. As noted above, coinciding with Manager Shen's ascendancy, in 1992 Yangjia became a kind of special economic zone that could offer preferential policies for foreign investors, similar to those offered in the Zone. Dalian Municipal Government and

Jinzhou District Government ratified this new zone as Dalian City Yangjia Economic Development Small Zone (*Dalian shi Yangjia jingji kaifa xiaoqu*).

Currently Yangjia stands as an example in the Dalian area of how a village can enter the international economy and gain international cooperation, based on collective-owned development of the Jinyang Corporation. Manager Shen believes that collective development is much faster than investment on an individual basis. Every year they take some of the profits and keep it for the collective and the collective's expenses. Some of this is distributed as bonuses and some is kept for further investment in infrastructure. In 1994, when the collective took back land from people to develop industry, it gave 8,000 RMB to every person whose land was involved.

Now in the village's 1.44 sq km, there are twenty-eight enterprises, ten of which are foreign-invested projects. These include a large Sino-Malaysian joint plywood manufacturing venture, construction of machine parts, production of wood chopsticks and frozen seafood for export to Japan, and a dairy[20] and a Japanese sake brewery. Most land in the village has already been used for nonagricultural activities, but they have determined that some kinds of agricultural production are, in fact, quite profitable. Manager Shen is now talking about buying land in the mountain areas and converting it to both a tourist area and an orchard, which would offer higher profits than growing grain or vegetables. Yangjia will invest in the roads, parks, swimming areas, and fishing facilities. They call this a new economic development area, or *xinde jingji fazhan qu*. With its position near the big city, Yangjia can rely on the city's influence, but poorer rural areas must use this kind of village development and investment. Planners want to engage locals in a step-by-step process whereby small towns invest money in developing the poorer inland areas, Shen explained.

Landscape Changes

Although the process of urbanization, especially "folk" conceptions of it (see Guldin, chapter 3 this volume) often is defined as the construction of tall buildings and the disappearance of "agricultural" green space, Yangjia is an exception to this. Originally, Manager Shen was driven by the image of Hong Kong and hence had planned to build sixty apartment buildings in the 1.44 sq km of land available. But then the mayor of Dalian, Bo Xilai, encouraged him to use the image of Singapore rather than Hong Kong to develop a healthy urban atmosphere: "Do not strive to be largest, but strive to be best" (*buqiu zuida, dan qiu zui jia*) is a commonly heard phrase in Dalian. Mayor Bo has relied on the Singaporean model particularly in terms of the city's environment and the establishment of new green space. After hearing this, Manager Shen changed the development strategy and decided to build only twenty-eight large apartment buildings. He also made a point of showing us the green space, which includes 5,000 trees along roads and pathways and 60,000 sq m of grass. Only 1 more sq km remains to be built up as an industrial area. Mr. Shen also is proud of their "zoned" development, which separates functional areas: the industrial area, the commercial and trade zone, and the residential section.

Lists of land-use planning and infrastructure development reveal that the village includes 520 *mu* of agricultural land (1 *mu* = 0.0667 hectares), 800,000 sq m (equal to 1,200 *mu*) of industrial land, and 260,000 sq m of residential and public buildings. Infrastructure and facilities development includes 10,200 m of water lines and 7,500 m of sewage lines, 6,000 m of roads, and 40,000 sq m of centrally heated space. The clinic building has two doctors and covers 100 sq m, and there is a larger hospital 2 km from the village. An old folks center has 250 senior citizens and covers 200 sq m. At the time of our visit, they were preparing to build a new five-story, European-style school building. "We want it to be even better than the ones in the city." The plans include a sports arena and larger local hospital as well.

Such land-use changes are not just edifices, but have a significant impact on residents' lives. For instance, we met an elderly couple of seventy-seven and seventy-five years old whose families had been working the land in the area for about 300 years. But now "there is no more land," so their children find work, often temporary, in jobs such as construction, local factories, and carpentry. The village gives them an old-age pension of 100 RMB per month per person (those over eighty receive 115 RMB), but if it is not enough their children also provide money.[21] The local government hopes to increase the pension to 150 a month by 1997, and to 200 a month by the year 2000. Cleaning or beautifying (e.g., sweeping the streets) after retirement can add another 200 RMB a month to one's pension.

Population and Migration

The total current population of the Yangjia area is 1,700 local residents and 1,500 outsiders, which breaks down to 1,900 agricultural registrations and 1,300 nonagricultural registrations. Significantly, the majority of the residents have agricultural registrations, but there is "no more land" to farm. Currently there are 503 people of working age in the village—233 men and 270 women—but only 50 people do agricultural work on a daily basis. Three hundred work in industry and the remaining 153 are in various service industries. In addition, there are 780 in-migrant workers in factories and about 100 technical workers.

Many of the in-migrant workers are hired by the joint-venture and foreign-owned factories in the nearby Zone. This has caused some friction with local residents, who feel they are losing higher-paying factory jobs, especially those for young women. "The outsiders get the good jobs in the Development Zone because they have more education than the local girls," our seventy-seven-year-old interviewee told us. Many of the foreign enterprises require a certain level of education, usually either junior or senior middle school, to work in their factories. Apparently many young women from Pulandian District, Zhuanghe District, and even Heilongjiang Province are living in the Yangjia area where rent is cheaper than in the Zone and taking these jobs. "We don't have much to do with them. They come here just for work. If there is no work they go. . . . If they don't do anything illegal and they come here to work, we welcome them," she said as she backed off of her critique. "We are all Chinese and they come here so they can have money to eat." Later on in the interview she complained that many of these young women come here to have more children too, and the local government cannot control them all (*guanbuliao*).

The Urbanizing Experience in Yangjia

In the past three years the collective has built 850 units of residential space in apartment buildings, totaling 60,000 sq m of housing. Half are for local residents and the other half are for sale to in-migrants. Local residents and in-migrants who have lived here for a long time can buy a home for 800 RMB per sq m, but newly arrived outsiders must pay 1,350 RMB per square meter. One hundred and twenty local people already have moved out of their original one-story houses into the new buildings. "Old people are not willing to live in the big buildings," we were told by the elderly woman who *did* want to move out of her single-story, traditional courtyard home. "Here we burn coal," which makes things very dirty, she explained as she prodded the local official about when they would be allowed to move. Although they bought a color television four years ago, they are waiting to move into the big building before buying a refrigerator. In general she and her husband are pleased with life today: "I didn't realize it could be this good; all the big factories are great."

If a family's housing space does not exceed 20 sq m per person, then all heating and gas costs are paid by the collective, but if it is more than 20 sq m, then the family must pay 6 RMB for the winter. The average in Yangjia is 20 sq m, which is quite high compared to the average of 8 sq m in Dalian

City proper and a national rural area average of 14 sq m per person. The collective provides housing for all nonagricultural *hukou* holders, for technicians, and for those who went into the military and have come home to Yangjia. Military returnees are given jobs as well.

When we inquired about electrical appliances such as televisions and refrigerators—common products in urban households, we were told that people all have these now and that now they are buying new ones and upgrading to larger, color TVs. This is a new way of doing things for the *nongmin* (farmers); in the past, people would use something until it was broken, Mr. Shen explained, but now even if a television is not broken they will buy a new one and upgrade. The majority of expenditures are for buying and decorating homes, however. Mr. Shen estimated that there is a 50 percent bank savings rate as well.

Emphasizing Education for Development

Yangjia is also a special place because it uses the talent and high technology of the cities. For instance, people there rely heavily on graduates of Dalian's Light Industry Institute and Yangjia has sent many people to Dalian's Foreign Language Institute for training. In addition, as a local leader, Shen has worked to distinguish Yangjia by emphasizing local education and "raising the level" of residents. In order to attract more foreign investment, he believes the village must raise its level—the technical level of the enterprises—and increase beautification of the area. To reach this goal, the village will provide bonuses to local residents who want to get an education beyond senior middle school. Finding those who have graduated from senior middle school even in Jinzhou City is not easy, so this is a significant incentive for a village like Yangjia. If the student wants to study in a secondary specialized school (*zhongdeng zhuanke xuexiao*), the village gives the individual 1,000 RMB after graduation, and if the student wants to study for a three-year (*dazhuan*) or four-year bachelor's degree (*benke*), the village will give 2,000 RMB. The village has local study classes as well, but these focus mostly on foreign trade and customs issues because of the number of joint-venture projects here. In addition, Manager Shen relies on the city for highly educated and trained technicians and managers.

The combination of emphases on education, on attracting foreign investment, and on beautifying the village makes Yangjia an interesting example of the rural urbanization process. Manager Shen engages the policies offered and has taken advantage of the village's unique position between two larger urban arenas.

Yangshufang: Farmer-Initiated Urbanization

Yangshufang (70 km from the Zone and 35 km from Pulandian City) is an example of farmer-initiated and self-reliant economic development and urbanization that works "to urbanize a rural area and to make townspeople out of farmers" (Dayang Nongmin Cheng Planning Office 1993: 2). Originally, a woman named Li Guilian, who started a local garment enterprise, suggested to the Dalian Municipal Government that Yangshufang *zhen* designate an area as a farmer's town (*nongmin cheng*), which would rely on investments from the enterprise's profits. After the Municipal Government agreed, the decision was ratified by the province (1993) and Yangshufang became one of the small industrial zones (*gongye xiaoqu*)—the first to be established by an enterprise rather than by the government. In this sense it is referred to as a model (*moshi*) and as an experimental site. The terminology is confusing, but the term *nongmin cheng* refers to the rural residents' self-motivated development efforts to build "a countryside metropolis" (*xiangcunli de dushi*) (Liu et al. 1994), while the term *gongye xiaoqu* is used to denote the special policies provided by the municipal and provincial governments for that *nongmin cheng* area. The *nongmin cheng* (6.6 sq km), considered an "experimental site" by the State Council, is part of greater Yangshufang *zhen,* which covers a much larger area (20 sq km).

The most important conditions the farmer's town status granted for Yangshufang are being able to keep local taxes and reinvest them locally rather than giving them to Pulandian City, and being able to make its own international contacts and engage in international trade instead of going through the provincial foreign trade bureau. The local leader who accompanied us explained that there are limits on what the state can do for a village, so if the rural residents do it themselves, they can expand and develop faster. Furthermore, there is a greater incentive to make the money back faster if it is your own investment than if it is the state's money. Clearly, it is the combination of investing the town's own money (enterprises and individuals) and privileges from the state that is fueling local development (Ji Liu, and Yang 1994).

Like Beile and Yangjia, this village was very poor owing to limited and not very fertile land. From the late fifties to the early sixties, one day's work on the land reaped only 5–6 *mao* and there were no other economic options. When land was redistributed with the household responsibility system, each person received, on average, 2.5 *mu*. The average salary before 1979 was 250 RMB a year, and the main crops were corn, peanuts, and rice. Households also raised animals, but each family would have only one pig, for example, and eat half of it themselves at Spring Festival. Animal husbandry was not meant as a money-making venture.

Li Guilian, a local director of the Women's Federation and a secretary of the Party committee in Yangshufang, tackled these problems by organizing a small group of women to work together in a house, making clothes for other local people. She went to the town leader and told him she wanted to open a collective-owned clothing workshop that did not need a large initial investment, was labor intensive, and did not require high technology. He agreed. This was the beginning of what is now known as Dayang Group (officially established October 1979), the largest exporter of garments in the Dalian area. Then in 1985, just as the Zone was starting, Li Guilian applied to open enterprises there, the first starting in 1987. Now it is extremely difficult for a township enterprise to move into the Zone, as that area focuses on foreign investment projects. Li Guilian's leadership role is different from those of Manager Chi and Manager Shen, however, because she recently gave up her position as leader of the township and now focuses only on Dayang Group. We return to this issue below.

The Dayang Model of Development and Industrialization

At present, Dayang Group encompasses forty-eight enterprises that the fifty-one-year-old founder, Chairwoman Li, grew from the original workshop in sixteen years. They have twenty-six joint-venture companies, nineteen of which are in clothing (75 percent) and work with three independent Japanese companies. They also have six domestic cooperations (*neilian*), twenty-two of their own investments, 7,000 workers, 100 foreign customers, and relations with twenty-five countries. All of the enterprises are either in Yangshufang or in Dalian's Zone. In addition, they have opened three branch offices, in Hong Kong, Japan, and Russia. Dayang also is well respected for sending employees abroad for training and to Dalian schools for study, as well as working to attract specialists from the city. The impressive expansion of Dayang Group has made Yangshufang a place of great interest in Dalian.

There is a well-known legend of Dayang's beginnings: In the winter of 1981 a representative of an American company came to China to look for a place to make western suits. He first went to a state-run enterprise in Dalian, but found it was difficult to do business there. He urgently needed to get 24,000 suits made (or so the legend goes), but this enterprise had just sent its employees off on their annual Spring Festival vacation. Li Guilian heard about the visitor and said they could do all the pattern cutouts for him in three days and three nights. The American already had bought his ticket to leave Dalian, convinced that there was no way he could get the suits made there, but Li Guilian managed to keep her promise and went to the airport to see him before he left, asking him to come back and view the cutouts. He had not believed "a peasant could do it." At that time the roads out to Yangshufang were quite bad, but he made the trip and saw all of the patterns hanging in the workshop. He looked at the quality and agreed to sign a contract to make all 24,000 suits here, bringing Dayang its first U.S. customer. Chairwoman Li then fostered a good relationship with the foreign trade bureau so they would tell international customers that if they wanted to make money they should go to Li Guilian.

Problems

Yangshufang helps us to understand what a "farmer entrepreneur's" concept of urbanization is. Many officials have great expectations of what they can and should accomplish, but as Liu Zhongquan and his university colleagues argue, it is not a problem-free or necessarily strong vision of urbanization. Industrial development in the town and by the Dayang Group in general is very strong, but urbanization of rural areas cannot rely solely on industrialization at the expense of agricultural development and mechanization (see also Ji et al. 1994).

Because of this lack of attention to aspects other than Dayang Group's development, Liu and his colleagues were disappointed with the *nongmin cheng's* urbanization progress since their last visit several years before. Other than the main road through town and the separation of functional areas, the local leaders had not pushed forward their well-intentioned original urbanization plan.[22] In particular, Liu was not satisfied with how farmers were dispersed in small family plots wasting labor, nor with the lack of mechanization in agricultural production. In addition, Yangshufang has the problem of letting land that has been bought for industrial use remain unproductive while waiting for building to start. Agricultural production, Liu believes, should continue rather than letting large tracts of land sit idle.

Yangshufang also had not been a market center, that means there was no historical transportation network feeding into the town. Nor was there a finance system in place, which has plagued development as well. For example, the trade center, which had investment by the government and was meant to serve as a garment and fashion market for surrounding communities, was empty when we visited—all of the products, sellers, and buyers had already moved to Pulandian, about 40 minutes away. Apparently buyers from outside the area (e.g., Changchun or Harbin) go directly to the factories to buy what they need, and local people have their own connections with the factories. The market opened May 27, 1994, and it took only one year to determine that Pulandian's market was much better. They started moving products over to that market and now use part of the building as a warehouse for beverages and shampoo.

As in the other two field sites, we were told that before Yangshufang got its new classification, there were no tall buildings, all the roads were dirt, and all of the residents had agricultural *hukou*—signs of no urbanization or development. Before 1992 most of the area was fields—over 80 percent—but now in the 6.6 km *nongmin cheng* development area, only ten percent is agricultural. Similar to the Zone and other "new city areas" (*xinshiqu*), Yangshufang is proud of its functional divisions, which have separate industrial, service sector, and residential/cultural areas.

Population and the Hidden Urbanization of Blue Hukou

In 1993 Yangshufang began supplying the farmer's town *hukou,* or blue *hukou* (*lanpi hukou*), and experienced a 50 percent population increase. The official *hukou* booklets have red covers, prompting this new, quasi-official urban *hukou* to be identified on the basis of its blue color. Official agricultural to nonagricultural *hukou* transfers are noted in the red-covered *hukou* booklet and are limited by a government quota every year. That process is different from this one, where local administrations decide on the number and manage these households locally as long-term residents. Theoretically it is a nonagricultural *hukou* that is used only at the township level, but in the national statistics the blue *hukou* is still counted as agricultural. These blue registrations need to be incorporated into urban statistics and could be camouflaging many "urban" lives. In 1995, however, Liaoning Province did begin trying to distinguish between the agricultural population and the township population (which includes the blue registrations and official urban and agricultural registrations) in 100 experimental sites.

Methods such as the blue *hukou* are meant to keep rural people in the "rural" areas by smoothing migration between towns of a similar classification but not migration to larger cities. It is also a way that a locality can manipulate policies to attract more workers from outside the village and build up a small town. If an in-migrant buys a home, has fixed work (e.g., in a factory or store), and has a set salary, then the local government can give him or her a blue township *hukou.* if the individual works in a township enterprise for several years, he or she could pay a comprehensive fee (*peitao,* usually 2,000–3,000 RMB) for infrastructure and other investments and then receive a blue registration. It is also possible that if the collective buys a person's farm land for development, then the town will find work for the person in an enterprise or in the service industry and that person's *hukou* becomes a blue *zhen* registration.

Such blue *zhen* documents are different from a temporary registration, being a kind of permanent registration that also offers benefits. Benefits such as easier access to work for one's children in the local area, including opportunities to go into the military (which is attractive for its salary and technical training). If there is a job opening, the town will give it to the child of a blue *hukou* holder before giving it to an outsider; moreover, children can go to local schools, housing is easier to get, and building one's own home and buying land are permitted. Furthermore, if the in-migrant starts a service company, he or she will receive tax and other business benefits as a blue *hukou* holder.

The local population in Yangshufang's *nongmin cheng* is over 4,000; including the 670 outsider temporary *hukou* holders, the total exceeds 5,000. Official (red) nonagricultural *hukou* holders account for 1,100 residents, while 2,000 have the blue registration. (The greater Yangshufang *zhen* area has a population of about 30,000 people.) Noteworthy, of the 670 temporary *hukou* holders, 65 percent are single women with agricultural registrations who work in the garment factories. There are no limits on outsiders' bringing family members to Yangshufang. The local leader did say, however, that in general outsiders should be young, under twenty-five, have a middle school education, and be healthy. If the in-migrant has technical training, then the local government will provide housing and will help find work for accompanying family members.

There are over twenty people with city *hukou* (Pulandian, Dalian, Zone) who work in the Dayang Group. These people are either managers or technicians. They have been there for about five years, attracted by the higher salaries, housing (many live in the Zone), and benefits. Most are translators (ten total, including Japanese, Korean, Russian, and English) and master's degree holders with training in international trade and law.

In a small village next to the *nongmin cheng,* there is an interesting migration trend that suggests new arrivals are finding ways around some of the requirements for the privileges of blue *hukou* holders. An old man in the village told Liu that there are 110 households in the village, 40 of which are in-migrants, and that the young women go to work in Dayang Group's factories, but that most of the men still work the land. The reason the town has so many migrants is that people can build simpler and less expensive homes than they could in the farmer's town, but they can still work in Dayang's factories. Apparently, when the local village leaders apply for house-building rights they do not tell the government officials that the builder is an outsider. Most of the outsiders do not have enough money to build the fancy houses required by Yangshufang's official city plan, but they can afford motorcycles or bicycles to ride into town to work.

As we passed some old homes that were to be demolished, the local administrator directed our attention to the buildings across the street that were being built by blue *hukou* residents. The first floor was meant to function as a store or some other service company (e.g., car repair), and the family would live above. People are allowed to build only according to city plans and requirements and must invest their own money.

Factories and Salaries

As we have argued for Beile and Yangjia, the nonagricultural work and increases in salaries are important variables in the processes we are investigating. We visited factories, most belonging to Dayang Group, both in Yangshufang and in the Dalian City Zone (70 km away). Contracts usually run three years, and workers in the first garment factory visited receive 7,500 RMB a year average in the area. The salary, however, is based on work completed (piece rate compensation), which also means the workers sew for approximately nine hours a day. Upstairs there were two workrooms filled primarily with young women sewing clothes. In the Japanese independently financed enterprise (*duzi qiye*), all 287 workers were in light blue tops and dark bottoms. Seventy percent of the workers were women and only men used the larger pressing machines. Salaries are the same, but men receive a small health allowance because of the chemical odors associated with pressing. All equipment comes from Japan and the clothes are all exported to Japan—this is only a processing site. The salary here is related to individual worker production and is higher than at the joint-ventures by as much as 40 percent, which along with imported machines and management style, is identified as a benefit of having independent Japanese companies in the area. Work hours are five days a week, from 7 to 11 A.M. and 12 to 4:30 P.M. The factory will fire workers if they are late or are caught sleeping on the job. Air conditioning and fans are provided for the summer time, so that people are less likely to sleep during the hot weather.

The Dayang Group's five businesses in the Zone have a total of 2,000 workers,[23] 40 percent of whom are men and 60 percent women. Contracts run ten years in the garment businesses, but if no one disagrees, workers can leave prior to the end of the contract; they have the freedom to come and go. The average salary is 10,000 RMB a year (salaries are piece rate), which does not include a bonus calculated on the basis of profits (what they call dividends). The average extra dividend is 1,000 RMB a year, but white-collar workers receive a higher number of these "shares" (5,000 to 20,000 RMB) on top of their regular salary than do factory workers.

The local administrator in Yangshufang explained that office workers' salaries differ significantly, depending on responsibility. Top leaders earn around 60,000 RMB a year and vice directors earn 40,000 RMB a year. A department director may earn 20,000–25,000 RMB a year, while common office workers earn 12,000–15,000 RMB a year. When asked about previous salary levels, the administrator responded that before 1984, the salaries were not good, but then he nervously looked over at the Dalian official to see if he could say such a statement. They then agreed that after 1987 salaries went up, especially when the Zone started to be developed, special policies were begun, and more customers came in. As noted above, in 1979 the average salary was 250 RMB a year, but in 1992 it was 1,275 RMB and in 1995 it was 3,300 RMB per capita.

Conclusions

The emphasis on local leaders is not new to China studies, but with these three examples we argue that any study of the current urbanization process must consider the entrepreneurial skills of the leaders and how they use regional reforms and develop economic relationships. Our first example of rural industrialization and urbanization in the Dalian area is noteworthy because it has taken advantage of a major infrastructure investment project by the provincial government to promote growth in the area, which in turn prompted the Municipal Government to reclassify Beile as a *zhen* along the Shenyang-Dalian Expressway and to provide it with attractive investment and development policies as a *jingji jishu kaifaqu*. Local leaders also took a long-term view of how they could benefit from their location along the expressway and decided to build the 46,000 sq m commodities market after determining local needs. Beile has used its market to encourage further development of its agriculture, industry, and trade. Interestingly, when asked which policies were most important to him and for the development of his village, Manager Chi replied it was not one policy that was important but the general freedom to do what they want—that all of the policies from the government were good.

Yangjia, on the other hand, is a model of relying on foreign trade and investment, and of emphasizing the educational level of its citizens. But like Beile, the vision and leadership skills of the village leader/company general manager are critical to the area's physical and lifestyle changes. In addition, its closer relationship with Dalian city (both geographically and culturally) has affected the vision of what an urbanized and modernized Yangjia should be like. Manager Shen shied away from building another Hong Kong–type area that he now claims would be chaotic (*luan*). The Singapore model of an urban environment is not just influencing large cities like Dalian or the new city area near Suzhou, but is also causing physical changes in villages of a few thousand people. Clearly the flow of information, images, people, and capital is affecting people's daily lives, as well as their dreams and visions.

Finally, it is important to distinguish the success of Dayang Group from that of Yangshufang's farmer's town. Researchers and some officials are disappointed that Yangshufang has not kept up with the expansion of Dayang Group, yet it is an interesting example of how "farmers" see themselves when they are in the driver's seat of local development. More accurately, they strike a balance between the right of the government to lead and respect for the rights of the enterprise and its urbanization plans. The local administrator in Yangshufang emphasized how they must rely on individual strength and the investment of in-migrants like those with the blue *hukou,* in addition to money from the government. Relying only on themselves or the government was not realistic; they had to attract foreign investments as well in order to build up the area.

When comparing these three sites, we were struck by how important the individual leader was, not only in manipulating government policies and setting a vision for the future of the local community but also in influencing the residents. Whether it was Manager Chi in Beile, Manager Shen in Yangjia, or Chairwoman Li at Dayang, the leader projects an aura of authority. We are not suggesting that all urbanization changes are due to or determined by local leaders, but perhaps leaders have much to do with determining which areas begin the urbanization process early. Clearly the reforms in the Dalian area, such as establishment of the small industrial zones, Mayor Bo Xilai's desire to build a thriving metropolitan region, and state efforts to engage surplus labor in nonagricultural activities, are critical elements of this process. Also, late-twentieth-century capitalism and increasing transnational investment, as well as today's steady flow of modern images and people, must be accounted for in our reflections on the meaning of urbanized lives and the urbanization process in "rural" areas.

Notes

1. On initial visits to Yangjia and Beile, two officials from Jinzhou District Commission of Rural Affairs also accompanied us.

2. Although our three field sites do not rely primarily on heavy industry township enterprises, an excellent example of this is Hongqizhen in a suburb of Dalian, near the airport.

3. For an interesting perspective and the history of rural enterprises across China, see Zhou 1996.

4. For an interesting study of gender issues in rural north China, see Judd 1994.

5. Ethnoscapes reflect the increased presence of "tourists, immigrants, refugees, exiles, guestworkers, and other moving groups and persons" in the world today. While Appadurai does not intend to argue that no stable communities or networks exist today, he does argue that "the warp of these stabilities is everywhere shot through with the

woof of human motion, as more persons and groups deal with the *realities of having to move or the fantasies of wanting to move* " (1991: 192, emphasis added).

6. If the state ratifies a village as a town, then it is called a *jianzhi zhen,* or designated town.

7. Until recently, it has been almost impossible to remain in cities without an official *hukou* because grains were not available on the open market and because the Public Security Bureau would send the migrants back. Now, however, the *hukou* system has been relaxed somewhat and people are flooding into cities. Officially, people are able to stay in a city where they are not registered for three months or longer with lodging permits, but many are disobeying these rules to stay as temporary and contract workers. For those interested in calculating urbanization levels, it is important to determine whether the statistics include people who do nonagricultural work in cities, but have a "rural" household registration.

8. As of March 1996, the city was reported to have a total population of 5.3 million, 2.5 million of whom were urban residents. The city proper covers 2,415 sq km (Yang 1996).

9. Yet Sit also argues that the invitation to foreigners to invest in areas of former colonial rule, such as Dalian's Economic and Technical Development Zone, is a process of "pseudo urbanization:" "The port zone and the new suburban industrial estates tend to be export processing zones where cheap labour is used in assembly or processing work for foreign multinational enterprises. Such uses of land reflect the subordinate relationship that still exists between these cities and their ex-colonial ruler or dominant outside power" (1985: 3).

10. For an insightful discussion of the term "urbanization" for the process in China, see Guldin 1992 and chapter 3 in this volume. Most useful is the way he has distinguished among townization, deagriculturalization, and citization.

11. The expressway is 375 km long, 137 km of which run through the Dalian area, and is sometimes called the "Number One Road of the Divine Land" (*shenzhou diyi lu*) (Yang 1996).

12. The Jinlian Company produces the needles, supplying 90 percent of the market in all of China.

13. Ten years ago they were growing wheat, corn, and fruit here, and using ox-drawn carts to plow the fields. To emphasize this point, our host, Manager Chi, explained that he himself was a farmer who had received only six years of education before becoming the general manager of the collective and head of the township government. Since the reclassification to *zhen* status was so recent, Manager Chi still is called *cunzhang,* but his title should change soon. He is also the director of the group that oversees the small development zones. Mr. Chi was the secretary of the village as well as a militia team leader in the past. This combination of having received some education and having some leadership experience helped propel him to the top position. On the relationships among local cadres, market exchanges, and peasant entrepreneurs, see Nee 1989.

14. It is ironic to note that in a certain sense, and to a small degree, "markets" have been able to accomplish what Mao called for through patriotic duty and/or required by administrative fiat—that is, urban registration holders going to "rural" areas. I would like to thank Neil Diamant for pointing this out.

15. Although it is common to talk of salaries in monthly amounts, these numbers were provided to us in yearly sums.

16. See the argument in Kate Xiao Zhou's book *How the Farmers Changed China* regarding the lack of subsidized goods for rural residents when the household registration system was put into place. She argues that "the availability of coupons became a mark of urban class status. With an urban *hukou,* one received *liangpiao* (food rationing coupons) for food, staples, and nonstaples, all at a subsidized price. . . . Through the rationing system (especially grain rationing), *hukou* divided the Chinese people into two

main groups: urban and rural" (1996: 34). See also Chan 1994 on the relationship between subsidies and *hukou* status.

17. This is an interesting combination of a socialist welfare system and a paternalistic reproduction of gender roles and hierarchies in policies and attitudes, particularly in "finding him a wife," Hoffman argues. More research needs to be done on how local administrations' policies and regulations reinforce and/or challenge existing notions of gender roles and symbolism.

18. Respect for the elderly, resonating with Confucian ideals, was a topic we often heard and that was expressed in the village by providing 36 RMB a month (80–100 RMB per month for cadres) in old-age pensions for men over sixty, and women over fifty-five. Also, in 1992 they arranged a trip to Beijing for the elderly citizens, which is part of the "Old Folks Day" (*laoren jie*) that started in 1990. A sixty-two-year-old woman told us that a total of eighty-six people went; they took soft sleeper trains to Beijing and came back by air. In 1994 they arranged a trip to a hot springs in Liaoning Province, and for Old Folks Day the collective takes the elderly out for an annual meal. "Every year they give us gifts, and last year we ate sea cucumbers, prawns and fish," a sixty-eight-year-old man remembered.

19. Previously, Yangjia's main economic activity was agriculture—corn mostly and a few vegetables. In 1980 the average salary was 340 RMB a year, but in 1995 it was 3,800 RMB per person (including children and elderly). After the reform era began, Jinzhou became a city, which now has a population of about 80,000, and the larger Jinzhou District has a population of 290,000.

20. The dairy is 90 percent owned by a Japanese company and the Chinese manager of the processing plant, a former professor at Liaoning Normal University, was hired through a job advertisement. The milk itself comes from collective and private dairies in Jinzhou.

21. Like Beile, Yangjia arranged a trip to Beijing for the older residents, in addition to other Old Folks' Day activities. One hundred and thirty-five people went to Beijing, and remembering the trip brought our seventy-seven-year-old interviewee to life: "It was great!" she exclaimed. "We took soft sleepers to Beijing for eighteen hours, and then a car took us to the hotel. We all showered, changed clothes, and then went to eat. At every meal we had ten dishes and a soup. Beautiful! . . . At breakfast each person had two steamed breads, rice porridge, vegetables, and two eggs. Two eggs alone is enough for us." Manager Shen went to see them once, she remembered, and he also saw them off at the train station and met them at the airport when they came back.

22. In 1993 the town's planning office published a detailed outline of local goals, including production numbers, agricultural development, roads, and utilities. The report also explains that a farmer's town is a place where residents have stable work, salaries, and material and cultural living conditions (see Dayang Nongmin Cheng Planning Office 1993).

23. Pulandian District, home of Dayang's headquarters, has many unemployed surplus laborers so the local labor bureau sends them to the Zone's labor office, which then sends them to Dayang—thus most workers are from Pulandian. Dayang does accept individual introductions from employees and contacts, too.

References

Appadurai, Arjun. 1991. "Global Ethnoscapes: Notes and Queries for a Transnational Anthropology." *Recapturing Anthropology: Working in the Present.* Santa Fe, NM: School of American Research Press.

Chan, Kam Wing. 1994. "Urbanization and Rural-Urban Migration in China since 1982." *Modern China* 20 (3): 243–281.

Clausen, Soren, and Thogersen, Stig. 1995. *The Making of a Chinese City: History and Historiography in Harbin.* Armonk, NY: M.E. Sharpe.

Dayang Nongmin Cheng Planning Office. 1993. *Dayang nongmin cheng jianjie* (Dayang farmer's town brief introduction), July 30, 1993.

Fincher, John. 1990. "Rural Bias and the Renaissance of Coastal China." In G.J.R. Linge and D.K. Forbes (eds.), *China's Spatial Economy: Recent Developments and Reforms,* pp. 35–38. Hong Kong: Oxford University Press.

Goldstein, Sidney. 1990. "Urbanization in China, 1982–87: Effects of Migration and Reclassification." *Population and Development Review* 16 (4): 673–701.

Gui Shixun and Liu Xian. 1992. "Urban Migration in Shanghai, 1950–88: Trends and Characteristics." *Population and Development Review* 18 (3): 533–548.

Guldin, Gregory E. 1992. *Urbanizing China.* Westport, CT: Greenwood Press.

Hua Hua. 1995. "Towns Form Bridge Between City and Farm." *China Daily,* October 16.

Ji Xiaolan, Liu Zhongquan, and Yang Baixin. 1994. *"Guanyu Dalian Yangshufang 'nong-min cheng' ruogan wenti tantao"* (An inquiry into the problems facing Dalian's Yangshufang "farmer town"). Paper presented to China National Meeting on Rural Industrialization, Urbanization, and Agricultural Modernization (*Quanguo nongcun gongyehua chengshihua nongye xiandaihua yantaohui*). Huadu City, Guangdong Province, May.

Johnson, Graham E. 1993. "The Political Economy of Chinese Urbanization: Guangdong and the Pearl River Delta Region," in Greg Guldin and Aidan Southall (eds.), *Urban Anthropology in China,* pp. 167–204. Leiden: E.J. Brill.

Judd, Ellen R. 1994. *Gender and Power in Rural North China.* Stanford: Stanford University Press.

Linge, G.J.R., and Forbes, D.K. (eds.). 1990. *China's Spatial Economy: Recent Developments and Reforms.* Hong Kong: Oxford University Press.

Liu Zhongquan, Ji Xiaolan, and Chang Baixin. 1994. *Dalian xiandai chengzhen tixi yu jiasu quyu chengshihuade zhanlue xuanze* (Dalian's strategic choices for city and town systematization and rapid urbanization). Dalian, China: Dalian Urban Economy Working Group.

Ma Rong. 1992. "The Development of Small Towns and Their Role in the Modernization of China," in Gregory E. Guldin (ed.), *Urbanizing China,* pp. 119–154. Westport, CT: Greenwood Press.

Nee, Victor. 1989. "Peasant Entrepreneurship and the Politics of Regulation in China," in Victor Nee and David Stark (eds.), *Remaking the Economic Institutions of Socialism: China and Eastern Europe,* pp. 169–207. Stanford: Stanford University Press.

Sit, Victor. 1985. "Introduction: Urbanization and City Development in the People's Republic of China." In Victor Sit (ed.), *Chinese Cities: The Growth of the Metropolis Since 1949.* Oxford: Oxford University Press.

Solinger, Dorothy. 1985. "Temporary Residence Certificate Regulations in Wuhan, May 1983." *China Quarterly* 101: 98–103.

Wang Hui. 1996. "Remedy Needed for Rural Migrants." *China Daily,* March 29.

Wang, Mark Yaolin. 1995. "Invisible Urbanization in China: Case Study in the Shenyang-Dalian Region." Paper presented to Western Division, Canadian Association of Geographers, March.

Whyte, Martin K., and Parish, William L. 1984. *Urban Life in Contemporary China.* Chicago: University of Chicago Press.

Yang Baixin. 1996. *Urban Development of Dalian, China.* Beijing: China Architecture and Building Press.

Yue Xin. 1996. "Mass Media Enter Rural People's Lives." *China Daily,* March 5.

Zhou Daming. 1993. "An Approach to the Problems of Population Movement and Cultural Adaptation in the Urbanizing Pearl River Delta," in Greg Guldin and Aidan Southall (eds.), *Urban Anthropology in China,* pp. 205–215. Leiden: E.J. Brill.

Zhou, Kate Xiao. 1996. *How the Farmers Changed China: Power of the People.* Boulder, CO: Westview Press.

7

Rural Urbanization in China's Tibetan Region

Duilongdeqing County as a Typical Example

Gelek and Li Tao

Beginning in the late 1970s and early 1980s, China's rural areas embarked on the road to urbanization under the influence of the great tide of reform and the policy of opening to the outside world. Has Tibet, a broad, interior region on the southwestern borders of the fatherland, been swept into this urbanization tide? What progress has been made? What are the influences of urbanization on Tibetan society, its economy, and its culture? In November 1993, we made a case study of Duilongdeqing County in the suburbs of Lhasa to find answers to the above questions.

I. Definition of Urbanization and the Basic Situation in Duilongdeqing

The concept of urbanization is controversial in China and abroad. Different disciplines have different approaches. Geographers claim that urbanization is a territorial transformation, while demographers say it refers to the extent of concentration of rural population in the cities, and economists emphasize urban economic centers and their development and expansion to nearby rural areas. In short, urbanization includes three developments:

1. The shift of rural population into urban districts; large numbers of agricultural population becoming nonagricultural; and the continuous rise of urban population as a proportion of the total national population.
2. Changes in the status of cities and expansion of their sizes. For in-

183

stance, expansion of old city limits to include neighboring rural areas, or changes in the character of certain communities to become new cities or towns.

3. The expansion of urban economic relations and lifestyles—gradual adoption of the urban way of life in the rural areas and changes in rural living standards in the urban mode.

Scholars of urban studies currently pay a great deal of attention to the first two points but often neglect the third. In this respect, the American anthropologist Gregory Guldin has pointed out that urbanization does not simply mean more and more people living in cities and towns; it is also the process in which the urban and nonurban areas of a society increase communication and ties.[1] That is to say, with the reciprocal influence of cities and rural areas upon each other and mutual contact and integration of urban-rural cultures, an integrated social ideal has been generated that includes elements of both the rural and the urban civilization. This phenomenon is "rural urbanization." In the wake of rural urbanization comes a narrowing of the urban-rural gap; the structure of rural productive forces, its production and management, income level and structure, way of life, ideas, and thinking become increasingly close to and in unity with that of cities. In this chapter, we will illustrate the rural urbanization process in the Tibetan region through the changes that have occurred in Duilongdeqing.

Duilongdeqing County is located on the western outskirts of Lhasa, the capital of the Tibetan Autonomous Region. The county seat is only 14 km from the center of Lhasa. Most of the county lies in the Yaluzangbu river valley, on the southern bank of the Lhasa River and the banks of a tributary, the Duilong zangbu. On the northwest, the county borders on the north Tibet grasslands; on its southeast, it forms part of the southern Tibet river valley. Two southeastern ridges of the Nianqing Tanggula Mountains meander to the north and south of the county, giving it two different types of climate and natural resources. In the main, the county is topographically in a high plains valley region with its western part high and eastern part low. The highest sea elevation is 5,500 m, the lowest 3,640 m. Annual mean temperature is 7 degrees Centigrade, with the January temperature ranging to below -10° C. Annual rainfall is 440 mm; in the autumn alone, the rainfall reaches 310 mm. Natural resources are abundant, including rare animals and plants as well as medicinal herbs such as river deer, deer, otter, brown bears, leopards, black neck cranes, blue Tibetan horse-chickens (*Crossoptilon*), Chinese caterpillar fungus, fritillary bulbs, and snow lotus.

Duilongdeqing (which in Tibetan means "Joy on the Heights") has a long history. As far back as the time of Songzanganbu, it was economically developed by the Tibetan kings as the "granary" of Luoxie (the capital Lhasa). Agriculture was predominant in the region along with some livestock raising. In 1992, the county had an area of 2,600 sq m and had jurisdiction over 12 *xiang* (townships), namely: Qiusang, Deqing, Langba, Maxiang, Naga, Gurong, Yangda, Dongga, Jiare, Naiqiong, Sangda, and Liuwu, comprising 90 administrative villages. Total population of the county was 33,581 in 6,500 households, of which 31,181 or 6,128 households—94.28 percent and 92.29 percent, respectively—engaged in farming. Around 90 percent of the total population was Tibetan. Residents of other nationalities were concentrated in the county town.

II. Labor Structure and Population Movement

Before the 1980s, most of the rural labor power in Duilongdeqing County, as elsewhere in the autonomous region, farmed and raised livestock; only a very few engaged in subsidiary occupations. The structure of the rural labor force was monolithic. In the wake of reform and the opening to the outside, this structure has begun evolving toward diversification. Peasants and herdsmen have ventured into industry, construction, transportation, commerce, food and beverages, finance and insurance, culture and education, and health. (See Table 7.1.)

The laboring population engaged in farming and livestock-raising has decreased year by year. Between 1984 and 1992, its proportion in the total labor force decreased by 10 percentage points. The number of people in other occupations has steadily mounted, by contrast, especially in transportation and posts and telecommunications, as well as those who left home to work outside: from 2.49 percent and 4.54 percent, respectively, in 1984, rising to 5.6 percent and 8.39 percent in 1992. The number of people engaged in commerce, food and beverage and other service trades has also risen rapidly—from 139 in 1984 to 218 in 1992. As the table shows, not only does the industrial work force make up a small proportion of the total but it is dropping drastically. In the mid-1980s, the county had cooperated with inland regions to build many types of county-, *xiang*- and village-run factories and processing plants. Due to poor management and lack of resources, virtually all closed down. In 1992, the construction work force had also decreased as compared to 1988, when it was expanding rapidly to meet the needs of Lhasa's "43 engineering projects." In the near future, however, the construction work force will resume its expansion.

In short, transportation, construction, commerce, food and beverages and other services are the industries that changed the structure of the rural labor

Table 7.1

Structure of and Changes in Duilongdeqing's Rural Labor Force
(Unit: one person)

	1984	%	1988	%	1992	%
Labor force total	16,283	100	17,100	100	17,556	100
Primary sector (agriculture, husbandry, forestry, fishery)	14,686	90.19	14,100	82.46	14,274	81.31
Industry	—	—	300	1.75	107	0.61
Construction	125	0.77	400	2.34	239	1.36
Transportation, posts & telecomm.	405	2.49	700	4.09	984	5.60
Commerce, food & bev., services	139	0.85	200	1.17	218	1.24
Culture/education, health	188	1.15	200	1.17	227	1.29
Xiang administrative personnel	—	—	—	—	33	0.19
Finance/insurance	—	—	—	—	1	0.01
Absentee labor	740	4.54	1,200	7.02	1,473*	8.39

Source: Provided by the Duilongdeqing County Planning Commission and the Lhasa Statistical Bureau.
*3,000 in 1993

force of Duilongdeqing County, and in fact of all the Tibetan region.

As for labor force who had left home, that is not, strictly speaking, in the same category as those who have turned to other occupations. They do, however, occupy a unique position within the rural labor force, being large in number and swift to grow. Our surveys showed that the numbers that have gone elsewhere are far greater than those statistically estimated. In villages close to cities where transportation is convenient, 50–60 percent leave their homes for outside work during the slack farming seasons. Ninety percent of them end up in Lhasa and 5 percent in Rigeze, Tibet's second-largest city (a few hours' car ride from Lhasa). The rest go to Zhangmu,

Yadong, Geermu, and inland areas; not a few are in Nepal or India. When away, these people are engaged in transportation, construction, or business, or are carpenters, painters, stonecutters, *qingke* wine brewers, or odd-jobs men. This is a growing force in the county that cannot be ignored.

III. Changes in Production and Management

During the urbanization process, the first areas to change in the villages are usually the production and management modes. Duilongdeqing peasants had worked in nothing but farming and livestock-breeding for centuries; their modes of production and management were traditional and backward. Since reform and the open policy, not only has the economy diversified into the nationality handicrafts industry, transportation, construction, commerce, food and beverages and other services, but traditional modes of farming and livestock-raising have also changed enormously. Furthermore, this process seems to have quickened significantly since 1993.

According to statistical data, there are currently twenty-eight township enterprises in Duilongdeqing, including cement factories, a limited holding company for mineral water, and a comprehensive welfare services company, as well as factories manufacturing or processing traditional Tibetan *hada* (ceremonial silk scarves), vermicelli, and cakes of roasted barley flour. As to sources of financing, besides investment from the county and *xiang* as well as individuals, cooperation has spread into areas outside the county or autonomous region in order to raise all funds possible. For instance, the Lianying Cement Plant in Dongga township was jointly financed by the township and the Economic Development Company of Gansu Province's Township Enterprise Bureau. The Yangda Mineral Water Company Ltd. was a joint venture among the county Economic Development Corp., Yangda *xiang,* the Geothermal and Geological Team of the Tibetan Autonomous Region, and the region's Geothermal Development Company. The investment ratio among these entities was 43:19:33:5. The Dongga Comprehensive Welfare Services Company was financed by the Civil Administration of Lhasa with 110,000 *yuan.* As to the size of enterprises, Duilongdeqing has large ones with millions of *yuan* in investment and several hundred workers, as well as smaller ones with several thousand *yuan* investment and a handful of workers. In short, the rise and rapid development of township enterprises in Duilongdeqing was a major factor in changing the rural production structure.

Diversification has brought even greater changes to Duilongdeqing's rural economy. Hinging on the needs of Lhasa, it has branched into many industries including transportation, processing, gathering, subcontracting, commerce, food and beverages, and services. According to county government statistics, up to September 1993, 4,291 people were employed in these industries, or 25 percent of the county's rural labor force. Farmers in the county owned altogether 329 automobiles (thirty-four of which are vehicles for hire), 159 large- and medium-sized tractors, and 610 manual tractors, most of which are concentrated in townships close to Lhasa, including Dongga town, Yangda *xiang,* Naiqiong *xiang,* and Jiare *xiang.* Dongga town alone had 103 automobiles; in Xiachong Village, virtually every family owned a tractor (including manual ones) or an automobile. These cars and tractors carried out farm and subsidiary products and brought back agricultural means of production and daily articles. They were also used by neighboring state factories or farms or townships for transportation, going as far afield as Geermu and Zhangmu port to carry freight. Some rural dwellers bought large or compact passenger cars to enter the transportation business, ferrying passengers to Lhasa, Qushui, Zedang, or Rigeze, thus increasing income, facilitating commuting for the masses, and enhancing the link between town and country. At present, riders can get a peasant's *zhaoshou ting* (hitchhiker's) cab for a fare of one *yuan* for the few dozen minutes' ride between Lhasa and Duilongdeqing.

Processing is also relatively well developed in the various *xiang.* In Naiqiong, a dozen peasant families started a flour mill and half a dozen families opened a noodle factory. Between the two, local wheat was milled into flour and made into noodles, which were sold in the county as well as Lhasa. In Jiare, a group of disabled people and financially strapped families organized a woolen mill, the products of which were sold to carpet-making factories. This brought them a sizable income.

In recent years, snack shops and sweet tea shops have sprung up everywhere. In Naiqiong alone, there are four tea shops and one snack shop. The *xiang* head, a young woman, took the lead in setting up a sweet tea shop, which we visited at the conclusion of our survey. Business was extremely good. Customers were discussing business, eating noodles (Tibetan sweet tea shops also provide Tibetan noodles), or playing mahjong. We saw elderly *po-la* [Tibetan for "paternal grandfather"] in their sixties and seventies as well as children of five or six years. In some *xiang,* peasants are running pool halls and video arcades. The proliferation of snack shops, sweet tea shops, and video games in the rural areas will no doubt have a big influence on the rural mode of production.

A major source of income for rural dwellers in this county was going outside the local area to work and subcontract. In the beginning of the reform era and the open policy, this was one way the rural economy went about primary accumulation. With economic development, higher productivity, and the enlargement of labor surplus, the number of rural dwellers working outside the local area rose rapidly.

Table 7.2

1993 Outputs of Subsidiary Occupations in Naiqiong *Xiang*
(Unit: *yuan*)

Occupation	Transportation	Construction	Handicrafts	Noodle-making	Flour milling
Revenue	189,492	46,310	5,436	1,822	6,959
Occupation	Qingke wine-making	Retail stores	Eggs	Forestry	Stone quarrying
Revenue	1,200	3,380	1,645	550	16,204
Occupation	Adobe making	Other		Total	
Revenue	2,200	750		275,948	

Source: Provided by Naiqiong. The *xiang* has seven villages with 726 families (724 of which were agricultural households) and 3,193 people (3,173 of which were in the farming sector).

Rather than listing the many areas of diversification in the county's rural areas, we will provide a table of the output values in one *xiang*. (See Table 7.2.)

The rise of township enterprises and growing economic diversification not only did not affect farm and livestock production, but enhanced the county's swift economic development. This was due to a more prosperous rural economy, which gave rural dwellers the wherewithal to improve their management level and increase output. (See Table 7.3.)

The table clearly shows that between 1980 and 1992, despite the decrease in cultivated acreage and in acreage under farm crops due to urbanization, the growth of agricultural output far exceeded that of the prior twenty years; further, the types of farm crops also diversified. This was chiefly the result of the changes in the production and management of agriculture and livestock-raising.

In agriculture, the county's farmers increasingly adopted scientific methods, and many volunteered to take courses in science and technology. In 1992, 5,930 rural dwellers, or 92 percent of the rural households, participated in such training. Naiqiong set up a Science Popularization Association, and the *xiang* head personally assumed the chairmanship. Members came from all the local villages. The updating of ideas was instrumental in changing the outdated traditional management mode. This was shown in the following:

1. Active popularization and use of new and improved strains. In many remote Tibetan areas even today, peasants used to the old ways reject new scientific ways. In Duilongdeqing, the reverse was true. Peasants voluntarily exchanged the seeds they had at home with new strains at the region's

Table 7.3

Structure of Agricultural Production in Duilongdeqing County

Cultivable land		1952	1976	1980	1984	1989	1992
Total		8.8	11.05	9.66	9.65	9.62	9.60
Acreage under farm crops (Unit: 10,000 mu)	Total	8.49	10.50	9.66	9.64	9.57	9.57
	Qingke	3.70	4.28	3.84	4.05	4.06	5.01
	Wheat	0.43	3.93	3.11	2.22	2.23	2.57
	Peas, beans	2.38	1.92	2.04	2.51	2.16	1.22
	Misc. grain	1.80	0.01	—	0.38	0.63	0.32
	Rapeseed	0.18	0.33	0.33	0.29	0.35	0.31
	Vegetables	—	—	0.30	0.07	0.07	0.04
	Other	—	0.03	0.04	0.12	0.07	0.10
Grain output: (Unit: 10,000 catties)	Total	824.20	2,831.59	3,181.34	3,193.86	3,529.70	4,439.78
	Qingke	377.40	1,130.37	1,254.93	1,626.29	1,797.99	2,547.56
	Wheat	40.85	1,173.30	1,363.06	964.01	335.31	1,499.71
	Peas, beans	231.35	525.08	563.35	540.18	548.48	343.61
	Misc. grain	174.60	2.84	—	63.38	149.92	48.82
Rapeseed		9.18	50.31	50.03	58.83	64.75	62.04
Vegetables		—	—	104.32	149.38	N.A.	34.61
Other		—	18.43	—	0.64	N.A.	9.58

Source: Figures come from *Lhasa in Progress, 1952–84* and *Statistical Data on the National Economy in Lhasa, 1989* published by the Lhasa Statistical Bureau, and *Compilation of Farm and Livestock Production Statistics, 1992* published by the Duilongdeqing County Planning Commission.

Agro-Technical Institute. In 1992, 79,000 *mu* of county land, or 87.8 percent of total farmland planted to grain, were planted with new strains.

2. More use of fertilizers, including both organic and chemical fertilizers. With rising family incomes, farmers could afford to buy more chemical fertilizers. This year, despite short supplies, each *mu* in the county still averaged twenty-eight catties of chemical fertilizer; in 1984, by contrast, the average was nineteen.

3. A higher degree of mechanization and expanded acreage under mechanized farming.

4. Greater emphasis on irrigation. Large-scale irrigation projects have been built in the past few years in the county using a combination of fund sources including investment by the country, the collective, and the individual. In 1992, with the 112,000 *yuan* provided by the autonomous region's Water Conservancy Bureau, the 250,000 *yuan* appropriated by the county, and funds from individuals, the county repaired or built many irrigation ditches, water-discharge outlets, and ponds, built new river dikes, and upgraded low-yielding farmland.

5. What is most noteworthy is that, because many county peasants were either working in the cities or in the tertiary sector and because they now had the financial capability to do so, they hired friends and relatives locally or from other counties to come and help out in the fields. This usually took place during the busy sowing, harvesting, or threshing seasons. After the work was done, they went back outside to earn money, leaving the elderly, the weak, and women and children to weed and water the fields. This phenomenon was particularly common in villages where transportation was convenient.

Animal husbandry made up only a small part of the county's agricultural sector. Management's function was mainly to control the number of livestock so as to alleviate fodder shortage, adjust herd structure, enhance quality, and speed up the fertility rate in order to raise the commodity price.

IV. Rural Dweller Income Levels and Structure

With the reform of traditional production methods, great changes have also taken place in the income levels and structure of Tibetan farmers and herders. The income level of those in Duilongdeqing has mounted sharply due to the promotion of scientific methods, higher efficiency, and diversification of the production structure. (See Table 7.4.)

Since the advent of reform, not only has there been rapid growth in the income levels of farmers and herders, but also a big change in income structure. Income from agriculture and/or livestock-raising are no longer the sole income source of a farming or herding family. The proportion of income from the tertiary and secondary industries has increased since 1980 (see Table 7.5 on page 193), and in villages near cities, the income from industry and subsidiary occupations has far surpassed that from agriculture and livestock-raising.

V. Changes in Lifestyle

In the process of rural urbanization, significant changes took place in the rural dwellers' mode of production, their living standards and quality of life

Table 7.4

Duilongdeqing Farmers' Per Capita Cash Income

Year	Per Capita	Year	Per Capita	Year	Per Capita	Year	Per Capita
1959	67.39	1968	96.57	1977	154.17	1986	377
1960	74.88	1969	91.97	1978	172.12	1987	352.36
1961	78.82	1970	103.34	1979	175.96	1988	369.48
1962	86.61	1971	111.12	1980	217.49	1989	415.52
1963	92.14	1972	111.33	1981	201.48	1990	441.95
1964	99.07	1973	124.51	1982	253.88		
1965	105.39	1974	141.57	1983	255.51		
1966	106.45	1975	135.25	1984	392.57		
1967	102.36	1976	144.56	1985	498.94		

Sources: Figures taken from *Duilongdeqing County's Compilation of Statistical Data, 1959–84* and yearly editions from 1984 to 1991 of *Statistical Data of the National Economy in Lhasa, 1984–91*.

were immeasurably enhanced, and the gap between town and country was increasingly narrowed.

Let us first examine the rural dwellers' consumer spending. According to a random sampling of thirty rural families in the county by the Rural Socio-economic Investigation Team of the Tibet Autonomous Region (the Rural Investigation Team, for short), per capita spending on consumables in the rural areas was 306.18 *yuan* in 1985 but rose to 608.36 *yuan* in 1992, making up 51.17 percent and 67.10 percent of total per capita spending, respectively, in those two years. This shows not only a rapid rise in rural dwellers' living expenses but also the increasing proportion of consumables in family consumption. With respect to the various items under household expenses, although consumable items still predominate, the proportion of expenses on durables rose steadily during 1985–92, by a total of 0.68 percentage points. At the same time, the spending ratio of different items of rural dwellers' livelihood consumption also changed. (See Table 7.6 on page 194.)

In Table 7.6, we are comparing Duilongdeqing rural dwellers' and Lhasa residents' different areas of household consumer spending during the same year or consecutive years. For some items, the gap was smaller in the early 1990s as compared to the mid-1980s. Some points of explanation are necessary:

Table 7.5

Changes in Duilongdeqing Farmers' Income Composition
(Unit: 10,000 *yuan*/%)

	1986		1988	1990	1992	
	Amount	%	Amount	Amount	Amount	%
Total rural income	1,474.01	100	1,677.23	1,913.14	3,373.11	100
Primary sector	1,128.95	76.59	1,321.78	1,409.07	2,634.53	78.10
Agriculture	770.74	52.29	913.60	999.57	2,030.51	60.20
Forestry	5.40	0.37	2.34	3.59	21.63	0.64
Herding	156.37	10.61	181.99	167.95	337.00	9.99
Sub. occup.	196.44	13.33	223.85	237.96	245.39	7.27
Fishery	—	—	—	—	—	—
Secondary sector	27.61	1.87	62.14	54.08	87.50	2.59
Industry	13.47	0.91	28.63	30.05	51.14	1.52
Construction	14.14	0.96	33.51	24.03	36.36	1.08
Tertiary sector	317.45	21.54	293.31	449.99	651.08	19.30
Transportation	203.29	13.79	222.06	355.67	507.86	15.06
Commerce, food, beverage	34.70	2.35	25.07	35.95	77.24	2.29
Services	14.56	0.99	7.25	11.45	8.36	0.25
Other	64.90	4.40	38.93	46.92	57.62	1.71

Source: Figures provided by the Lhasa Statistical Bureau.

1. Because of the open policy on grain and edible oil in recent years, which led to a big rise in the prices of staple foods, the proportion of food expenses of urban dwellers in 1991 was higher than in 1985.

2. Particularly worth noting is the fact that, in 1985, there was a rush in Lhasa to buy home appliances and build private housing, bringing up the proportion of expenses in the two areas of daily articles and housing. Looking at 1980 to 1992, city residents' daily article expenses showed a tendency to rise. As most city residents lived in public housing, their rent was included in noncommodity spending.

Table 7.6

Comparison Between Urban and Rural Household Consumption
(Unit: %)

		Rural Inhabitant 1985	Urban Resident* 1985	Rural Inhabitant 1992	Urban Resident* 1991
Total livelihood spending		100	100	100	100
Expenses on durables		1.16	3.08	1.84	5.58
Expenses on consumables		99.62	96.92	98.16	94.42
Item-ized spend-ing on consum-ables	Food	76.28	57.26	69.29	66.98
	Clothing	13.84	14.47	11.35	16.88
	Housing	2.04	3.42	3.98	0.1
	Fuel	2.11	1.91	8.14	1.29
	Daily articles	5.73	21.93	7.25	14.48

Source: Tibet Autonomous Region Statistical Bureau, *Data on the Livelihood and Commodity Prices for Lhasa Residents, 1985–90*; *Data on the Livelihood and Commodity Prices for Residents of Townships in Lhasa Municipality, 1991*; *Data Obtained from a Random Sampling of Rural Households in the Tibet Autonomous Region, 1985*; and *Annual Compilation of Statistics on Duilongdeqing Residents, 1992.*

3. In recent years, rural people began to buy, rather than supply their own, fuel, thus causing a sharp rise in the fuel cost category.

The narrowing gap between urban and rural consumer spending demonstrates rural-urban convergence in thinking in regard to consumption. This change is directly affecting and guiding people's behavior. Let us now examine in more detail the way of life of rural dwellers in clothing, food, housing, and articles of daily use.

Food

For the longest time, food customs were monolithic in rural Tibet, with the major foods being *tsampa* (roasted *qingke* barley cakes) and beef and mutton. Very few vegetables were eaten and there was little variety—turnips, potatoes, and Chinese cabbage [bai cai or bok choy—Ed.]. In famine years, people ate wild vegetables. Since the third plenary session of the Eleventh Central Committee, the rural economic situation has improved, and food and drink have become much more diversified. For instance, we visited Bazhu's family in the Number Two Brigade of Naiqiong *xiang*'s Number Three village and asked them about their meals. The lady of the house, Bianbazhuoga, told us: "In the morning, we generally eat *mantou* [steamed bread] and drink buttered tea; occasionally we also eat *tsampa*. Noontime we often eat noodles. At supper, we have rice and fried dishes, sometimes also noodles. What kind of fried dishes? Lots: vermicelli, broccoli, cucumber. . . . Basically what they eat in the cities." From what we discovered, *mantou*, noodles, rice, and stir-fried dishes were the daily fare in rural families in Naiqiong and throughout Tibet. Changes in this area in rural Tibet were manifested in the following four ways:

Change in Staple Food Structure and More Diversified Nonstaples

In the past, rural Tibetans ate mainly *tsampa*, but more and more they like noodles and rice. In villages closer to the cities, such as Naiqiong and Liuwu, noodles and rice are the staples, with *tsampa* relegated to special occasions. In the past, peasants seldom ate vegetables and fruit. Now these frequently appear on the dining table. Of course, expenses for nonstaples have also gone up. According to the Rural Investigation Team's data, in 1985, the county's rural dwellers spent 81.56 *yuan* per capita on staples and 68.05 on nonstaples; by 1992, the former had become 145.04 and the latter 179.74. Between 1985 and 1992, the consumption of such traditional Tibetan foods as beef and mutton dropped, but that of fruit and other new types of food rose by a large margin. (See Table 7.7.)

Increasing Diversity in Food Preparation

Due to improved communications with other areas, new ways of preparing food (primarily urban ways) had spread to the rural areas. New cooking utensils and fuel, plus rural food processing, all contributed. For instance, a dozen noodle factories had sprung up in Naiqiong, and this completely eliminated manual noodle making. It was then possible to eat noodles of different lengths, widths, and shapes.

More Dining Out

According to statistics of the Rural Investigation Team survey, in 1985, the per capita expense of peasants in the county for eating out was 2.62 *yuan*. By 1992, this had tripled to 8.17 *yuan*.

Table 7.7

Changes in Rural Food Consumption in Duilongdeqing County

		1985		1992	
	Unit	Amount Consumed	Amount Purchased	Amount Consumed	Amount Purchased
Vegetables	kg	31.11	0.86	20.98	2.25
	yuan		1.18		3.13
Bean products	kg	—	—	0.46	0.46
	yuan	—	—		1.55
Vegetable oil	kg	2.7	—	2.79	—
	yuan		—		—
Pork	kg	0.73	0.08	0.35	0.32
	yuan		0.29		2.16
Beef, mutton	kg	13.36	4.51	10.42	3.56
	yuan		12.86		21.62
Cow/goat milk	kg	17.70	—	32.28	—
	yuan		—		—
Eggs	kg	0.41	—	0.53	—
	yuan		—		—
Sugar	kg	2.30	2.15	1.31	1.30
	yuan		4.25		4.43
Confectionary	kg	0.34	0.38	0.69	0.69
	yuan		1.26		2.76
Pastries	kg	0.36	0.41	0.25	0.37
	yuan		0.78		0.98
Fruit	kg	0.10	0.08	0.90	0.90
	yuan		0.16		1.66
Tea	kg	4.60	4.18	28.91	28.91
	yuan		12.38		9.26
Tobacco	cartons	15.46	10.73	18.32	18.42
	yuan		5.90		18.14
Liquor	kg	23.38	0.03	36.87	0.13
	yuan		1.79		0.31

Source: Data provided by the Rural Investigation Team of the Tibetan Autonomous Region.

More Commodity Food Items Were Bought

From 1985 to 1992, the quantities bought and expenses paid for all food items except beef and mutton had risen. They demonstrate the rise in rural-sector purchasing power in the wake of economic development. Further, the social division of labor in the rural areas was more clear than before, the self-contained nature of the rural economy had been thoroughly eliminated, and there were more urban-rural economic ties. Finally, the flourishing market economy provided the conditions for this phenomenon. Small retail stores had opened all over, interspersed with rural markets. Naiqiong peasants no longer had to go to Lhasa or the county town to buy vegetables; they could get them in the village from peddlers who were dependents of workers in neighboring contracting teams or factories or mines. In this *xiang*, peasants grew some vegetables in the summer for their own use but generally bought them in the winter.

Clothing

In the past, rural Tibetans generally made their own woolen fabrics and brought in tailors to make clothes in the off-season. This was also true of Duilongdeqing, although better-quality items were purchased or ordered from Shannan. At that time, whether male or female, young or old, the vast majority all wore Tibetan costume. Later, people began to feel that working in heavy woolen clothing was not as convenient as working in Han clothing, and the more open-minded began to don Han clothing. With the advent of reform, in line with changes in rural thinking and affordability, more and more people changed to Han clothing. In the rural areas today, especially near cities, few young people can still be found wearing Tibetan clothing, which has become a kind of ceremonial dress for the elderly or for people during the New Year or holidays. Young women who put on Tibetan dress at New Year's often complained of backaches from the heavy weight of the long skirts. In the villages we visited, people had begun to consider Tibetan clothing too *tuqi* ("hickish"). Relatives who came visiting in such clothes were often a source of embarrassment. With the change of clothes, rural people began to have a wider choice of fabric and tailoring styles. The native Tibetan woolen fabric is now seldom used. Cotton, synthetic fibers, flannel, and silk are bought from the stores, even for making Tibetan costumes. Tailors no longer come to people's homes; customers go to them. More and more, rural Tibetans like to buy ready-made clothing. (See Table 7.8.) In 1992, the quantities of shirts, pants, and shoes bought by Duilongdeqing's peasants were far greater than that in 1985. From Table

Table 7.8

Changes in Rural Clothing Purchase Patterns

	Unit	1985	1992
Cotton cloth	meter	3.05	2.26
	cost in *yuan*	12.84	10.48
Of above,	garments	1.35	0.67
cotton clothing	cost in *yuan*	11.90	8.39
Synthetic fabrics	meter	0.27	1.62
	cost in *yuan*	1.89	17.09
Of above,	garments	0.10	0.84
clothing	cost in *yuan*	1.64	17.60
Nylon fabric	meter	0.14	0.02
	cost in *yuan*	2.28	—
Of above,	garments	0.03	0.02
clothing	cost in *yuan*	1.01	0.27
Silk and brocade	meter	0.08	—
	cost in *yuan*	0.79	—
Of above,	garments	0.05	—
clothing	cost in *yuan*	0.73	—
Flannel/woolen	kg	0.02	0.68
knitwear	cost in *yuan*	0.33	0.80
Nylon shirts/pants	garments	0.02	0.02
	cost in *yuan*	0.16	0.07
Cotton jersey	garments	0.01	0.22
shirts/pants	cost in *yuan*	0.12	1.95
Leather shoes	pair	0.36	0.45
	cost in *yuan*	5.64	8.93
Sneakers	pair	0.68	1.37
	cost in *yuan*	3.60	9.95

Source: Tibetan Autonomous Region's Rural Investigation Team. Data obtained from *A Random Sampling of Rural Households in the Tibetan Autonomous Region 1985* and *Annual Compilation of Statistics on Duilongdeqing Residents 1992.*

7.8 we can also see that, prior to the 1980s, peasants chiefly wore cotton clothing; in the 1990s, however, due to rising incomes, they chiefly wore synthetic fibers. (Note: Unlike in the industrially developed West, in China where agriculture predominates, cotton fabrics are still cheaper than synthetic fibers.)

From the changes in clothing styles, use of fabrics and tailoring, one can also see that rural Tibetans had gradually departed from self-sufficiency to reliance on cities and industry. According to the survey of the Rural Investigation Team, per capita spending on clothes was 42.21 *yuan* in Duilongdeqing's rural areas in 1985, of which 40.59 *yuan* was in cash. In 1992, per capita spending was 67.77 *yuan,* all of which was in cash. This demonstrates that while country dwellers were still making part of their own clothing in the mid-1980s, they were paying cash for all clothing in the 1990s.

Housing

Rural housing conditions also improved with economic development. Beginning in the 1980s, a building boom exploded and by 1990, 70 percent of the county's rural residents had moved into new houses. Per capita living space quickly expanded. Between 1985 and 1992, on average, living space increased by 1.75 sq m, the per capita value of such space being an extra 813.09 *yuan.* In contrast to the crude simple dwellings of the past, houses built in the 1980s were lavish and decorative. Modern construction materials such as concrete and cement were used. From interior to exterior, rural houses were no different from urban ones. Furthermore, great changes had also taken place in rural living facilities. No longer were people casually relieving themselves outside, but instead were using hygienic bathrooms. Fuel was now provided by wood, solar energy, and electricity in place of the cow and sheep dung and dried grass of the past. Liquefied fuel had appeared in a few homes. With frequent trips out of town, peasants loved to bring back new gadgets which they displayed in their homes. In the rural homes we visited, interior decoration had become much closer to urban styles.

Use

According to a sampling by the Rural Investigation Team of articles of daily use in Duilongdeqing homes, in 1992 per capita consumption of daily articles rose by 147.8 percent over that of 1985. Types of articles found also differed: More was being paid for recreation and books and periodicals. (See Table 7.9.) More rural homes now had modern home appliances and other articles. (See Table 7.10.) During the early 1980s, most peasants here had never seen a TV; in some remote areas, it was still unknown. In 1992, many families owned TV sets, especially those in villages near Lhasa. In Xiachong village, Liuwu *xiang,* 70 percent of the families owned color TVs

Table 7.9

Changes in Consumer Spending Structure

	1985		1992	
	Per capita outlay *(yuan)*	Percentage of total	Per capita outlay *(yuan)*	Percentage of total
Total expenditures	17.47	100	43.29	100
Daily necessities	16.64	95.25	36.33	83.92
Recreation	—	—	5.46	12.61
Books, magazines	—	—	0.07	0.16
Other	0.83	4.75	1.43	3.30

Source: Same as Table 7.8.

Table 7.10

Changes in Per Capita Durable Goods Owned

	1985	1992
Sewing machine	0.03	0.05
Clock and/or watch	0.12	0.23
Electric fan	—	—
Washing machine	—	—
Electric refrigerator	—	—
Motorcycle	0.07	—
Radio	0.09	0.09
Television	—	0.03
Cassette recorder	0.02	0.08
Camera	—	—

Source: Same as Table 7.8.

in 1992. Black-and-white sets were being gradually eliminated. Modern appliances had replaced traditional ones. Electric blenders had replaced butter tea urns—modernizing a centuries-old traditional process in Tibetan homes.

The modernization of every facet of daily household items was no doubt a direct factor in changing lifestyles.

Cultural and Recreational Activities

In the past, villagers loved to gather after work to sing and dance, drink *qingke* liquor, and play Tibetan cards and dice. Yet at that time, village cultural life allowed few other choices. With reform and the open policy, recreational activities have become much richer in form and content. This included watching TV and videos, listening to radio broadcasts, playing pool and video games, participating in karaoke programs, social dancing in clubs, drinking tea at sweet tea shops, and playing mahjong. By 1992, almost all forms of recreation found in cities were found here.

With the changes urbanization brought to rural clothing, food, housing, goods, and transportation, Tibetan villages in the 1980s and 1990s acquired an entirely new lifestyle. The backward and confining nature of their past life and rural self-sufficiency had completely disappeared. Agriculture was now dependent on industry, on the outside world, and on the cities.

VI. Rising Cultural Quality and Changing Values

Changes in the human being—enhancing of cultural quality and updating of value concepts—are important manifestations of social change. With economic development, Tibetan peasants and herdsmen themselves had changed dramatically, as shown below:

1. *The general raising of cultural and educational levels of farmers and herders.* Before the peaceful liberation of Tibet, culture was a prerogative of the slave-owning and religious clergy strata. After the liberation, the party and the government instituted compulsory education and campaigns to wipe out illiteracy, greatly raising the cultural and education level among peasants and herders in Tibet. In the 1960s and 1970s, however, most rural inhabitants were indifferent to formal education, and they had to be forcibly inculcated. In the 1980s and 1990s, with the modernization of production and the economy and increasingly frequent contact with the outside world, the masses of farmers and herdsmen began to embrace education with a rising awareness of its importance. They actively participated in the campaigns to wipe out illiteracy. In 1993, over 5,000 Duilongdeqing people

attended language classes and technical training classes in agrotechnology, vegetable growing, and hog-raising. This started a new wave. A peasant in his thirties or forties told us: "I didn't use to speak the Han language and got ripped off by businessmen in the interior." They not only learned the Han language, but also English and Hindi. Aboard minibuses owned by Duilongdeqing rural inhabitants, one could often see ticket sellers speaking fluent English with foreign passengers; village women in their forties or fifties hawked their goods to foreign visitors with a few words of English.

Farmers and herdsmen today are concerned not only about their own education, but that of their offspring. In the early period of reform when land and livestock were returned to the peasant households for management, most families kept their school-age children at home to take care of smaller children or graze the livestock. Despite compulsory education, teachers had to attract students to school with a daily attendance stipend, despite which the attendance rate remained low. During the late 1980s and early 1990s, when people began to realize the importance of education, they not only willingly sent their children to school but tried to get them the best education in good schools. Some "Ten Thousand *Yuan* Household" (wealthy) families in Naiqiong, for instance, sent their children to nearby schools for the children of workers and miners, or even to Lhasa at great expense. When state education funds were low, they made donations or built or repaired school buildings and bought educational equipment themselves. According to 1988–90 data, donations amounting to 260,000 *yuan* were made by county residents to renovate twenty-six local, community-run elementary schools. In the same period, state appropriations amounted to only 70,000 *yuan*.

2. *Changes in ideas about marriage and children.* In the 1960s and 1970s, due to the mammoth gap between urban and rural living conditions, the "dream husbands" of peasant girls were national-level cadres (*guojia ganbu*) who had an "iron rice bowl" filled with "the emperor's grain." They longed to leave the rural areas and become nonfarming urban dwellers. It was not easy, however, for a simple farm girl who had never left home to find a city dweller. That was why servicemen from the rural areas were all the rage; they had a good chance of promotion in the services and were assured of good jobs as nonfarming residents after demobilization. In the 1980s, along with the narrowing of the gap, conditions for the selection of marriage partners changed drastically. The pull of urban dwellers lessened and "specialized households" working in farming, raising hogs, or doing business in the rural areas became priority marriage targets. One motivation for young fellows in the rural areas to get rich through their own efforts, in fact, was "to get rich and find a good wife."

Planned birth is a difficult task to implement in the Chinese hinterland. The state exercises a special policy in the Tibetan rural areas of allowing three children per couple. Our investigation in Duilongdeqing yielded surprising results. In Naiqiong, for instance, most of the young people indicated they wanted only two children, with no preference for male or female. They did not want too many children to take care of and support. Bazhu's family, our key informant, had two boys, one five years old and one eleven.

3. *Change in religious beliefs.* During the early period of reform villages experienced a "religious fever," with peasants going to the temples or monasteries and worshiping whenever they had time. Some postponed farm work to join religious activities. All family income after necessary living expenses for the year was donated to the temples or monasteries. Lamas recited sutras at illnesses, deaths, or marriages. This situation has quietly changed. With higher family incomes, religious expenses did not dwindle but increased, but at the same time, more money was used to expand production. Lamas were still invited to perform rites at large-scale marriages and funerals, but it was more a prestige and wealth display expressed through custom. Heartfelt devotion to religion decreased. In some families, patients were first sent to hospitals. They asked lamas to perform rites only when that did not work.

4. *Appearance of new social relationship circles and the strengthening of information exchange.* Social circles built around monasteries, villages, or kin had existed for a long time in rural Tibet. With reform and changes in production and lifestyles, peasants had a lot more communication with the outside world and the once conservative and closed social circles of the past broke up, to be replaced by new modern relationships. Groups formed around common economic interests, rather than blood or similar surnames, as the boundaries between "clans" and "tribes" have been surmounted. Relations between different households in a community, too, changed. For instance, the few families that first had TV soon became gathering places for the whole village. When more families acquired TVs and VCRs, elders of the entire village continued to gather at one home to watch Tibetan-language films. Videos dubbed in Tibetan, such as *Journey to the West, Water Margin,* and *Magistrate Ji,* were special favorites. Young women gathered at another home to watch romances and dramas. Young men preferred martial arts films. In addition, sweet tea shops had also become centers of village activity, where young and old, male and female gathered. (A few years earlier, women had been ridiculed for patronizing these shops.) Here they relaxed, met members of the opposite sex, talked business, or exchanged information. These shops had become places for villagers to go for entertainment and to get in touch with others.

In regard to communication between rural and urban Tibetans, since the peaceful liberation of the region, the serfs had become the masters of their own destinies. Many had become national cadres and changed from rural to urban residents. In the 1960s and 1970s, because of the huge urban-rural gap, city people did not have much to do with their rural relatives apart from financial aid. In the 1980s, along with the development of the tertiary sector in the cities, urban residents began to invite in their relatives and help them set up businesses in the city. The latter's monthly incomes were now often higher than those of national cadres, and they turned around and helped their city relatives financially. One of us made a survey of Balang Street in Lhasa and discovered many individual business people to have been rural inhabitants whose city relatives helped them rent housing and/or set up businesses. Once they settled down, more rural relatives were brought over. Ties with city dwellers thus became increasingly close. The social circles of the farmers and herdsmen expanded constantly. Not only had the communication mode among farmers and herdsmen themselves changed and become more frequent, their relations with city residents had also become much closer.

Through increased communication with the outside world and media channels such as the TV, VCR, and Tibetan-language newspapers and magazines such as the *Tibetan Daily* and *Tibetan Science and Technology,* rural Tibetans are increasingly up-to-date with information. We discovered with surprise that peasants in Naiqiong were extremely savvy about market supply and demand in Zhangmu port.

5. *Formation of the concept of a commodity.* In the self-contained, closed and backward rural areas of the past, the concept of commodity exchange was extremely weak. In the last dozen years, however, the change in rural production and management modes has enhanced the farmers' and herdsmen's social sophistication. Those who worked out of town had to hire other people to work on their own land, or they covertly rented out the land that they had contracted (state policy forbade assignment of land). Whatever the form, the essence was that the exchange mode was one of commodity exchange. From our survey, we found that most people who bought vehicles in Duilongdeqing saved up the money from working elsewhere. Their first vehicle was generally an old-fashioned Dongfeng truck, for which they would hire a driver at 7 or 8 *yuan* per day (food and lodging supplied). They would learn to drive from this driver and take over in a year. After they earned more money, they would sell the old truck and buy a new one. Some other people would first work in a family with a vehicle as the driver's assistant. They could earn up to 5 *yuan* a day and learn to drive as well. After a time, they bought and drove their own vehicles. The pur-

chase or trading of cars, hiring of drivers, or helping out in learning to drive all showed sound business sense. The formation of this commodity concept is an indispensable condition for entry into a commodity society.

VII. The Urbanization Mode of Tibetan Villages

In the above, we have analyzed changes to Tibet's villages in the structure of productive forces, production and management modes, income level, lifestyles, and farmer/herder values. We can thus definitively state: Tibetan villages have already entered the urbanization process. The level is low compared to interior and coastal China, however, and the process is still in its start-up stage. After more than a decade of development, though, the urbanization model of rural Tibet has begun to form. That is, with the reform and opening to the outside policies of post-1980 in China, productive forces in rural Tibet have been released, impelling a large mass of surplus labor to shift to the cities into construction and other industries. The money earned by such outside work provides the "primary accumulation" for rural economic development, with which came changes in production and management styles. The rise of a diverse economy comprising rural transportation, construction, commerce, and food and beverage industries not only brought wealth to peasant families but also to the *xiang* and townships—the collective and the county. This provided the start-up capital for township enterprises. Township enterprises, in turn, concentrated scattered rural capital and capital from other places, provinces, and even foreign countries. This further stimulated the rural economy and raised the inhabitants' income level. Rising incomes raised rural living standards and promoted changes in the rural way of life, bringing the once self-sufficient rural lifestyle closer to its urban counterpart, which depends on consumption. Farmers' and herdsmen's values and consumption patterns have also moved closer to those of city residents. In addition, rural cultural quality has improved, which further promoted production and the economy. Urbanization first takes place in villages close to cities and convenient to transportation. Their development will influence more villages to embark on urbanization. Thus, a unique path to rural urbanization has been found in Tibet.

The changes brought about by a short dozen years of urbanization far exceed those experienced in scores of years or centuries in the past. In a few years, peasants' incomes have risen manyfold. Diversification has replaced traditional farming and livestock-raising, which had predominated for thousands of years. Modern urban lifestyles have replaced the self-contained and traditionally closed lifestyle of the past. The concept of commodities has replaced conservative and backward rural thinking. In short, urbanization has integrated rural with urban culture, giving birth to a new, more ideal type of culture which contains elements of both rural and urban civilization. It has brought social and cultural changes unimaginable before.

Naturally, confronted with such abrupt social and cultural changes, Tibetan villages as communities are facing the problem of how to make the transition from the traditional to a new urban life and how to rebuild community order. Farmers and herdsmen, as individual members of these communities faced with a new cultural system far removed from the one they knew, have the problem of how to absorb the new culture while retaining elements of their former culture. The two patterns merging into one will no doubt be an uneven process. Some worthwhile elements of their former culture may be discarded while not-so-good ones may be preserved. This includes, for instance, the discarding of traditional singing and dancing at wedding ceremonies while mahjong games become widespread.

Nonetheless, the positive side of urbanization no doubt outweighs the negative. Rural urbanization is a shortcut, an indispensable path, to the economic development of our nationalities' regions. We must do our best to guide and promote this road, first in villages close to cities and convenient to transportation, so that they can promote overall rural economic development.

Note

1. Guldin, Gregory Eliyu, "An Urbanizing China," in Guldin (ed.), *Urbanizing China*. Westport, CT: Greenwood Press, 1993, p. 5.

Part IV

Social Dimensions of
Rural Urbanization

8

An Investigative Report on the Migrant Population of Caitang Village, Xiamen Special Economic Zone

Lan Daju

Anthropologists have lavished much attention on the Chinese urbanization process. In 1992, I had occasion to participate in a multisite project focusing on urbanization that was organized by Dr. Gregory Guldin of Pacific Lutheran University in the United States. I took part in an investigation of migrant population in Caitang village in the Xiamen Special Economic Zone.[1] This report describes how migrant populations are adapting to life and work in a new environment and other related issues.

I. Caitang Village

Caitang Village is located on the outskirts of Xiamen city on Xiamen Island, 10 km from downtown. It is linked with the city by a heavily traveled highway. The village has been in existence for over a century. Its earliest settlers came from elsewhere on Xiamen Island, from nearby Zengcuoan. The village currently [mid-1993—Ed.] has 200–odd families with 1,196 people. It is divided into two natural villages (*ziran cun*) and has five villagers' groups (*cunmin xiaozu*). Traditionally an agricultural community, prior to the implementation of the responsibility system in the 1980s, it was Xiamen's vegetable supply source—the entire village grew vegetables for Xiamen's consumption. Even today, one can see large tracts of farms and dry land on the edges of the village, giving one the feeling of being in the countryside.

Since 1979, when economic reform and the open policy were put into effect, Caitang has experienced significant social and cultural change. In the beginning of that period, Caitang had no migrant population to speak of, but since then urbanization has proceeded apace and attracted many outsiders.

Economic reform has certainly been quite successful. In 1978, the village's group output was over 300,000 *yuan*. By 1991, this had risen to 5 million *yuan,* and by 1992, 18 million *yuan.* In 1984, per capita income was under 800 *yuan,* and this had increased to over 2,000 *yuan* by 1992. Both the production and living standards of the community had risen significantly.

A major change in the lives of Caitang inhabitants was turning from farming to business. Before 1978, as a fruit and vegetable supplier, the village had had a sales representative in the Xiamen Municipal Vegetable Company, to which it sent fresh vegetables daily and brought back fertilizer. With the development of the Xiamen Special Economic Zone (SEZ), local people started manufacturing companies, businesses, or services. They contracted to run twenty-odd small enterprises that had originally belonged to the commune and production brigades. Many went into real estate in areas lying between their village and the city. Taxicab drivers made daily runs into the city. As the farmland in this area was not permitted to go fallow, most villagers leased their land to outsiders to till or simply arranged for others to take over the responsibility. From what we were told, the largest number of villagers engaged in transport. Many drove taxis or small vans, of which the village owned about a dozen, in addition to eight cars. Some villagers rented out their vehicles while running factories or stores themselves.

The community actively solicited outside capital. They improved the investment environment by building basic facilities, including water, power, roads, and communication in order to attract more outside capital. At the time of our study, the place already had eight enterprises with foreign capital (four each from Taiwan and Hong Kong). Joint ventures with investment from local and other domestic sources numbered eleven. In 1990, the first Taiwan enterprise, the Xiamen Haoli Industrial Arts Company Ltd., was set up. It manufactured children's toys, which were sold abroad. The village authorities helped foreign investors as much as they could by providing water and power and security protection, for which they received appropriate compensation.

Material conditions had greatly improved. During the 1970s, living standards here were much lower than those of Xiamen residents. Marrying a daughter off to the city was a real coup. The situation was now different. As early as 1984, per capita income had reached 700 *yuan,* the highest of the nineteen production brigades on Xiamen Island. Currently, Caitang ranks third in rural economic development among all rural areas on the island. It was the first provincial-level "civilized village" (*wenming cun*) in Xiamen city. The Caitang village head told us that life here was no different from that in Xiamen city. As a matter of fact, some intermediate technical school graduates preferred to join the agricultural population (*fei zhuan nong*) rather than remain in the nonagricultural ranks; they preferred to work in the village's enterprises rather than take posts in city enterprises.

Village shareholding companies gave out dividends of 2,000 to 3,000 *yuan* per shareholder per year. In 1992, the village administration took in revenues amounting to 1.15 million *yuan.* In 1993, the amount was over 1.50 million *yuan.* The village authorities had control of these funds and used them to improve community welfare. The laying of water pipes cost 300,000 *yuan* in 1992; expansion of school buildings, 1 million *yuan.* Villagers got 80 percent of medical care free. Everyone had insurance, half of which was paid by the village. Villagers paid no taxes on land they farmed; taxes were paid collectively by the village. The village head also told us that a wide thoroughfare was being planned and much old housing was going to be renovated.

As a matter of fact, every village family had already built new houses, some luxurious. Most now had gas for cooking. Every home owned a refrigerator and a color TV set. Seventy families had installed telephone lines; in addition, there were 100 beepers, and some people even possessed cellular phones. There was a karaoke lounge, video room, and a caroms pool hall—all creating a village entertainment and recreation center.

A significant feature marking Caitang's urbanization was a large influx of people from outside, hitherto unknown in the village's history. After learning about the village's background, we began to delve into the main topic of our research.

II. Migrant Population: The General Situation

Caitang had about 1,000 migrants, almost equal to the number of natives. They came from Fujian, Jiangxi, Sichuan, and other provinces, with the majority from Fujian primarily and Jiangxi running second.[2] Migrants who rent housing from locals included those who originally worked for foreign enterprises but later found other employment.

According to our survey, most migrant workers were between the ages of 17 and 30. A few vegetable growers from outside were between 20 and

Table 8.1

Ages of Caitang's Migrant Population
(Incomplete statistics, 1993)

Age/No. of people	Age/No. of people	Age/No. of people	Age/No. of people	Age/No. of people	Age/No. of people
17/6	18/11	19/27	20/18	21/14	22/10
23/10	24/5	25/11	26/5	27/1	28/5
29/1	30/4	31/1	32/2	33/0	34/0
35/2	36/1	37/1	38/1	39/0	40/0
41/2	63/1				

41. (See Table 8.1.) They all arrived in Xiamen between April 1990 and May 1993. From incomplete statistics, among the third batch of migrants, five came in 1990, twenty-two in 1991, eighty-four in 1992, and 197 in 1993.

Migrant workers were employed by different Caitang companies or participated in different lines of work. (See Table 8.2.) The Xiamen Haoli Industrial Arts Ltd., one of the bigger local companies, belonged to Taiwan businessmen and manufactured children's industrial arts products for export. It hired over 700 migrant workers and only two Caitang natives. The reason few natives want to work there had to do with its long hours, strict management, and none-too-high wages. Nonlocal business people preferred to hire outside laborers because they came from economically backward interior regions, had low expectations on wages, and were easier to manage. Natives were like "local snakes" (*di tou she*); i.e., they had more influence locally and were harder to manage. The majority of the people we surveyed were migrant workers who were employed in this company.

To work in Caitang, migrant workers first had to apply for temporary resident permits from Caitang authorities. According to government regulations, temporary residence could be obtained only after specified procedures. Once approved, migrants were eligible to work in local factories or companies. They went mainly into three types of enterprises: 1. enterprises with outside capital, such as the Xiamen Haoli Industrial Arts Co.; 2. collectively contracted holding enterprises, such as the Caitang Hot-Plating Co.; and 3. individually owned private enterprises, such as the Caitang Paper Carton Factory. A few migrant workers did temporary jobs such as bricklaying and freight transport.

Table 8.2

Employment of Caitang's Migrant Population
(incomplete statistics, 1993)

Company (line of work)	No. employed	Company (line of work)	No. employed
Haoli Industrial Arts Co.	350	Auhua Co.	13
Huli Industrial Arts Co.	13	Hongan Co.	6
Huate Co.	4	Fouhua Industrial & Trading Co.	2
Yaohua Co.	2	Caitang Paper Carton Co.	3
Xingxingzuo Toy Factory	2	Siji Porcelain Factory	2
Hongchang Co.	2	Wang Aiguo's worksite	2
masons	12	tofu makers	7
vegetable growers	9	Caitang Hot-Plating Factory	1
Xiamen Chemical Plant	1	Xiamen Bicycle Plant	1
Chen He Paper Factory	1	Juxiang Garment Co.	1
Jincheng Co.	1	vehicle drivers	1
hairdressers	1	other	6

The following describes some ways in which migrant workers found employment in Caitang's enterprises: (1) Heard about a hiring opportunity from people from the same town or friends, applied, passed necessary examination, and got hired; (2) had townspeople or friends already working in an enterprise and got hired through these connections without any examination; (3) students of vocational schools, led by teachers, went to different enterprises in groups and got hired *en masse;* and (4) got hired purely through one's own efforts.

III. Sampling Survey of Migrant Population

In order to find out more concretely the situation of Caitang's migrant population, we used the convenience sampling technique, a form of the nonprobability random sampling method, to interview fifty people, twenty-five males and twenty-five females. The following are our findings:

1. Motive for Coming to Xiamen

A. Native Place

	Fujian	Jiangxi	Sichuan	Guizhou	Hunan
Male	7	16	1	1	—
Female	15	9	—	—	1

Most of the 50 came from Fujian and Jiangxi, a few from other inland provinces. According to our survey, of those who came from Fujian, most were from Pinghe, Liancheng, Zhangpu, and Yunxiao.

B. Time of Arrival in Xiamen

	1988	1991	1992	1993
Male	1	—	10	14
Female	—	2	3	20

Apart from a few who arrived earlier, the majority came after 1991. This relates directly to the development of the area.

C. Work Experience

	Have work experience	No work experience
Male	13	12
Female	6	19

Not a few left their native places to work outside for the first time. A number had had experience in working in Guangdong, Zhejiang, or other places in Fujian.

D. Marital Status

	Married	Single, Have Fiancé(e)	No Fiancé(e)
Male	6	2	17
Female	3	—	22

Some of them were married couples; the majority were single. Most came after graduating or dropping out of middle school. Many of those interviewed indicated that marriage expenses being as high as they were, they had to earn some money first before considering such a step.

E. Motive for Coming to Xiamen

	Earn money	See the world	Mixture of both
Male	8	2	15
Female	8	8	9

The motive was either to earn money or see the world. Many wanted to see the world while young, while learning a trade and earning some money.

F. Sending Money Home

Basically, migrant workers showed a sense of responsibility toward their families. Apart from what they needed for daily life, they sent surplus money home either to help the family, save up for marriage, or to lay aside for future business. They all realized they were there to work, not to enjoy a life of ease.

Response	Amount (yuan/mo.)	Proportion of monthly earnings
Men:		
Send every extra penny home	100	1/3
Have not yet earned money	N.A.	N.A.
Have not yet earned money	N.A.	N.A.
Send extra money home	200	2/3
Intend to send	200	2/3
All used up	N.A.	N.A.
Have sent 4/5 times	200 at a time	2/3
Intend to send	ca. 100	1/3
Send part of earnings	100	1/2
Have not earned any money	N.A.	N.A.
Only enough for oneself	N.A.	N.A.
In training, no income	N.A.	N.A.
Send half home	200	1/2

Depend on monthly income	250	2/3
Sent 900 *yuan* last year, none yet this year	N.A.	N.A.
Intend to	50	1/5
Just entered factory, earning only ca. 200 *yuan*	N.A.	N.A.
Send some home	100–200	1/2
Mother, wife, family all here	N.A.	N.A.
Depend on amount earned	N.A.	N.A.
Send	100–200	1/2
Send	150	1/2
Don't need to; save up	N.A.	N.A.
Send when earn more	N.A.	N.A.
Not yet, plan to	N.A.	N.A.
Women:		
Send when more left over	200–250	1/2–2/3
Never	N.A.	N.A.
Send	500–600/yr.	N.A.
Send	500–600/yr.	N.A.
Send	500–600/yr.	N.A.
Have not earned any money yet	N.A.	N.A.
Have not earned any money yet	N.A.	N.A.
Have not earned any money yet	N.A.	N.A.
Will send when have money	100	1/3
Have not sent yet, plan to	100	1/3

Have not sent yet, plan to	100	1/3
Have not sent yet, plan to	100	1/3
Only if left over, maybe	N.A.	N.A.
Intend to	200	2/3
Don't pay food, lodging here; send every bit	200+	100%
Don't pay food, lodging here; send every bit	200+	100%
Have sent	150	1/2
Have sent	150	1/2
Have sent	150	1/2
Send some	150	1/2
Send some	150	1/2
Sometimes	100	1/4
Sometimes	100	1/4
No money to send yet	N.A.	N.A.
Will send when earn more	100	1/2

2. Work conditions

A. Cultural Quality

The educational level of all interviewees was at or below senior middle school. This factor determined that they could only do simple operations and manual labor and would make low wages. A low cultural level also affected their ability to adapt to a new environment quickly and actively.

	Male	Female
Illiterate	0	3
Learning to read/write	0	1
Up to 4th grade primary school	2	1
5th or 6th grade primary school	1	4
Junior middle school	12	11
Senior middle school	10	5
Intermediate vocational school	0	0
Senior vocational school	0	0

B. Employment Channel

	Open exam	Friend/relative referral	On own	Exam + referral
Male	2	13	1	9
Female	9	7	1	8

The most common pattern in getting hired was first to be referred by friends or relatives and then pass the requisite exam, or obtain news about hiring and apply. Referral by friends or relatives seemed to be an important channel for migrants, who were unfamiliar with the local hiring situation.

C. Priorities in Hiring Considerations (Response Frequency)

	Age	Will be obedient	"Have culture"	Have technical skills	Other
Male	14	19	21	21	4
Female	3	9	19	22	2

In hiring, primary considerations on the part of enterprises were education ("have culture") and skill level in addition to honesty and obedience.

D. Time Necessary to Become Skilled Laborers

	1 week	2 weeks	3 weeks	1 month	2 months
Male	10	2	0	10	3
Female	11	0	0	13	1

Since categories of work for migrant workers were usually not complicated, most were able to acquire the necessary skills within a month. Enterprises often set aside the first month as a training period, and employees were paid at a lower rate during that period.

E. Monthly Wages (Yuan)

	200–300 y.	300–400 y.	400–500 y.	900–1,000 y.
Male	13	4	6	2
Female	14	11	0	0

Most migrant workers were earning under 500 *yuan* a month. A few who drove vehicles earned up to 1,000 *yuan*. Wages were lower for females as compared to males. According to our survey, monthly expenses for food and lodging came to about 100 *yuan*. At the end of a year, deducting expenses, each could save an average of 2,000–3,000 *yuan*.

F. Relationship with Superiors (Response Frequency) (as Revealed by How the Worker Addressed a Superior)

	Directly by name	By title	By title & surname
Male:			
Working hours	1	11	11
After work	2	10	12
Female:			
Working hours	1	16	6
After work	1	16	6

Form of address was decided by relationship with a superior. If the superior's rank was not too high or the person was friendly with the worker, the form of address was casual—stricter during working hours and less so after work. Toward high-ranking executives (such as general managers or factory directors), the form of address was usually by title whether during or after work. [Usually, calling someone by both surname and title would be the most formal of these three forms of address—Ed.]

G. Attitude toward Commands from a Superior

	Complete compliance	Have reservations
Male	21	4
Female	22	3

Most workers realized their own positions; they either "obeyed" their superiors or became "fried squid" [i.e., were fired—ed.]. They had no other choice. Enterprise management also emphasized that managers kept their distance from employees.

H. Employment Stability

The relationship between employees and the enterprise was loose. Workers came and went, which gave enterprises little stability as far as workers were concerned. Many workers quit and as many more came in.

	Much stability	Not much stability	Don't know
Male	2	17	6
Female	6	17	2

3. Spare-Time Life

A. How After-Work Hours Are Spent (Response Frequency)

	Male	Female
Doing housework	1	3
Rest/sleep	17	22
Watch video	1	0
Play caroms	3	0
Wash clothes	4	13
Hang out	8	4
Read books	4	7
Watch TV	3	2
Talk/play cards/mahjong	4	0

Rest or sleep, washing or talking, took up the major part of workers' spare time. They often had to work intensively 12 hours a day including overtime and only wanted to rest after work. They had little time for recreation.

B. *Visiting Local Scenic Sites*

	Have visited	Have not visited
Male	14	11
Female	19	6

Most utilized their days off to visit scenic spots in the vicinity, demonstrating their need for outdoor life.

C. *Watching TV*

Some watched only because TV was accessible and some did not because it was not accessible. More often, people had no time to watch. Martial-arts films were favorites. Knowledge gleaned about social realities from this source was extremely limited.

	Watch often	Not so often
Male	12	13
Female	10	15

D. *Drinking Out*

	Regularly drink out?	
Male	2	23
Female	1	24

The goal of migrant workers was to earn money, and therefore they were reluctant to spend money on food and alcohol. A night out drinking was an occasional "luxury."

E. *Knowledge about Current Clothing Fashions*

	Knowledgeable about clothing fashions	Not clear about fashions
Male	10	15
Female	8	17

Some of the migrant workers kept up with social fashions; some did not. This may have to do with the length of time of their stay in Xiamen. It may also be because they did not pay attention to things that were of no immediate interest to them.

4. Social activities and contacts

A. With Whom

They basically hung out with people from their home districts (*laoxiang*) or former schoolmates. People from the same *xiang* or school often came to Xiamen together. They had little contact with locals. Migrant workers had little social activity except to hang out on the streets in small groups of two or three. Only a very few made friends with locals, and friendships were very limited. Most did not make friends, had language difficulties, and were unable to penetrate local social life.

	Most interaction with whom?			
	Laoxiang or schoolmates	Work place friends	Caitang people	Xiamen relatives
Male	22	1	2	—
Female	21	1	1	2

B. From Whom Do They Borrow Money (Response Frequency)

	Friends	Relatives	Boss/ coworker	Bank	Loan association	Usurers
Male	18	13	5	10	0	1
Female	8	10	2	12	0	0

Most considered borrowing from friends or relatives first, then banks. (Some considered banks because they had connections there.) They gave little consideration to coworkers or bosses since relations were seldom that close, or a loan association among their peers because of the risks involved, or usurers because of the high interest rate. Some had never even heard of the latter two sources. In migrant worker circles, friends were mostly townspeople or former schoolmates. Blood and geographic ties were the major social links.

C. Views on Differences, If Any, with Locals

	Significant differences	Little or no differences	Unclear
Male	22	3	0
Female	10	5	10

The majority clearly perceived differences with locals in many ways (language, food preference, living standards, etc.). Some claimed to not perceive or realize any difference. This was because most migrant workers had not been accepted into local social circles and lacked understanding of the social situation locally.

D. Self-Description of Social Role (response frequency)

	Male	Female
Migrant population	23	24
Local	0	0
Mobile migrant population	16	18
"Blind flow" (*mangliu*)	2	5
Temporary migrant population	24	24
Migrant laborers	20	17
Temporary urban population	5	7
Urban laborers	9	8
Rural laborers	17	11
Temporary rural population	10	15

Migrant workers were generally able to separate their role from that of locals and were clear about their outsider status. Many did not understand the meaning of "blind migration" (*mangliu*), or whether they were temporary urban or rural population or laborers. This had to do with their level of cognition as well as the situation in Caitang itself. Actually, they were little bothered by such things; all they knew was that they were out to earn money, and that was enough.

5. Choices and Preferences

A. Comparison between Urban and Rural Life

	City life better	Rural life better	Same
Male	15	3	7
Female	10	2	13

Half considered urban life better, the other half was divided between preferring rural life or considering the two about the same.

B. Preference for a Place of Residence

	Buy apartment in city	Build house in village	Don't know
Male	8	17	0
Female	6	18	1

Seventy percent preferred to build a house in the countryside. Actually, urban life was attractive to everyone; the choice for "building a house in the village" stemmed from a realistic assessment of their situation. Being hired laborers, they dared not even think of buying an apartment in town.

C. Preference for Work Location

	Home district	Caitang
Male	24	1
Female	16	9

Eighty percent chose to work in their home districts; 20 percent in Caitang. If wages were the same, people preferred to work in their native places because of friends, relatives, and a feeling of security.

D. Willingness to Do Farm Work

	Unwilling	Willing
Male	14	11
Female	17	8

The majority were unwilling to work on the farm even if the income was good because the work was hard. Some were willing because they said you only worked hard in the busy seasons, and because farm laborers had more freedom as compared to factory workers, who were subject to strict supervision.

E. First Preference in Investing Money

	Build house	Go into business or open factory	Don't know
Male	2	23	0
Female	2	19	4

If they had enough money, most would choose first to go into business or open a factory rather than build a house. This showed a strong wish for business, which was common among migrant workers. According to a news report in the June 16, 1994 issue of the *Xiamen Daily,* in recent years many young men and women who had earlier left Sichuan to work elsewhere had gone back home with the money they had earned, the production and business skills they had learned, and the information they had acquired to go into the individual or private economic sector to contribute to the improvement of their home towns. Over 100,000 such former migrant workers are now owners of individual or private businesses. They have provided employment for a surplus rural labor force of 200,000.

F. Ideas on One's Destiny

	Fate in one's own hands	Fate in hands of destiny
Male	19	6
Female	16	9

Seventy percent felt their fate was in their own hands; 30 percent left their fates to "destiny." Two possible factors influenced their ideas: life experience and work experience in Xiamen.

G. Favorite Type of Songs (Response Frequency)

	Male	Female
"Red Sun"	9	5
Nostalgia about native place	10	6
Rock music	13	7
Minnan folk songs	6	14
Cantonese songs	3	4

Preference for songs has to do with current social trends. Generally speaking, these migrant workers had diverse tastes; most liked popular tunes. Their preference was somewhat limited by language. ["Minnan," or the

Southern Min area, is the language/cultural region of eastern Guangdong, southern Fujian, and Taiwan—ed.]

IV. Some Perceptions Based on Comparisons

Anthropologist Zhou Daming of Zhongshan University, in his article "Population Shift in the Pearl River Delta and the Question of Cultural Adaptation,"[3] explored some questions concerning migrants' adaptation to urban cultures. I would like to make a simple comparison in regard to Xiamen's migrant worker population.

A. Attitude toward Urban Life

Migrants in the Pearl River Delta who were once part of the agricultural population but who had changed to nonagricultural resented urban life. They felt themselves looked down upon by city people, could get only unskilled work, received low wages, had to pay for everything, and shouldered heavier burdens of life than at home. Young people could not find marriage partners. They therefore thought rural life better than urban life. These attitudes were similarly reflected among Caitang's migrant worker population (see the "Choices and Preferences" section above). They felt that urban living standards were higher, goods were plentiful, one could get anything if one had the money, and transportation was convenient; they also felt, however, that compared to rural life, the air was not as refreshing, the food and vegetables not as fresh, and the pace of life too fast. In the countryside, moreover, people are less anxious, are relatively free, and are more open and caring. Therefore, many felt rural life was not inferior to urban life.

B. Adaptability to City Life

Zhou Daming was of the opinion that the migrant workers in the Pearl River Delta had their own way of adapting to the city. They did not do so by accepting the local culture. Generally, they arrived in groups comprising people from the same villages, or friends or relatives. One person led the group and spoke for it. Inside the groups, the customs of the home towns were preserved and internal unity prevailed. They clearly knew that they were there to work and earn money, not to settle down permanently. Professor Zhou felt this enabled them to live at peace temporarily, but they did not have the feeling of being masters of their own fate or that of belonging to the community, and this was not "genuine adaptation."

This situation also applied to migrant workers in Caitang. They also arrived in groups with their townspeople, lived in the same houses, and took care of each other. All they wanted was a place to stay and earn some money. They knew they would not be there long. That was why they were critical of urban life and rural life remained their standard. Their only purpose was to earn money and send it home, thus discharging their responsibility to their parents. Their hope was to be able to go into business or open factories at home and become small business owners. They were thus not too observant of local life, and did not feel obliged to learn the local language or make friends locally. All they wanted was "money and rice." As long as someone hired them and gave them work, they would have "rice." They did not have to become "Xiamen people," because they would be leaving.

C. Relationships with Local People

Tension existed between locals and migrants in the Pearl River Delta. Migrant workers generally worked hard and lived frugally, contributing to the local economy. But the work they did was simple physical labor at low pay, and this made them objects of local scorn. Locals complained they had driven up food and vegetable prices and threatened community safety. Migrants complained of low wages and poor working conditions.

While in Caitang, we had occasion to observe the subtle relationship between locals and outsiders. The place needed a migrant labor force to develop its economy and provide locals with extra income through rent from lodgings. On the other hand, locals were afraid of outsiders, looked down on them, and considered them mean—hence not people to make friends with. They cited examples in the papers of crimes committed by migrants. Outsiders envied the locals' living standards while disliking them; they thought the locals had a superior attitude merely because they had more money. The relationship between the two was quite subtle: a sort of mutual using while rejecting each other.

Notes

1. For a more comprehensive report on Caitang, see Chapter 5.
2. Of those surveyed, we foung the following distribution—Fujian: 280; Jiangxi: 106; Henan: 9; Sichuan: 19; Hunan: 11; Anhui: 4; Zhejiang: 2; Guangxi: 2; Jiangsu: 2; Shaanxi: 1; Unknown: 8.
3. Zhou Daming, *Urban Anthropology*. Beijing: Huaxia Publishers, 1990.

9

Investigative Analysis of "Migrant Odd-Job Workers" in Guangzhou

Zhou Daming

Beginning in the 1980s, wave after wave of migrant laborers have poured out of the countryside in search of work, and the Pearl River Delta, including Guangzhou, was the first to be affected. In 1988, the delta's migrant laboring population reached 2 million. In 1989, it was 3 million, in 1990, 4 million, in 1991, 5 million, in 1992, 6 million, and in 1993, an estimated 10 million or more.[1] Migrant laborers take jobs shunned by local people, jobs which pay low wages and are of low social status but which are labor intensive and in poor work environments. This author has divided such migrant laborers into four types: those with professional skills, those who work in enterprises, those who work in agriculture, and odd-job workers (*sangong*).[2] This classification is the conventional, traditional one.

"Odd-job workers" refers to people among the migrant laboring population who "freelance." They are not licensed as individual business proprietors, nor are they legally employed by different enterprises. They work in a variety of jobs, roughly divided into the two following categories. In the first category, they mainly sell their physical labor, similar to day (short-term) laborers. They do whatever jobs bosses give them, including moving earth, bricks, digging, and shoveling. Such workers are usually hired for short periods by foremen in charge of urban road, sewage, or gasoline piping projects. They make up the labor reserve. In the second category, laborers are handicraftsmen who work exclusively in one occupation or another, such as carpentry, bricklaying, shoe repairing, bicycle repairing, cotton fluffing, etc. They are widely dispersed and have a lot of mobility, and are hence hard to count, but the total number is not small. According to a 1988 Shenzhen estimate, the area's *sanwu* population (most of them odd-job workers) numbered 200,000.[3] The Guangzhou figure probably greatly exceeds this number.

From the end of 1992 to the beginning of 1993, this author organized an investigation into the migrant workers. Participants included nineteen undergraduate students of the [entering] 1991 class of Zhongshan University's anthropology department and three teachers who attended the university for advanced training. Participants were divided into eight groups, each focusing on a topic listed in our outline. The method we used was interviews and questionnaires, the data obtained were then discussed and summarized. This was the basis of this chapter, which therefore relies on the work of many people to whom I wish to render thanks at this time.

The survey was very limited. First, time was limited because we had to use after-school hours and were able to survey only some places in the vicinity. Second, funds were limited, thus restricting the number of samples we were able to collect. We had planned to interview 120 people and actually ended up interviewing 146. Eighty-two useful questionnaires were received. No tracking study was possible. Third, due to limitations on the objects of our survey, we were unable to do random sampling and had to "follow the vine to get at the melon"—to make friends with one person and then widen our circle of interviewees. Fourth, on considerations of security, we forbade students to look into illegal activities. Fifth, there is the question of timeliness—two years had elapsed before this chapter was written. This author has noticed, however, that no other chapter on migrant odd-job workers has appeared during this period, which gives this particular article some value in uncovering facts about people living at the bottom rung of society.

I. Odd-Job Worker Communities

In Guangzhou, most odd-job workers lived in integrated urban-rural areas on the periphery of the city center.[4] This author had the opportunity to survey a few of these communities. People from the same region lived together, forming "villages within villages." They included, for instance, "Zhejiang village," "Hunan village," "Sichuan village," and "Xinjiang village." Below is a description of "Sichuan village" on the southern bank of the Pearl River in the Haizhu District.

Located beside the Xiaogang River, this community was under the jurisdiction of Lianxing village (which comprised two production teams) and was extremely convenient to traffic. With the Hai-Yin Bridge now completed, people can walk directly into downtown by just crossing the bridge. At the time of the study, the environment was poor, with a chemical plant releasing large amounts of pollutants into the water. The Xiaogang River, some 20–30 meters wide, poured into the Zhujiang River. When the tide was in, the waters rose, but when it receded, silt and garbage were exposed and gave off a stench when exposed to the sun. All low-lying areas beside the vegetable fields were filled with trash. For many years, docks and warehouses storing building materials had sat along the banks. About a decade ago, more docks and warehouses were built, and outlets for construction materials sprang up along a two-kilometer track. The need for temporary workers grew, and more and more odd-job workers poured in. In recent years, with increasing numbers of Guangzhou residents remodeling their homes, odd-job workers have had no lack of work. Villagers and migrants in the village told us that as many as 5,000 migrant workers were now living there. We were at first skeptical about this, figuring that the place was too small to hold that many people. But this was the figure everyone gave us. After visiting the dwelling places of some of those migrants, we began to believe the figure to be pretty close to the truth.

In this "Sichuan village," most of the odd-job workers came from Sichuan Province. The majority were "brickers" (*nishui lao*) doing construction and repairs or transporting materials (and, of course, whatever else the boss wanted them to do). In the mornings, they waited on the streets, docks, or in front of warehouses to be hired. At noon, they ate box lunches. After dark, they went home to temporary dwellings that the dock or warehouse owners built on the narrow riverbanks or under the dikes. The dwellings were extremely cramped with only about 10 sq m of floor space. Like cages, they each had three levels inside; each level had six openings, each opening leading to a space about the size of a sleeping berth on a train, although not as high. Usually, two openings were saved to put the belongings of the twelve to sixteen occupants. The "cages" were built of brick, and a person crawled through an opening to his space to sleep, pulling a curtain over his opening. The entire unit had only one small window, and when the weather was sultry, the situation could be imagined. Each occupant paid 30 *yuan* rent a month.

Workers from other places in Guangdong lived better, mostly three to four people renting a room. The units provided no toilets, kitchens, or baths. People set up makeshift stoves at the foot of the walls outside with bricks or discarded oil barrels, on which they cooked with huge pots or woks. Twigs were used for fuel. They were not choosy about what they ate as long as they had enough to fill their stomachs. They bought the cheapest rice and vegetables possible. I watched seven or eight of them eating one day and saw each holding an oversized rice bowl, piled high with rice topped by red-hot peppers and fatty pork. A forty-inch pot over the stove was still half full of cooked rice. The laborers usually made their own breakfasts and bought their lunches at eateries in Guangzhou catering especially to their business. We researchers went into one such place and bought some lunch. "Each plate consisted of three *liang* of rice, a plate of stir-fried vegetables, plus a few slices of none-too-fresh fatty pork, costing 1.5 *yuan*. An odd-job worker told us: 'Although the quality is not high, the quantity is adequate and the price low, so we often eat here.' As they spoke, they were puffing Duobao cigarettes which cost 90 cents a pack. Their clothes were cheap but durable." (Excerpt from notes taken by a member of the survey team.)

Without toilets, people urinated wherever convenient and defecated near the river behind some paper boards. They bathed themselves under outdoor taps, often fully clothed, thus washing both themselves and their clothes. Dirty water and refuse were splashed on the ground or dumped into the river. There was no electricity in the units, and with only the feeble light from one small window, the inside was perpetually in semidarkness. We were told, however, that they had no need for lights since they did everything outdoors after dark, whether talking, standing, eating, or playing chess or cards under the street lights, and went inside only to sleep. That was okay as long as the weather was good, but when it rained, they could only stand outside under the overhanging roofs or crawl in to sleep.

Odd-job workers owned only a few simple production tools. Their most valuable asset was pedicabs, followed by foot-pedaled transport vehicles. People chipped in to buy them. Other tools included mason's tools, pails, burlap sacks, and shoulder poles. A few were gang bosses wearing beepers, avowedly to "find jobs with." Most workers had formed into fixed groups of three to five, a number of groups forming a cluster. Several groups worked the larger projects together. Wages were divided equally in the group, with a little extra for the one who got the job for the group. They also ate together and divided meal costs equally.

Going out during the day, jobs were not always easy to find. One earned something when one was lucky and returned empty-handed when one was not. Staking out a fixed location to await hiring was not easy either. It often involved maintaining good relations with warehouse or store owners and doing odd jobs for the bosses for free, who might then refer a client or two. There also had to be coordination among the workers. Fights frequently broke out over jobs and territories. Moreover, good relations had to be maintained with city management personnel. In some areas, security personnel exacted monthly fees from each starting at 5 *yuan*. If the fee was not paid, the culprit was either driven out or beaten up and put in the repatriation center. Moreover, the local "black society" [criminal underworld—ed.] had to be dealt with. Gang members extorted money on a daily or monthly basis, and the workers had better watch out for their lives if they failed to pay. Besides rent, the workers had to pay a temporary resident registration fee and the security personnel's "protection fee." The security personnel were from elsewhere in Guangdong and didn't dare bully locals, so they made people from other provinces their targets of choice.

One young fellow we met had a bandage around his head with blood seeping through. He was around 25. He told us he was a veteran of the army and had been stationed in the Guangzhou Military Region some years ago. After leaving the army, he became an odd-job worker here and had stayed for six years now. He smiled with nostalgia when he talked about working here a few years ago. Jobs were plentiful and wages were good; restrictions were few. He was able to put aside some money, and went home and got married. He returned here to earn money to build a house. He sighed as he told us that work had become much harder to find. There was too much competition, wages were low, and too many extortions. He had found no work for the past dozen days, he said, and still owed "territory fees" and "protection fees." He had hardly enough to travel back home. That noon, the local gang had asked for his "territory fee," which he was unable to pay. He talked back a little and had his head cracked open. Tears came to his eyes as he spoke. He told us that as soon as he made enough for travel, he was going home to Nanchong, Sichuan Province. Life was a little hard at home, but it was better than roughing it out here.

Another young man told us he considered himself lucky when he compared himself to some other workers. The man who slept in the cubbyhole above him, a fellow Sichuan native in his forties, used to be the Communist party secretary in his production brigade. This man organized a group of them to come here to "seek the road to wealth" and they had been here a few years now. The local mafia took "particular care" of this man because he used to be a party secretary and demanded from him several times the monthly fee as compared to others. Moreover, because he was older and got tired faster, he had a tough time finding jobs. So he barely made enough. He didn't want to go home yet either, because he was afraid of ridicule. A few days ago, he was down on his luck and was caught by city management workers who fined him 150 *yuan*. As he was unable to come up with the money, he was given a beating and sent to a shelter. The other Sichuan workers eventually pitched in 300 *yuan* and got him released. He had been laid up for the last three days. As we talked, the party secretary put his head out of his cubbyhole to look at us. He was dark and thin, with a headful of gray hair. He pleaded with us: "Please write about this!" thinking we were reporters. When I told him we were not, he sighed hopelessly and went back to sleep.

Odd-job workers with relatively stable incomes rent housing from the villagers. Villagers here lived spaciously. Some owned three to five houses, some two or three, mostly multistory buildings. They rent out extra space at relatively high prices. A two-bedroom apartment cost 500 *yuan* per month and a single room 150, utilities not included. Three or four odd-job workers would share an apartment. Though rent was high, they could save a lot of trouble because the landlords helped them to get temporary resident permits, and security and city management personnel would by and large leave them alone. Such renters were mostly handicraftsmen or those illegally doing business. A deposit had to be put down before renting, which put it beyond the means of most "brickers."

A young man from Zhejiang, a nodding acquaintance I had seen around for a dozen years, also lived in this village. He came from Jinhua. When I first got to know him, he was unmarried. Later on, he went back, got married, and built a house. His younger brother followed him to Guangzhou and worked in the shoe repair trade. Now the brother, too, was married and had built his own house back home. His brother-in-law subsequently came to Guangzhou, and the three families, each with a child, shared a two-bedroom apartment with kitchen and bath at 600 *yuan* rent. The brother-in-law was also a skilled shoe repairer and repaired umbrellas. He told us that there was more business in umbrella repairs than shoe repairs. During the rainy season, he could make 500 *yuan* a month. His wife also had a small business and the couple together sometimes made over 1,000 *yuan* a month. Life was okay for them here and they had nicer houses waiting for them at home. They planned to save some more money and go back and start a shoe manufacturing factory, so that they no longer had to leave home. Besides, their children were growing up and they wanted to send them to school. "We may repair shoes, but our children are going to college."

Many private factories had also sprung up in the village, some owned by locals, others by migrants. Many were housed in private homes, so the working environment was not too good. Workshops were small and lacked ventilation. Women migrants worked here, for the most part. One garment workshop had several dozen sewing machines set up in one room in addition to a few cutting tables, where more than fifty female workers toiled. All available space was piled high with bolts of cloth and finished products, and one had to pick one's way to cross the room. There were a few small, barred windows. One narrow path led away from the front door, so if a fire or some other emergency arose, the results could be imagined.

Villagers were sympathetic to the migrants, knowing how hard it was for them to leave their homes. Migrant workers were also very friendly to villagers. They said they had to be since they were the outsiders. By contrast, relations among groups of odd-job workers from different provinces or areas were constantly marred by conflict. We witnessed a bloody fight among Sichuan natives wielding knives and throwing bricks. There were many injuries. Sichuan natives also fought with natives from Hunan, who lived not far from them. Group fights were generally over business and territory.

Most of the empty space in the village had been requisitioned by the government and was undergoing construction. Land along the riverbanks had been leased out, chiefly to build warehouses and yards for building materials. Owners had also built a lot of temporary dwelling houses here which, besides those they used, were rented out. The "cages" described earlier belonged to this type. The village's main street was lined by shops—mostly restaurants, grocery stores, or construction material outlets—by and large owned by villagers. They did a brisk business because of the rising population.

II. Analysis of Questionnaires Returned by Odd-Job Workers

Although we received a total of 146 questionnaires, only eighty-two gave appropriate and useful answers to our questions and constituted effective samples. Questions were both open-ended ones and multiple-choice.

1. Basic Characteristics of Odd-Job Workers

Table 9.1 shows the majority of odd-job workers to be males, chiefly belonging to the 18–24 and 25–30 age groups. Those age groups made up 76 percent of the sample. The reason for this was that odd-job workers had to do heavy physical labor, with some danger, and the work was dirty. Workers over 40 were all doing carpentry or cotton fluffing (we did not come across anyone older than 55). Most of the women repaired shoes or sold food.

Because young adults made up the majority, the educational level of these workers was not low. Only 6 percent were illiterate, most of them were men over 40 or women. Almost 50 percent were of junior middle school level, although most were dropouts and few graduated from either junior or senior middle school. From what we observed, most of them were able to read newspapers and books and do simple calculations. A few could speak some sentences of English.

Sixty-seven percent of the male odd-job workers were single. In the 18–24 age group, only one female was married, the rest were not. Fifty-seven percent of the single males or females belonged to families (including parents and siblings) with five to seven members and 9 percent to families with more than eight members.

Table 9.1

Basic Sample Data

Sex

Males	76	92%
Females	6	8%

Age

18–24	39	48%
25–30	23	28%
31–39	10	12%
40 and over	10	12%

Education

3–6 grade	17	21%
7–9 grade (j.m.s.)	40	49%
10–12 grade (s.m.s.)	18	22%

Family size

3	11	13%
4	10	12%
5	25	30%
6–7	22	27%
8 and over	7	9%

Marital Status

Age	Married	Single
18–24	1 (3%)	38 (97%)
25–30	9 (39%)	14 (61%)
31–39	8 (80%)	2 (20%)
40 and over	9 (90%)	1 (10%)
Total	27 (33%)	55 (67%)

2. Types of Work Odd-Job Workers Did

Odd-job workers did many different jobs, making them hard to classify. (Table 9.2) Some workers told us that they "don't know what type of work we do—whatever is available." We ended up listing that as a separate item on our questionnaire because it was such a common answer. It truthfully reflected their situation. They went out early in the morning and stood by the roadside in groups of two or three, holding up a sign (brick, tile, or cardboard) saying "repairs, transporting earth." Actually, of course, they did

Table 9.2

Types of Work* Done by Odd-Job Workers
(listed according to decreasing frequency of responses)

1. Whatever available	11. Painted
2. Transported stuff	12. Repaired cars
3. Transported earth	13. Scavenged
4. Pushed carts	14. Sold box lunches
5. Did repairs	15. Sold *dabing***
6. Repaired shoes	16. Sold fake invoices
7. Fluffed cotton	17. Traded documents and vouchers
8. Did construction	18. Dug earth
9. Did maintenance/repairs	19. Sold popcorn
10. Did carpentry	

*From 146 samples.
**A pancake-like flat bread—ed.

whatever the day brought. For instance, the Zhujiang Film Studio hired extras or transport workers daily. After a while, a labor market formed in front of the filming site with a crowd of workers waiting to be hired. Competition was fierce although the pay was low. Few odd-job workers stuck to only one job. Shoe repairers, for instance, also repaired umbrellas and sold soles and polish. Carpenters often did painting and even bought up old furniture which they restored and sold. Scavengers not only scavenged but stole. In short, odd-job workers resorted to all kinds of ways to make a living.

3. Point of Origin and Motivation of Odd-Job Workers

Most odd-job workers came from the provinces of Hunan, Sichuan, Jiangxi, and Zhejiang. From Hunan and Jiangxi, the largest number came from the southern areas abutting Guangdong. From Sichuan, most came from the central and eastern parts, and from Zhejiang, the area of Jinhua. (Table 9.3)

For the way in which such workers came to Guangdong and the reasons why, see Table 9.4. The largest number reported that they came on their own, while the next-highest group came by recommendation of *tongxiang* (district-mates) or friends. Few came at the invitation of relatives. My observations, however, showed that the majority of them arrived in groups. What they referred to as "friends" were actually tongxiang. The major reason cited for coming to Guangzhou was that reportedly "You can earn a lot of money here."

The "reason for coming to Guangzhou" was an open-ended question, but

Table 9.3

Provincial Origin of Odd-Job Workers

Hunan, 49	Guizhou, 6
Sichuan, 47	Henan, 5
Jiangxi, 12	Jiangsu, 4
Zhejiang, 10	Tibet, 2
Guangxi, 8	Other, 3

Total of 146 respondents

Table 9.4

How and Why Odd-Job Workers Came to Guangzhou

Manner of arrival in Guangzhou	Reason for coming to Guangzhou
By themselves 28 (34%)	Earn more money in Guangzhou 29 (35%)
On advice of *tongxiang* 27 (33%)	Not enough land or work, too many people at home 22 (27%)
On advice of friends 15 (18%)	
On advice of relatives 10 (12%)	Guangdong has more work 19 (23%)
Other 3 (4%)	Other 8 (10%)

Total of 83 respondents

the response was surprisingly concentrated, bearing out the traditional theory of "push-pull." For the "pull," through the media and other channels, most "knew" that Guangzhou was an open city where work was plentiful and the pay was high. The "push," on the other hand, was provided by the fact that, at home, land and work were scarce as compared to the population. The provinces where many odd-job workers originated all had dense populations. In many of the responses to our questionnaires, people said that average per capita cultivable land at home was under half a *mu*, which left a lot of surplus manpower. Township enterprises were not developed, much less the tertiary sector. There were few employment opportunities, and this forced them to look outward. From Table 9.1, we can see that the majority of odd-job workers were young single males and we discovered that the reason they came to Guangzhou was to earn money to get married. Because of the strict household registration system, they knew they would not be able to settle down in Guangzhou, so except for handicraftsmen like shoe repairers and carpenters, most earned some money and went home, got married, and never came back. In China today, the cost of a wedding for a young man in the rural area has risen sharply, creating a lot of pressure on the man to earn enough money to build a house and get married. Some of the workers came to Guangzhou because of the frequent natural disasters that hit their areas. Some students came because they were frustrated at having failed senior middle school entrance exams; this was another source of "push."

4. Working Conditions

Migrant odd-job workers took the heaviest, dirtiest, most tiring and low-paying jobs, which locals shunned. Yet such work was indispensable to a city, and the migrants filled a vacuum. The vacuum first appeared in the mid-1980s, and because of lack of labor for such jobs, the pay was relatively good. Within a few years, however, with the influx of people from outside, a huge labor reserve had been created and a buyer's market had now appeared. Old-timers now talked about "the good old days" when the money was easy and sighed about times getting harder.

A. Monthly incomes. According to the questionnaire responses, handicraftsmen had relatively stable incomes, averaging 300 *yuan* a month, with actual incomes surpassing this figure. Incomes of other odd-job workers fluctuated between 120 and 300 *yuan*. The less fortunate barely made the rent and meals.

B. Hiring method. Most sat at a stationary spot waiting for people to hire them. On the streets of Guangzhou, you could see groups of three to five waiting for work. Others went around looking for work in residential areas or marketplaces. A third channel was referral by friends and relatives.

C. Working hours. Most came out in the morning and went home at night. Sometimes a job lasted fifteen hours; sometimes no jobs were found. Hours varied according to occupation. Handicraftsmen worked relatively stable hours; others had no fixed hours, working whenever there was a job.

Overall then, most odd-job workers felt their work was none too easy; there was too much competition and undercutting of wages. By comparison, though, handicraftsmen made somewhat better money.

5. Living Conditions

Odd-job workers led a relatively hard life with poor housing and food. They had no recreation to speak of.

A. Housing. The majority shared living space rented from the villagers or lived in illegal housing. Groups of eight to ten young men typically shared one room. Sometimes a family rented one room and a number of families shared an apartment. A few stayed at low-cost inns and hostels, where each paid for a double-decker bunk space. Scavengers lived in whatever shelters they could find.

B. *Food.* Most made their own breakfasts and suppers. People who shared a room also boarded together, chipping in to buy rice and other food and taking turns in preparing meals. Families made their own meals. Most people made no lunch. They either bought fast food or ate in the cafeterias of the work place. Average monthly food expenses came to 90–120 *yuan.* Since most dwelling places did not provide kitchens, simple brick stoves were set up at the foot of outer walls and twigs were used for fuel. Meals were simple—a big pot of rice and a dish. The cheapest foods were bought.

C. *Illness and injury.* Since most were young and able-bodied, illness was uncommon. Minor illnesses were ignored. When someone was truly sick, he returned to his native place. In our investigation, we found one man who had been sick in bed for three days. He never went to the hospital and had no money to travel home. Injuries from work were not treated in hospitals. One man was bleeding heavily from a head wound. He went to the hospital to stop the bleeding, and wanted to leave immediately afterwards. We paid the hospital to suture his wound.

D. *Free time.* Migrant workers had little free time. After a day's hard work, they usually got into bed and slept. Most of the answers we got from our question: "What do you do in your free time?" were "sleep." This made up 60 percent. Other answers we got were "play cards," "hang out on the street," "talk," "read books and newspapers," and "watch a movie/video," in that order. Some replied that their only pastime was to "watch the people passing on the street."

Since nobody owned a TV, the major source of news for these workers, besides an occasional movie/video, was newspapers. Some of them went to the park, a shopping mall, or a night market once in a while. Most had never visited a park or mall or even heard about Guangzhou's well-known scenic spots.

E. *Language.* Since they were all from other provinces, they all spoke their own dialects; among themselves, they spoke their local tongue, but when others were present, they switched to *putonghua.* Most, however, could not speak the Cantonese dialect, although a few said they understood and spoke it a little.

Odd-job workers maintained little communication with people in their home districts. Besides sending home their earnings, they sent an occasional letter. Since few had mailing addresses, they received no mail. They seldom returned home for visits. A few went home for the spring festival; some had not returned home for years.

6. Informal Organizational Structure

Unlike ordinary individual laborers, odd-job workers did not belong to any formal organizations. Being unorganized, how did groups and individuals communicate and adjust to each other? Did they belong to informal organizations? We devised some questions in this area to find out.

A. *Work relations*. Fierce competition existed among workers in the same occupation. People fought to get business by undercutting each other's prices. The sharpest competition occurred over territory, especially some of the better hiring spots. Among people from the same area, usually whoever arrived early got the spot, and if disputes broke out, an unofficial leader would arbitrate. When disputes broke out among people from different areas, fights were frequent. The hiring boss always had the final say. Nobody disputed him, obviously because of possible reprisals and other problems.

B. *Relations with people from other areas*. Most migrant laborers from the same areas (*tongxiang*) arrived in droves. They lived and worked together. One worker might be linked to a network of 200–300 *tongxiang* from the same area. Workers had little contact with people from other areas. Each little community had a relatively fixed territory. West of Xingang Central Road, for instance, was the territory of the Sichuanese. East of that road was the territory of the Hunanese. When disputes arose over work or territory and could not be resolved, gang fights broke out, using knives and clubs. Such fights were never reported to the city management or public security bureau, because both sides would be fined and/or repatriated.

Handicraftsmen were basically divided by trade. For instance, Zhejiang people chiefly repaired shoes. Jiangxi people fluffed cotton and did carpentry. Henan people put on acrobatic shows or scavenged. Tibetans bought and sold coupons and certificates. There was little conflict of interest among people from different areas here.

C. *Among tongxiang, to whom did people listen?* Many respondents avoided this question, or answered that everybody was equal. Actually, some people spoke with more authority. In groups of three to five, for instance, one person usually negotiated the price. Although the others also had a say, once the price was determined, they all listened to the negotiator. This person was the de facto head of the group. Usually, this person was a good talker and had stayed in Guangzhou longer. Among large groups of people from the same area, there were a few leaders who arbitrated disputes. When we asked: "Why do you listen to so and so?" The usual answer was: Because so and so is fair; he has a group of supporters; or he is more experienced.

We learned of the existence of local underworld gangs from our conversations with the odd-job workers. One was a Sichuan gang calling itself the "Knives." Its size was unclear, although some said it had seventy to eighty members and others said 200–300. The Knives exacted 5 to 10 *yuan* per worker without exception on fixed dates in the month. Whoever refused or owed them was beaten up. One army veteran from Sichuan got his head broken because of this and had to get a dozen stitches in the hospital. The money was supposedly for the "protection" of the victims' territory. When some other group disputed the ownership of the territory, the Knives would try to settle the dispute by appeasement or beat the other group up. In eateries frequented by odd-job workers, we witnessed a couple of gang fights during which blood flowed copiously.

D. Pricing of labor. Despite the unorganized nature of the workers, prices asked for different types of labor were relatively uniform. The price asked for pushing a cart of sand, for instance, was 12–15 *yuan,* plus 1 *yuan* extra up each flight of stairs. Transportation of each bag of cement was 0.50–1 *yuan,* plus extra for stairs. Prices for shoe repairs and cotton fluffing were also at similar levels. According to the workers, cost, degree of difficulty, and time were the factors taken into account. A day's wages (eight hours) was generally 12–20 *yuan.* Each hour of overtime started at 1 *yuan.* The rule was to ask a high price, leaving room for bargaining. Thus they made more from inexperienced employers and less from savvy ones. So long as it was higher than cost, the deal was usually clinched.

7. Relations with Local People

Migrant workers lived and worked among the local people, hence relations between the two directly affected their livelihood.

A. Relations with Local Government

A strict household registration system was enforced. All migrant workers had to register and obtain a temporary resident permit, which was granted for three months up to a year. Re-registration was required at expiration. The local administration, therefore, inspected requisite documents periodically. Those who were undocumented or whose documents had expired were fined. We discovered during our investigation, however, that government inspection was not very regular. It was done most often before major holidays or large-scale activities (such as sports meets). All those who were inspected or being checked upon, no matter whether they violated regulations or not, would be fined. Inspecting entities included security personnel in the neighborhood or village committees as well as members of the public security stations.

B. Relations with City Management Personnel

In addition to regular public security personnel, cities have city management offices whose function is to keep order and take care of environmental sanitation. These offices regularly hire temporary workers, especially security workers. Of all people, the odd-job workers hated the security workers most, because their "inspections" meant extra money out of the migrant workers' pockets. If payment was not made, the tools of the offender were confiscated or he got a savage beating. Some were locked up and could be "redeemed" only with payments of 150–300 *yuan,* or they were sent to repatriation centers from which they were sent home. The majority of odd-job workers had been "fined" by such city personnel. Though most tried hard to avoid this, they did not always succeed.

C. Relations with Tax Workers.

Most odd-job workers had no contact with tax workers. This was because they had no fixed work or income and tax workers had no time for them.

D. Relations with Landlords.

Relations with landlords were generally good. As long as rents were paid on time, landlords left odd-job workers alone.

E. Relations with Locals.

Odd-job workers did not communicate much with locals except in the course of work, hence there was little conflict. Most migrant workers could not speak the local dialect. They felt locals looked down on them or pitied them. Some claimed locals were very good to them. This author thinks that, because of lack of contact and being completely enveloped by their own subcultures, the feelings of migrant workers toward locals were more assumption than fact. Some told us that whenever conflicts did arise, they were usually the ones who suffered because public security and city workers were always on the side of the locals.

8. Odd-Job Workers' Attitudes

This author designed a set of five questions to examine odd-job workers' attitudes toward Guangzhou and its people and their achievement motivation (see Table 9.5).

Table 9.5

Odd-Job Workers' Attitudes
(82 samples; %)

	Would be willing	No such plans	Unwilling
If possible, would you permanently live in Guangzhou?	34%	12%	54%
Do you plan to work in other places in Guangdong?	27%	10%	63%
Are you willing to become a temporary employee at a work unit or factory?	55%	29%	16%
	Agree	Hard to say	Disagree
Do you agree with the saying that "only those who suffer the most bitter hardships can go to the top"?	28%	51%	21%
Many people say Guangzhou people are very clever.* Do you agree?	41%	31%	28%

* "*Jing*" means "smart" but it also is somewhat pejorative, as "cunning."

This table shows that the majority of odd-job workers were unwilling to resettle permanently in Guangzhou. Their major goal in coming to the place was to earn money to spend at home—to get married, build a house, or to use as capital for future investment. When we asked about this unwillingness, most answered: "Because the land and people are strange to us"; "Because we can't continue doing heavy physical labor when we get old"; or "Because I prefer my native place."

The second question was designed to explore their motivation for keeping moving—the "ladder migration" in population movement. The response we got was that 63 percent were unwilling, 10 percent had no such plans. Based on what we heard, the reasons were the following: Some had already been to other places and found them similar to Guangzhou; and some felt that Guangzhou, being a big metropolis, provided more opportunities and the city management was not too strict. This showed that, without moving on, the migrant workers would settle in one place and form an ever more dense concentration.

The third question was to explore whether odd-job workers were willing to find a fixed job. Fifty-five percent were willing, but 16 percent were unwilling or did not comment. After further interviewing, we found that a part of them had already worked as temporary workers in factories (mainly joint and private ventures), found it too stressful, and left them to be on their own. Most of those willing to work in factories had never worked there, or had failed to find a job there. Factories liked to hire women over men. Some odd-job workers shook their heads over this: "To think that times have changed so much that women are preferred over men!"

The fourth question was to test achievement motivation. The result showed only 28 percent in agreement, 51 percent noncommittal, and 21 percent disagreeing. This reflected the odd-job workers' view that their situation was hard to change, and that they had to take what work and money they could find a day at a time.

The final question examined their attitude toward the local people. Our findings confirmed our own observations and interviews. Relations were good between most odd-job workers and the local people.

III. Questions and Discussion

Although odd-job workers represent but one mode of population movement, they have a unique way of adapting to their environment. In this author's view, odd-job migrants had developed subcultures of their own. In these subcultures, they communicated mostly with people from their native regions, spoke their native dialects, maintained their eating habits, lived in close community, and shared strong feelings for their home districts. In Guangzhou, such subcultures had not become integrated with the local culture. Migrant workers did not speak Cantonese or have any contact with Guangzhou people except for work; in work, the relationship was one of employer and employee, preventing other communication. That was why they had so little to say about the local people when asked. Though living in Guangzhou, they knew next to nothing about the city: who its mayor was, who the provincial governor was, what the scenic spots were. They could evaluate the locals only through feelings and impressions.

We had mentioned earlier a surprising answer we got from those we questioned, which was that the majority felt they were adapting well to life in Guangzhou. How could people doing jobs shunned by other people, living in dire conditions, and subject to unfair treatment and other problems feel they were adapting well? We feel the reasons are: First, they were addressing the question from a collective perspective. Having built relatively closed subcultures in a foreign place, the individual was insulated from directly experiencing the normal cultural shock. That is to say, they had little direct contact with the foreign culture. Clustered together like a soccerball, odd-job worker groups were kicked around from one culture to another without breaking up.

Second, there are different criteria for adapting well or not. Judging their living standards from our own, we are apt to see them as the most neglected stratum at the bottom of society. To them, since most came from economically backward or impoverished areas, labor conditions and living standards at home were not necessarily better. In Guangzhou, they could at least feed themselves and earn some extra money, so life was not all that bad.

Third, the Chinese like to save face, and this habit is especially strong among people from Hunan and Sichuan. It may be that they were putting the best face on things so that they would not be considered losers. This might not have been the chief reason, but it certainly was one reason.

The adaptation mode of odd-job workers is linked to their cultural characteristics as well as to the government's household registration system.

In China, the residence status of each child is registered at birth. Like a straitjacket, this status prohibits a person from freely moving to other areas. To a large extent, it decides his or her fate. The household registration system rigidly controls movement between urban and rural areas and between different regions. Beginning in the 1950s, waves of peasants had surged to the cities and factories and mines to seek a living, but because these moves were unplanned and unregistered, they were considered "blind population flow" (blind flow into the cities) and repatriated back to places they came from. Thus, surges of migrant laborers were dubbed "blind flows" (*mangliu*).[5] The term itself signified homelessness, filth, and ignorance, the lowest stratum of society.

This policy system led to the formation of odd-job workers' subcultures and to their isolation from the mainstream culture. The surges of migrant laborers, both in the 1950s and today, are the result of the interaction of push and pull. In leaving their homes for other places, Chinese peasants never question the reasonableness of the household registration system or feel that it can ever be changed. Instead, they suffer hardships passively and carry around with them a feeling of shame. They never forget their "alien" status or wonder if this status can be changed. The Zhejiang workers mentioned earlier, despite ten years of work in Guangzhou, had never thought of settling down. They sent their money home to build houses which they themselves could not enjoy. When forcibly sent home or refused permission to leave their native places, they never complained. Perhaps one day they will ask: "Why is it that we share the same land and sky, but we don't have the same rights?"

Because of the registration system, a fixed concept was born in government and society that surges of migrant laborers are disasters and the root of turmoil. Whenever such surges occur, they are stopped, dispersed, or suppressed. This makes it easier to understand why odd-job workers become the target every time the government "cleans up the city," although they toil for the least pay and are subject to all kinds of injustices.

Thus, reform and updating of ideas and concepts is the first step to resolving the problems of migrant workers (and especially those of odd-job workers). The more society develops, the greater the population movement. Surges of civilian workers are the outcome of societal growth. At the core of the problem is the need for policies that work. Past policies obviously did not. Migrant workers remained the targets of every cleanup. Why is it that the more odd-job workers are targeted, the more they grow in number? As analyzed above, it is because, on the one hand, of the push—more and more members of the labor reserve are joining their ranks—and, on the other, because of the pull—Guangzhou is truly a place that offers more opportunities. It is therefore the opinion of this author that it is not possible to prohibit the appearance of odd-job workers, because they fill an objective need in urban development. Their work has become an indispensable part of the urban economy and makes an important contribution to urban development.

In the wake of urban economic growth and rising living standards, popular concepts have changed. The need for this type of migrant labor did not arise in the past because of previous emphasis on there being "no distinction between superior and inferior jobs in the revolution" and on "the greatest glory belongs to the working people." In addition, the cities themselves had their own odd-job workers, who were making a fair living and had no opportunity to switch to other work. Since reform and the open-door policy, more job opportunities have opened up for urban odd-job workers, while the income gap between them and workers in other occupations has widened. This caused the majority of local urban odd-job workers to switch to other occupations, leaving a vacuum for new manpower. Moreover, urban development has also exacerbated the demand for odd-job workers in such projects as pipe-laying, ditch-digging, road construction and repairs, etc. Another great demand for odd-job workers comes from the residents who, with rising living standards, are remodeling their homes and need large amounts of labor. This vacuum has been filled by the migrant odd-job seekers. Since these trades and skills are necessary to cities and their residents, merely prohibiting them or expelling them is not going to work. On the contrary, management and coordination should be enhanced, such as establishing minimum per-hour wages, setting up agencies (such as moving companies) to provide information on supply and demand, and providing odd-job workers with protection from all the physical and illegal attacks they are prey to.

The most urgent problem at present is this lack of protection for the personal safety of odd-job workers. This was their greatest concern when talking to us, and we can summarize its dimensions as follows:

First, there is undue extortion of odd-job workers by various types of city management personnel. Almost every odd-job worker has been subjected to demands of 10 or 20 *yuan* from such personnel under various pretexts. If he refused, he would either be given a savage beating, or sent to the repatriation center.

Second, there is extortion by "local snakes" [local gang bosses—Ed.]. Odd-job workers generally have to get the consent of these gang bosses and pay them when they want a piece of territory. They hate this, but they are powerless. Such gang bosses have power, as well as connections. The aforementioned party secretary, for instance, had to pay them 4 *yuan* daily while others paid 1 *yuan* a day.

Third, there are some hoodlums and crooks among the odd-job workers who organize gangs to do nasty things. From what we heard, these are people born after 1970 who have no jobs or homes and refuse to work after coming to Guangzhou, hence resorting to illegal acts. They can steal a dozen bicycles in a night and sell each for 5–10 *yuan*. They also extort money from other workers and beat up those who refuse to pay. The public security organs do not pay much attention to such goings-on. Sometimes they arrest the whole lot, including the good and bad guys. The majority arrested are honest workers.

Fourth, there are fights among odd-job workers for work, especially among workers from different provinces and areas. Hunan and Sichuan workers are deadly foes and engage in many fights. Fights also happen among natives of the same area. The outcome is normally very serious, including injury and death. This is also ignored by public security.

Solving the problems here regarding their personal safety would also actually improve citywide security.

This essay cannot fully answer the question of how to manage and coordinate odd-job workers and ensure their personal safety, but the author would like to make the following suggestions: A unified management and oversight system should be established to control migrant population. At present, there is no single unified agency but a dozen. Unified action is taken in a desultory fashion. In locations where special agencies have been formed, the staff is inadequate, efficiency is low, and the attitude is poor. In addition, because of the lack of an oversight system and due to the inferior quality of enforcement personnel, instances of violations of the law, extortion, harsh treatment, and illegal arrests sometimes occur. It is therefore of the utmost urgency that management bodies should be overhauled, exclusive reliance on punishment and arrests should be changed, and the legal rights of every citizen observed.

In the final analysis, the problems of the odd-job workers can be resolved only when the government and all social strata adopt a fair and just attitude toward them—that is, when they recognize the fact that the work the odd-job workers do constitutes an indispensable and supplementary part of the urban economy and that they are contributing to urban growth. Despite the social problems they bring in their wake, in this author's view, we must not prohibit their existence, just as we cannot forbid auto manufacture simply because accidents happen.

Notes

1. No detailed statistics are available on the size of the migrant population in the Pearl River Delta. See Zhou Daming, "Population Movement in the Pearl River Delta," *Shehui kexue zhanxian* (Social Science Front) 1990:2, and "Research on the Migrant Laboring Population in the Pearl River Delta," *Shehuixue yanjiu* 1992:5, pp. 330–41.

2. Zhou Daming, "Distributional Characteristics and Classification of the Migrant Laboring Population in the Pearl River Delta" and "Review and Prospects of Economic Development in the Pearl River Delta," *Xueshu taolunhui lunwenji* (Collection of Seminar Treatises). Guangzhou: Zhongshan University Publishers, 1992.

3. Zhao Shili and Zhang Minru, "Population Shift and Mobility in Shenzhen," *Shenzhen daxue xuebao* (Shenzhen University Journal), 1990:1, p. 71. The "*sanwu* population" mentioned in that article refers to people without fixed jobs, without fixed abodes, and without valid documentation. The odd-job workers are included.

4. Zhou Daming, "Urbanization of Rural Communities on the Urban Periphery—A Study of Guangdong's Urbanization," *Shehuixue yanjiu,* 1993:6, p. 213.

5. Guo Shutian, Liu Chunbin et al., *Shihengde zhongguo—chengshihuade guoqu, xianzai yu weilai* (China in Imbalance—the Past, Present, and Future of Urbanization). Shijiazhuang: Hebei People's Publishing House, 1990. See pp. 14 and 31.

10

Rural Development and Social Security

Guo Zhenglin and Zhou Daming

Social security is a major factor in China's policy of separation of cities and rural areas, for which reason we deem it an important topic in the study of rural urbanization. Rural township enterprises are the motive force and pillar of rural urbanization; in looking into social security in township enterprises, we discovered that, in the Pearl River Delta, such enterprises are closely integrated with the communities in which they are located and that the social security systems of the two are actually one. To study the social security system in township enterprises, therefore, we must first study the system in the township communities. This can be said to be a characteristic of Chinese rural urbanization.

In China, the chief difference between holding an "iron rice bowl" or a "clay rice bowl" depends on whether or not a person enjoys the social security benefits provided by the state. The former include such people as public government functionaries and employees of state-owned enterprises. For them, the state takes care of all benefits from birth to old age, sickness, and death. These benefits total over 100 percent of their wages. Those holding the "clay rice bowl," on the other hand, such as peasants and entrepreneurs, take care of everything themselves. They do not enjoy any of the benefits enjoyed by those in the public sector. In the Pearl River Delta, the same situation is true. State functionaries such as township officials, teachers, and doctors, as well as employees of enterprises owned by the people as a whole or employees of large collective township enterprises, can enjoy social security provided by the state, which includes public housing, free medical care, labor insurance, and pension and retirement benefits. Rural dwellers and employees of township enterprises (the majority of whom are *mingong* rural nonfarm workers), entrepreneurs (*getihu*), and employees of private enterprises cannot enjoy state benefits and have to rely on their own efforts for security. This was why, once the conditions were ripe, rural communities experimented with setting up social security systems, thus breaking down the state system that privileges cities over rural areas.

Since 1978, the economy and culture of the Pearl River Delta have made tremendous progress, thus providing the material foundations and social conditions for setting up a rural social security system. At the same time, the labor force in the area, acting in its own interests, has also placed new demands on the question of social security. To meet this demand, township and village organizations have adopted different types of social security systems in line with their particular conditions. The following is a discussion of the various modes of township social security in the Pearl River Delta, and other related issues.

Currently, township social security in the Pearl River Delta is still in the process of changing from the traditional to newer modes. There are three major patterns, with the first two systems closely integrated with society. The other, which has recently emerged, is linked with the shareholding system.

I. Rural Community Pattern—Humen and Longgang

1. Humen Town[1]

Humen is located at the midpoint of the Guangzhou-Shenzhen Highway on the eastern bank of the Pearl River estuary. Since the Nansha ferry was opened to traffic, the township has become a major link between the eastern and western banks of the Pearl River. Humen's economy got off the ground with "*sanlai yibu*" (processing, assembling, and customized manufacture of goods from materials supplied by foreign clients and compensation trade). It developed rapidly with town industry in the lead and management district[2] and village industry as the foundation. With management districts as the unit, a community security system has been established. The precondition for the establishment of this system was a strong collective economy. Many of Humen's management districts are showing a GVIAO (gross value of industrial and agricultural output) of over 30 million *yuan* with profit standing at 10 million *yuan*.

Benefits for the individual are similar in all Humen's management districts. They are:

A. *Security for the elderly.* 30 to 50 *yuan* per person is given to all people over sixty. "Five Guarantee households" (the guarantees of food, clothing, medical care, housing, and burial expenses [which were granted to the very young, the very old, and the infirm by the old collective system—ed.]) are given other subsidies.

B. *Free education.* Kindergarten and elementary school are paid for by the management district; middle school and college are subsidized. Generally, stipends come to 300–400 *yuan* per junior middle student per year, 400–500 *yuan* per senior middle student per year, and 800–1,000 *yuan* per college student per year.

C. *Medical care subsidies.* The individual pays for the first 50 *yuan*. Expenses above 50 *yuan* are subsidized 50 percent by the management district. Special subsidies are given to those in financial difficulty.

D. *Financial difficulty subsidy.* The criteria for a family in "financial difficulty" change along with changes in living standards. For instance, in 1992, a family averaging under 1,000 *yuan* per person was considered eligible for not only financial aid, but also policy benefits.

In the area of collective welfare and public undertakings, all management districts are spending a lot on education, nursing homes for the elderly, public transportation, public health, and maintenance of social order. Longyan District, for instance, has already invested 6.5 million *yuan* in building elementary schools, improving school facilities, and raising teachers' salaries.

With regard to labor security in township enterprises, the major benefit comes in the form of labor insurance for workers and other employees. The enterprise pays the management district a household registration management fee, labor management fee, and labor insurance fee. The last is for work injuries. Besides wages, the enterprise also gives employees other forms of subsidies such as 60–85 *yuan* per person per month for food and 20–40 *yuan* for housing. Some enterprises subsidize employees for recreational and sports activities.

Enterprises at Humen's management-district level are mostly *sanlai yibu* enterprises, and as such, have attracted large numbers of migrant labor. In Daning and Longyan districts, for instance, outsiders outnumber locals by a four-to-one ratio. The districts, therefore, emphasize a policy of nondiscrimination in benefits. They also help employees organize sports and entertainment events, with good results. However, migrant employees can enjoy only part of the benefits provided by the enterprise and no community benefits such as pensions, retirement, schooling, etc. The huge difference between locals and migrants in social security benefits is one root cause of a profound clash between the two.

2. Longgang Township

Bao'an's Longgang Township is only 30 km from Shenzhen. Its industrial structure is similar to Humen's and is predominated by *sanlai yibu* with nearly 500 enterprises of this type. They pay a total of over 100 million *yuan* of conversion fees (paid by enterprises to the community to compensate for use of land and labor) a year. In agriculture, export-oriented poultry, livestock, and fish breeding predominate. Due to a severe shortage of labor, there are more than twice as many migrant laborers as local laborers.

Longgang was one of the earliest places in the Pearl River Delta to establish a social security system. The township government emphasizes community social security and has adopted forceful measures to ensure it. It has been cited as an "advanced unit" (*xianjin danwei*) for its efforts in this area. Benefits are similar to current ones enjoyed by employees of the civil administration, such as care for "Five Guarantee households," public assistance, disaster relief, priority relief for the poor, preferential treatment for family members of veterans and martyrs, and benefits for the disabled. One of the township's initiatives was setting up a "social welfare foundation" in 1984 with dual functions: replacing the civil administration in administering social security and raising and managing funds. The foundation has many sources of fundraising, the major ones being: profit from township enterprises; donations from Hong Kong and Macao compatriots and other donations from society; enterprises run by the foundation; and state appropriations. As they develop, township enterprises have become the chief funding source.

II. Suburban Community Pattern—Nanji Village's Social Security for Those Who Lost Their Land[3]

Nanji village is under the jurisdiction of Nangang Township in Huangpu District, Guangzhou. It is situated in an urban-rural integrated area. The Guangzhou-Shenzhen Highway passes through its northern sector, while the Guangzhou Economic and Technical Development Zone borders on its southeast. To the west is the Huangpu power plant. Nanji people say about themselves, "You can say we're city people but we're not like city people; you can also say we're village people but we have city resident status." This urban/rural character determines the community's social security system.

Nanji village has ten economic cooperatives [*jingji hezuoshe;* a subvillage administrative unit roughly equivalent to the old commune-era production team—ed.] under it with 1,700 households and 4,080 people. From the 1970s to 1988, the Huangpu New Port and the Guangzhou Development Zone requisitioned large tracts of its land. As a result, a large part of Nanji's agricultural population turned into a nonagricultural population (*nong zhuan fei*) and gradually acquired urban resident status while others in the village abruptly lost their land and livelihood while simultaneously receiving a great quantity of money. As a community, Nanji had to wrestle with two important questions: How to ensure the social security of those who had lost their land, and how to help Nanji villagers adapt to the changes?

The Nanji village party committee adopted the following measures: First, they instituted a reasonable distribution of land requisition fees so that this fund was not totally divided and used up. Individuals got relocation fees and the money for seeds. Part of the fund was managed by the production teams and part by the village party committee. Second, to prevent waste, the fund was divided in two, one half deposited in the bank (interest payments were divided and given to the individual) and the other used as investment. Third, part of the land was retained for self-development. Fourth, returns on investments were used for social welfare and other public benefits.

In conformity with the change in production mode, the village set up a social security system which did the following: First, a kindergarten and two elementary schools were built in the three hamlets. [Nanji village as an administrative unit comprised three "natural villages," each of which in turn was subdivided into a few "economic cooperatives."—Ed.] Second, bonuses were given for schooling. Teachers whose classes averaged a grade of eighty or above in entrance exams to higher-level educational institutions received bonuses, as did students who gained admission to senior middle schools or colleges. A nine-year compulsory education system was instituted. Third, the Nanji Hospital was set up in conjunction with the Guangzhou Workers' Hospital to give villagers medical care. Fourth, Nanwan Park, the biggest rural park in the Guangzhou area, was built. Fifth, a rest home for the elderly was opened. Sixth, every individual was given 200–300 *yuan* of living expenses per month (based on workpoints, the highest being ten points).

Nanji has a lot of funds, so it can afford excellent benefits. Villagers can live well even if they do not work. The community has tremendous cohesive power, which both facilitates community development and bonds villagers together for fear of losing good benefits. This is no doubt harmful to an individual's overall development and also directly affects social economic and social security development. Actually, Nanji's investments are insurance in themselves; they are invested in the construction of housing or warehouses, which are rented out. Sometimes, land is also leased. However, Nanji has not utilized to the full its superiority in funds and geographic location, and this will affect the future development of its welfare.

III. Shareholders' Pattern—Report from Tianhe District

The idea of turning from the community social security mode into a shareholders' mode is a new one, and it is still too early to fully assess its relative merits and defects. One preliminary answer, however, is provided by the experience of townships in the Tianhe District, which have experimented with it.

Tianhe is located east of Guangzhou and is known to the world for its sports center. It is a typical urban-rural integrated area. It has jurisdiction over twenty-two administrative villages comprising 196 "natural villages" with a rural population of 67,000. The community shareholders' cooperative economy promoted by the rural areas of this district had its roots in a series of practical problems brought about by rural urbanization. These problems include the change of its agricultural population into a nonagricultural population, the question of how to handle collective rural assets after urbanization, the problem of the loss of the cohesion that existed during the old economic mode, and the question of how to restrict rural officials. The issue at the core was the disintegration and regrouping of community social relations after urbanization, thus giving rise to problems in handling the collective rural economy and distributing collective welfare benefits.

We have seen above that what has enabled many townships in the Pearl River Delta to leave poverty behind and become rich are the transfer of land resources (i.e., the exchange of land for capital) and the development of township enterprises (including joint Chinese-foreign, cooperative, or exclusively foreign-owned ventures). The financial revenues thus received by some of the rural areas far exceed those of many cities. This has led to the change in thinking from traditional ideas of "leaving the land" (*tiao nong men*) to "holding onto the farm" (*shou nong men*). In the villages of Tianhe District, for instance, per capita net income in 1987 was 2,622 *yuan* and that of able-bodied labor was 4,442 *yuan*. During the same period, Guangzhou employees averaged 2,087 *yuan*. In the twelve villages that implemented a shareholders' cooperative system relatively early, the 1991 per capita net income was 4,594 *yuan* and that of able-bodied labor 7,650 *yuan*. In the remaining ten villages, the 1991 per capita net income was 3,168 *yuan* and that of able-bodied labor, 4,829 *yuan*. In the same period, that of Guangzhou employees was 4,090 *yuan*. This new urban-rural gap has made that part of the agricultural population that the government has asked to become "nonagricultural" unwilling to do so. They preferred to stay on in the villages rather than become city workers. Here, financial considerations were uppermost: city workers earned less than farmers, and they would lose excellent community benefits if they left. Moreover, the more people left, the better benefits the rest of the community enjoyed. Thus, it is now extremely difficult to persuade rural people to leave, to the point where some who had already left are trying to buy back rural status at the cost of 3,000 *yuan* each, so that they could again enjoy collective community benefits and social security.

However, "holding onto the farm" or "buying peasant status" could only fetter people to their original communities. They do not facilitate the latter's urbanization or the overall development of the individual. The community-type rural shareholders' cooperative system implemented in Tianhe helps to resolve these conflicts. Fundamentally, what it does is to incorporate in the cooperative economic organizations of the community certain features of the organization of assets and the management and distribution modes of the shareholders' system. It unifies the integration of labor with the integration of funds and maintains the principles of collective ownership of land, the indivisibility of collective assets, and the lion's share going to the collective economic organization. It turns liquidated collective assets into shares of two types, shares toward collective accumulation and shares to be distributed among community members. It also absorbs cash purchases of shares by members. Newly raised funds and the major part of revenue received by the shareholders' cooperative every year are used to develop the collective economy and collective welfare. Such a community-type shareholders' system is different from that in an enterprise in that shares are of three types: collective accumulation shares, shares for member distribution, and cash shares. The first makes up 60 percent of the total and the member shares (including cash shares) less than 40 percent. Member shares are "dry shares" which qualify them to participate in the management and revenues of the community's economic organizations.

In contrast to the original community social security mode, members in the community who had become nonagricultural can also receive "distribution shares" based on their contribution to the collective. That is to say, they are also eligible to receive community benefits. Of course, the number of shares—hence, income and benefits derived—differs individually based on grade of labor, contribution, number of shares bought, number of years in farming, and age. Concretely, Tianhe's system adopts a distribution mode based chiefly on labor supplemented by capital contributed. Primary distribution is manifested as the rural family's income from subcontracting and/or wages and bonuses received from collective economic organizations. This reflects the principle of "to each according to his/her work." The secondary distribution is based on shares. Dividends given members on their "distribution shares" also reflect the principle of "to each according to his/her work"; only dividends given for personal cash shares reflect dividends by capital.

With the implementation of the community shareholders' system, the community's social security benefits are linked to shares. The elderly and weak receive sizable pensions based on the shares they own. Even those who have withdrawn from active work can enjoy welfare shares; the community gives each around 500 *yuan* living expenses a month from its welfare fund. With development of the collective economy, the community is putting in extensive funds to develop collective welfare undertakings. They are realizing the socialist social security goal of providing all who need them with day care, schooling, medical care, and public assistance.

Overall, the above three rural township social security patterns in the Pearl River Delta collectively demonstrate a further improvement over the original rural social security systems of China. Their contents are basically the same as before, mainly community welfare such as infant preschool care, education and other public causes, care for the elderly and needy, and medical care. The manner of providing social security is also basically the same as before—it is based upon the community, chiefly the management district (equivalent to the previous era's production brigades). All major social security work is done at this level: local people raise funds, set standards, engage in public undertakings, take care of "Five Guarantee Families," and give assistance to the poor and needy.

Existing modes of rural township social security in the Pearl River Delta also have the following significant unique characteristics:

1. The level of social security and funding is keyed to profits earned by township enterprises. A secondary source is donations from overseas compatriots and government appropriations. The individual pays no fees or a small fee. The financing mode is fundamentally still one-sided.

2. With the management district as the basic unit, the benefits, medical care, and pensions enjoyed by community members come from the secondary distribution of the community's collective wealth. This reflects the closed nature of these systems.

3. These systems lack appropriate policy and legal guarantees. In many places, they were spontaneously formed. They lack a policy basis for their scope and manner of funding and distribution; many guidelines were randomly set. Thus, once collective wealth dissipates, these systems will disintegrate.

4. The township social security system integrated with the rural community shareholders' economic mode can overcome the closed nature of previous modes and facilitate industrialization and urbanization. Although still in an embryonic stage, it points out the direction for rural and township social security.

IV. The Conditions for Building Township Social Security and Some Related Problems

Rural development is without a doubt the fundamental condition for a social security system. In the Pearl River Delta, the internal conditions for township social security were rural industrialization and urbanization; the external conditions were a large army of low-wage migrant labor and enormous wealth from transfer of land. Donations by Hong Kong and Macao compatriots and overseas Chinese to aid community social and public welfare also played an exemplary role.

1. The Internal Conditions—Rural Industrialization and Urbanization

In the area of industrialization, the ratio of the output increases in the three economic sectors [primary (agricultural), secondary (industrial), tertiary (service)—Ed.] in the Pearl River Delta was 25.8 percent to 45.3 percent to 28.9 percent in 1980 and 14.2 percent to 49.9 percent to 35.9 percent in 1991. The average rate of increase in the primary sector was 8 percent, its proportion dropping by 11.6 percentage points; that of the secondary and tertiary sectors were 19.5 percent and 16.7 percent respectively, their proportions having risen by 4.6 and 7.0 percentage points respectively. This trend demonstrates that the delta has roughly completed the evolution from an agricultural to an initial-stage industrial economy. In this process, township enterprises have played an important role. The Gross Value of Industrial Output of the township enterprises in the delta's twenty-eight counties and municipalities in 1991 was 125.554 billion *yuan,* of which 76.3 percent came from diverse types of industrial enterprises not owned by the whole people ["owned by the whole people": i.e., nationally-run enterprises, including party organizations and enterprises—Ed.], mainly township enterprises. The swift development of these enterprises brought tremendous changes to the internal structure of the rural economy. The nonagricultural output share rose as the agricultural output proportion dropped, providing a powerful impetus to urban-rural integration and rural industrialization.

Second, in the area of urbanization, with economic growth, major breakthroughs have been effected in basic facilities such as transportation, communications, power, and city construction. A pattern of urban-rural integration has emerged as the division between cities and rural areas has become indistinct. In the Pearl River Delta, one can find a city (including designated townships) [designated townships, the *jianzhi zhen*, make up the lowest officially recognized urban rung in the official urban hierarchy—

Ed.] every 70 sq km. In the larger delta formed by Guangzhou, Shenzhen, and Zhuhai, clusters of cities with flourishing economies such as are rarely found in other parts of China have appeared. The Pearl River Delta can be said to have one of the highest rates of urbanization in the country.

With rapid industrialization and urbanization in this area, profound changes have taken place in the delta's socioeconomic relations, interpersonal relations, and ways of life. The traditional closed-off agricultural sub-culture has rapidly given way to an industrial culture. The social security system with the traditional family at the core is no longer able to satisfy the needs of social change. Industrialization and urbanization have posed a new challenge to the old, backward social security system. The times call for an entirely new rural township social security system.

The Pearl River Delta's industrialization and urbanization have caused enormous social pressure to build as the once rural population becomes urbanized. A tour of the Pearl River Delta will show farm and hilly land everywhere marked as "industrial village," "business village," "villa area," and "high-tech development zone." Large tracts of farmland are being converted into industrial and business zones and cities and towns. This means that large segments of the agricultural population have become nonagricultural, thus changing past lifestyles and social relations. Although the peasants received relocation funding for their requisitioned land, society still has to resolve the employment of these newly nonagricultural people and provide them with basic security in their lives. The original labor employment and social security systems are unable to accommodate them in such large numbers. Thus, development of township enterprises and communities has to provide employment and financial security to this great mass of farmers who have lost their land. Such internal demand for survival and development, in turn, provides great motivation for the faster development of rural township enterprises.

We can thus see that the swift progress of industrialization and urbanization, which reflect social progress, and the failure of the previous social security system both fueled the development of township enterprises and acted as a catalyst to the birth of new township social security systems based in the community. These were the internal conditions for the development of township social security systems in the delta.

2. The External Conditions—a Large Army of Low-Cost Migrant Labor

Rural industrialization in the delta began with labor-intensive enterprises. These not only quickly absorbed surplus local labor, but also large numbers of migrant laborers from outside the local area. The scale is mammoth.

According to estimates, migrant labor from outside the delta and Guangdong Province has already reached a staggering 10 million. This author divides migrant labor into four types: professionals, referring to professional/technical personnel of college level and above; enterprise workers, referring to enterprise employees (which constitute the majority of migrant labor); agricultural workers, referring to migrant laborers doing farming or livestock, poultry, or fish-breeding on the farms and in the families; and odd-job workers (*sangong*), referring to those doing different types of temporary jobs without fixed locations. Migrant workers are mostly rural people who have created enormous wealth for the delta localities. Their remuneration is no doubt much higher than what they could get at home, although compared to the commodity value they created, it is still very low. The swift growth of wealth in the rural communities of the delta has a lot to do with low-cost migrant labor.

In the Daning Management District of Humen Township (see chapter 4 above), mentioned earlier, the revenue for processing materials from foreign clients (conversion fees) in 1991 totaled 17.18 million Hong Kong dollars. In Longyan District, the 1990 conversion fees came to 32 million Hong Kong dollars. These funds were originally intended to be mainly distributed among enterprise workers, but are actually retained by the community. In Daning, the per capita average is HK$8,720 and in Longyan, HK$17,297. This gave the management districts sufficient funds to build up their rural areas as well as their social security systems.

In Longyan, all factories are included in overall planning. Village houses are built in the mode of a small city district. New concrete roads total 4,678 m. Parks and gardens line the streets, street lights and a sewage system have been installed, digital telephones and fax machines are working, and 470,000 *yuan* have been appropriated to build a rural market. A new cultural center, sports arena, and sanitation stations have been built. Six and one-half million *yuan* have been invested to build a modern school, which includes a kindergarten, dormitories for faculty and staff, a gymnasium, swimming pools, and soccer and basketball fields. A social security system similar to Daning's has been instituted with even better benefits.

At present, the various social security systems in the Pearl River Delta are working well. Where the conditions are good, most migrant populations are included, showing that their contributions form the material foundations for local social security.

3. Land Resources Development and Land Transfer

Development of land resources changed along with rural urbanization and industrialization. First, land began to be managed in diverse ways, including the planting of high-quality, high-price crops. More important, the value of the land increased with its transfer. In areas near cities, towns, and industrial zones—due to, on the one hand, improvements in the investment environment, and thus a natural rise of land values, and, on the other hand, land requisition by growing numbers of nonagricultural residents—large sums of money have poured in.

The transfer of land resources provided the start-up capital for township enterprises. In the Pearl River Delta, we can feel a new "enclosure movement." Although the farmers have lost part of their land, they received, in return, large amounts of capital. As revealed by our investigations, they did not divide up all the funds, as was done during the "land reform," but kept the major part to develop the collective economy and set up township enterprises and community welfare benefits. The primary sector is being replaced by the secondary and tertiary sectors. Such large-scale transfer will necessarily bring down the proportion of agricultural output in the local gross output, but it enhances the general economic development level. With the rise of real estate development, the value of land has skyrocketed. Rural dwellers living near cities and industrial zones have quickly become rich. Communities have gained the financial capability to set up social welfare and social security systems.

4. The Exemplary Role of Donations to Public Causes Made by the "Three Compatriots" (San Bao; i.e., Overseas Chinese from Hong Kong, Macao, and Taiwan)

The Pearl River Delta is the home of many overseas Chinese. Eighty percent of Hong Kong and Macao compatriots have relatives in the delta. Since 1978, when the "left" interference was eliminated and the government policy on overseas Chinese was implemented, the patriotic sentiments of these overseas Chinese have reached new heights. Many are making donations to their home towns to build public undertakings such as cultural and educational institutions, medical facilities, health and sports facilities, and roads and bridges. Others are donating to cultural, educational, or health foundations. They have also introduced concepts of social security to the delta to enhance public well-being. Governments at all levels responded by implementing a policy of setting up social security systems to "serve the people." Localities have made good benefits a benchmark of their policies, and that was another reason the social security system was widely established.

5. Problems

Above, we have discussed the conditions for social security in the delta. Below, we will discuss some current problems in the model.

We believe that the following problems should be addressed in regard to the pattern of social security in the Pearl River Delta. First, there is the question of equity. Currently, individual units or communities are responsible for existing systems. Richer units or communities are able to provide better benefits and poorer ones cannot give employees and individuals the good benefits they really need. Moreover, the existing systems put increasingly heavy burdens on the units or communities, becoming an impediment to their development. Second, there is the question of reciprocity. Existing systems are mostly unidirectional; that is, the government, unit, or community funds the benefits and individuals pay nothing and have no intention of paying. This can only breed dependence on the country and the collective; it does nothing to stimulate the individual's enthusiasm for work, as well as causing waste. Third, there is the question of prevention. Existing systems emphasize treatment and cure rather than prevention; they kick in only when something happens. This leads to great waste, an example of which is paying for workmen's compensation while neglecting labor safety.

Aside from this, the most important issue here is: Who is eligible to enjoy rural township social security benefits?

In the above, we have analyzed the larger social environment and related conditions for the development of the delta's township economy. It is not hard to see that, like rural township enterprises everywhere in China, township enterprises in the delta had developed through the cracks of the dualistic economic structure of traditional agriculture and modern urban industry. The impetus for its appearance and swift development came, on the one hand, from the rejection of surplus labor on the land in traditional agriculture and the pressures of low agricultural income. On the other hand, it came from urban industrial capital's rejection of surplus rural labor and a social security system that separated town and country.

From their inception, township enterprises had a dual characteristic: First, they provided employment opportunities for unemployed rural dwellers so as to alleviate the pressure on urban employment and social security created by large numbers of migrant peasants stripped of their land. Second, they offered a relatively low entrance threshold. Thus, employees of newly formed township enterprises were farmers who had lost their land, and whose welfare and other social security benefits were closely linked with their communities. Part of the wealth created by township enterprises is paid to the community for secondary distribution among its members. That is to say, only "official members of the community" are qualified to enjoy its social security benefits.

On the other hand, although the swift development of a township economy in the delta can be attributed to the hard work of the local population, it also involves the contributions of large numbers of migrant labor. The latter have, in fact, become the major labor force in most township enterprises. They do the heaviest, dirtiest, and most dangerous work. Moreover, they are also beginning to shoulder the heavy work on the farms. Not being official members of the community, however, they can only exchange their labors for wages or enjoy part of the labor benefits, but have no right to participate in the secondary distribution of the community's collective wealth, or community social security. In this, the delta's rural township social security system is similar to that in the cities. As the city social security system is closed to the rurally registered people, so are the rural township systems also closed to outside labor. The basis for qualifying for social security benefits, therefore, is not labor and the quantity of labor, but individual status (*shenfen*). In the cities, social security is granted only to people holding an "iron rice bowl"; in the delta, the only qualification is whether you are an official member of the community or not. As a member, a person is entitled to a slice of the collective economy's "big cake" even without contributing to it. Enormous differences exist between locals (agricultural and nonagricultural) and outsiders with respect to employment, social status, financial income, and welfare benefits. In social security benefits, in particular, the two form two distinct social groups, with the locals enjoying all benefits and outsiders none. The delta's social security systems have an exclusionary character and form closed systems of their own. This can only exacerbate tension between locals and outsiders. Such a unique social relationship is an external factor obstructing the region's social security development.

Note

1. See also Chapter 4 for a fuller discussion of Humen.
2. In Dongguan city (County) and other districts in Guangdong, the subcounty *xiang* has been redubbed a "management district" (*guanli qu*), the latest administrative label for the commune-era's "production brigade."—Ed.
3. See also Chapter 4 for a fuller discussion of Nanji.

Part V

Conclusion

11

Urbanization with Chinese Characteristics

Gregory Eliyu Guldin

Now fully into the post-Deng period, China's transforming society and social structure continue to blur the old distinctions between rural and urban existence. The reports in this volume point to a China which has permanently outgrown its peasant framework as a concatenation of demographic, economic, and social changes scramble the old patterns of the Chinese people's agricultural and rural lifeways. The rural-urban dualism which served as a structural barrier to urbanization and which was maintained, Zhou Daming tells us, by the *hukou* household registration system, by the social security system which delivered benefits to city-dwellers only, and by the land system wherein the state owned urban land and the collective owned all rural land, is breaking down. Urbanization, and particularly the urbanization of "rural" areas, is proceeding with vigor throughout the society and throughout most of the country.

Our authors also provide us with a good critique of Chinese definitions of urbanization, definitions that arose out of the Chinese reality of the *hukou* system as a mechanism of population movement control. Shi, Hoffman, Zhou, and Liu take to task the assumptions that urbanization means a concentration of people in the large cities, that it is limited to the official reclassification of *hukou* status to non-agricultural (*nong zhuan fei*), that cities always serve as the locus of all social and economic innovation, and that urbanization inevitably leads to prosperity and "development." Shi points out that the goal of migrants to cities is not to live in the cities *qua* cities, but to acquire what they perceive as "urban lifestyles." Such urban lifestyles can be found in towns as well as cities, and indeed, with townization, increasingly in villages as well.

Despite the ubiquity of the Chinese folk equation of urbanization with "development" and prosperity, it is more helpful for us to focus on the cultural dimensions of townization and citization, the twin processes of urbanization in China today. Such a concentration will enable us to see beyond the rampant misindicators of urbanization lurking in the official statistics founded on the *hukou* system. Our Liaoning chapter serves as a case in point.

Liu and Hoffman tell us that in Liaoning's Beile Township 2/3 of the local people retain agricultural *hukou* status but that fully 90 percent of them have left farming. These figures, furthermore, do not include the migrant population which comprises fully 40 percent of the total number of people actually resident in the district, and which is also overwhelmingly non-agricultural in work status, though not necessarily in *hukou*. In nearby Yangjia village, an old-timer comments that there is no more land to be farmed, that all the children are in industrial and service jobs, yet here too the majority is considered officially rural and agricultural. In the town, "blue *hukou*" holders as well as other migrant workers once again are not included in town population totals.

Recent country-wide surveys, moreover, indicate that this deagriculturization process is a national phenomenon. Rozelle, et al (1997) confirm the findings of Parish, Zhe, and Li (1995) that "rapid off farm growth has occurred" and estimate fully 34 percent of the rural labor force to have found employment off the farm as of 1995. Yet household registration figures indicate little of these employment and residence shifts.

Rural Urbanization Processes

Despite the inadequacy of the official statistical indicators, investigative reports both in this volume and elsewhere clearly document a widespread and thoroughgoing rural urbanization process—or, more precisely, processes. Urbanization encompasses a number of micro processes: villages becoming townlike in infrastructure, services, and lifestyle (townization) and towns becoming more citylike in infrastructure, services, and lifestyle (citization). The many cases of urbanization discussed in this volume can be seen as examples of one or the other of these two forms, and mostly the former. Three of the four rural urbanization types that Zhou and Zhang propose for the Pearl River Delta (city periphery rural urbanization, village and management district urbanization, and industrial zone-induced urbanization) can all be seen as townization. Shi and Lan's Caitang village urbanization, furthermore, is a good example of city periphery townization (combining Zhou's and Guldin's categories), as is Gelek and Li's

Duilongdeqing County's rural urbanization. Daning Management District's changes reflect Zhou and Zhang's second type, while the Shekou and other industrial and development zone cases, in turn, in effect create "instant towns" and should be recognized as a different variety of townization (industrial zone-induced). Lastly, Zhou and Zhang's fourth and final rural urbanization type, the extension of market towns, is more properly understood as an example of the citization process.

This exercise in categorization helps us do more than just organize neatly our data. It helps us understand the social changes on the ground and points us to significant changes in people's lives. With townization, the lifestyles of Anhai and Humen township residents have begun to change: they are leaving farming, purchasing their own food, buying their clothes ready-made, building new houses, and traveling further and more frequently. The pull to towns has diminished and the long-standing yearning for an urban *hukou* has not only decreased, it has been replaced in some districts by a desire, as in Shekou and Daning, to hold onto rural *hukous* for the benefits they may confer.

Townized villages are described by our authors as "integrated rural-urban areas" (Zhou and Zhang) where "amphibianized" peasants, neither rural nor urban, are constructing a new lifestyle amalgam—which calls to mind McGee's kotadesasi process in Southeast Asia. In this new pattern, even marriage strategies are changing; it is no longer as desirable as it once was to marry an urban *hukou* holder. Guo and Zhou also tell us that for some areas in the Pearl River Delta, rising economic prosperity has helped fund generous social security programs, thus allowing ostensibly "rural" areas to partake in what used to be exclusively urban arrangements. With the new shareholders cooperative system, distributions in rural areas may actually exceed urban payments, thus fueling the reverse desire for rural *hukous* and their attached superior wages and benefits.

Our authors also give numerous examples of the changes brought about by citization as well. Residents of Beile Town in Liaoning model their lifestyles after Dalian, while to the south, Humen Town looks to Guangzhou and Hong Kong. Zhou describes Humen as "a rural market town (*jizhen*) [becoming] a multifunctional city." In addition to lifestyle shifts, Humen is also making a substantial infrastructural investment in roads, transportation, energy, education, and recreation facilities. Even comparatively sleepy Xinqiao in Gaoyao, has begun the citization process, while the town of Nangang in the shadow of the Guangzhou Economic Development Zone is a bit further along that continuum. Government policy also promises to give such developments a firm push, as plans have been drawn up, Hoffman and Liu tell us, to encourage the transformation of *xiangzhen* into small cities of 30,000 people and above.

Roads to Urbanization

In striking contrast to many other global areas, this urbanization process in China has not been precipitated by a collapse of rural agriculture. On the contrary, our researchers tell us that those areas which have urbanized most rapidly are precisely those areas which have shown continuing agricultural strength. In both prosperous Guangdong and interior Tibet, agricultural productivity is up. This is occurring simultaneously with the feminization of agriculture as males in places as far apart as Duilongdeqing and Caitang leave agriculture to women and the elderly, returning to the fields only at the harvest or at other times of high labor need.

The decollectivization which made possible the release of labor power from the land has restructured the occupational structure and employment opportunities in these districts. Some people took advantage of their post-commune emancipation to migrate to other districts entirely, while others found ready employment locally in transportation and construction. In all of the districts studied, these two industries were the first to draw surplus labor and investment capital. Caitang saw a boom in building and construction in the mid-1980s spurred by its proximity to the Xiamen Special Economic Zone, while in Yunnan's Eshan County, the Hui villagers who specialized in transportation had prospered and urbanized to the point where 70 percent of households owned private cars in 1992 and residents there were rapidly townizing. In the hilly Yi area of Eshan County, by contrast, without these entryway economic developments, all of Gaoping *xiang* could boast of only one automobile, and that lone vehicle was the collective property of the village government.

For some districts, including some other nationality minority areas, still other mechanisms are used in their efforts to develop economically. Ruili in Yunnan, for example, is undergoing a rural urbanization process led by tourism and a brisk border trade. Although the immediate causes may differ, rural urbanization is causing similar lifestyle shifts there as well.

In some areas, these initial developments led to further economic breakthroughs which helped speed the townization process. Deagriculturization and the increase in rural incomes first led to a release of pent-up demand for services and goods, which in turn caused transportation and construction industries to boom initially, as we have noted above. The service sector then began to develop rapidly as well. Caitang followed such a process in the early and mid-1980s, but by the decade's end accumulated profits from these endeavors as well as investments garnered from abroad (Taiwan and Hong Kong) and elsewhere in China allowed the village to embark on the path of rural industrialization.

Capital from outside was indeed a key factor in the jump to the head of the prosperity and townization queue for districts such as Xinqiao and Daoyue in Gaoyao, as well as many sites throughout the Pearl River Delta. Zhou believes that Anhai's initial development edge over Humen was overcome in the early 1990s by the latter's superior connections to Hong Kong (and the adjoining Shenzhen SEZ). Moreover, with factories setting up shop and recruiting migrant labor (local males preferring to pursue non-factory entrepreneurial opportunities), the need for a wide range of service industries, from restaurants to hair salons, increased, and these new industries added their own demand for labor, construction, and materials.

These new service and industrial enterprises have taken a number of forms, ranging from state-managed, to collective-owned, to privately-operated. Some analysts, such as Eugene Cooper (pers. com.), have seen the very diversity of forms of production that has arisen at the township level as one of the keys to prosperity. Indeed, the multiplicity of enterprises at this level, including a wide variety of state, collective, and private ownership and management forms among themselves, has enabled districts to develop at their own speed and in their own way, as local conditions can best be bent to the needs of rural development. In this volume, Zhou Daming shows us how the form of enterprises, furthermore, can also help mold the urbanization process. In Anhai, he tells us, *lianheti* were the predominant form of collective enterprise, while in Humen, most enterprises were Management District (*Guanliqu*) or Town-run. In Anhai, most of the profits of the *lianheti* were directly distributed and privately consumed by the individual households making up the *lianheti*, leaving little left over for communal investments. In Humen, by contrast, with the *qu* and town governments major industrial players, a greater percentage of profits and taxes were utilized for infrastructural development. Privatization thus has discernible effects on the built environment;[1] one can notice the differences walking through the two towns.

Migrant labor streams are another key element of rural industrialization and urbanization. Although their labor is crucial to the profits amassed in the towns, villages, and cities where they live and work, they are systematically left out of the local social security systems of both rural and urban areas. Their living conditions were often quite poor in the districts our team surveyed, with the worst abuses occurring in those "cages" in Guangzhou which held 16–20 people per room. Exploitation of migrants is a fact of life, although this doesn't necessarily mean the *waidiren* receive the sympathy of the local people. In most of the districts, migrants had little contact with locals, and although by no means universal, antagonistic local-migrant relations were quite common. In areas with large numbers of migrants from different regions, furthermore, conflicts between groups of migrants over jobs and territory were frequent.

Discrimination against migrants fuels their desire to return home. Most had planned to journey "outside" for only a short while anyway, and difficulties of whatever sort help keep them to that original predilection. It is the dream of many to return home not merely wealthier than when they first set out, but as investors and entrepreneurs in their home towns. Migrants thus serve important social functions as catalysts of rural urbanization as they transfer capital and new ways of thinking to their home counties, set up entrepreneurial ventures in industry and service occupations back home, and continue to contribute needed labor to the industrializing projects of the already prosperous and urbanizing areas.

As a crucial dimension of lifestyle changes, job opportunities and occupational shifts can serve as good indicators of the urbanization processes. Whether an area is labor-exporting or labor-importing indicates how far the local economy has absorbed surplus agricultural labor by developing the secondary and tertiary sectors, and this in turn correlates with degree of townization. The dynamism of this process was demonstrated to us from one end of the country to the other. Yangjia village, only 30 km from Dalian, changed over from a labor-exporting area to a labor-importing area between 1992 and 1996, while Gaoyao in the outer Pearl River Delta was undergoing the same process during the same time frame. In southeastern coastal Fujian and the central Pearl River Delta, this changeover had occurred a decade earlier. Similarly, monitoring the sectoral distribution of labor power in the industrial, agricultural and service industries as the economies developed were also helpful on the ground indicators. Such percentages were more useful pointers to the changing lifestyles of the countryside than the official statistics on agricultural and non-agricultural *hukou*.

In poorer areas, such transitions have barely begun and rural urbanization is at a rudimentary stage. Non-Han minority nationality areas are likewise less likely to be undergoing as thoroughgoing an urbanization process as those of Fujian, Liaoning, and Guangdong, but townization and urbanization is by no means unknown in the national minority areas if the minority districts covered in this volume are any indication. In Duilongdeqing County in suburban Lhasa, for example, until recently the dynamic ripples pulsing through China's economy seemed to have completely bypassed the area. During the very time frame when Gaoyao and Yangjia were taking off, sectoral distribution in the county remained mostly static with agriculture continuing to monopolize production, decreasing only marginally to 80 percent of the total. Gelek and Li tell us, however, that by the early 1990s Duilongdeqing began to export its labor elsewhere, and in 1993, the number earning salaries outside doubled over the previous year. In villages close to cities, up to 50–60 percent of the labor force engaged in "pendular migration" (days in towns/city; nights in the village) during the slack season, contributing to an outmigration which not only was the first significant change in the local socioeconomic picture since the reform era began, but it was also the first substantial source of investment income in Duilongdeqing.

This "primary accumulation," as Gelek and Li refer to it, led the county to follow in the footsteps of other developing areas in the country as the service and transportation industries rapidly expanded to 25 percent of the productive total in 1993, up from 10 percent in 1992. With incomes and profits increasing, expenditures for daily necessities and staples have also increased, revealing that this modest prosperity in the county is still meeting pent-up demands for long-standing peasant staples such as food and housing—and religious obligations. Unlike districts further along on the continuum, the county's residents have just begun to diversify their spending into new consumer and investment options.

Duilongdeqing County is clearly at the early stages of a profound transformation, and on a number of fronts. Like its sister counties in the more prosperous areas, the county's residents have become city-dependent for key goods and services and will be drawn inexorably into an ever greater rural urbanization process. Unlike most areas of the country, however, this rural urbanization process is also bringing an embedded acculturative project as *Han* urban lifestyles spread to Lhasa's suburbs. This seems to be a common pattern in the nationality minority areas. Yet along with the Han acculturation, people have also poured those newly available *yuan* into religious activities and other markers of ethnic identity and maintenance. This may not be a bad outcome; a positive integration (partial acculturation within a cultural pluralist frame) into the larger society as living standards rise may be a worthwhile compromise goal as minority nationality individuals weigh the competing sirens of cultural nationalism and prosperity.

Zhou Daming helps us see the necessity for recognizing the need of different districts to follow different roads in their pursuit of the prosperous urban lifestyles they covet. He and our other authors help us contrast coastal and nationality areas as follows:

Coastal Areas	*Nationality Districts*
lack natural resources	abundant natural resources
densely populated	sparsely populated
little unemployment	much unemployment or underemployment

developed commercial traditions	some commercial traditions
industrial foundations	lack industrial foundations
remittances and investments from overseas Chinese	remittances and investments from outmigrants
rural industrialization → rural urbanization	tourism/commerce/transp → rural urbanization

Therefore, rural industrialization is not the road to rural urbanization and development (i.e., the acquisition of those coveted urban lifestyles) for all, even not for all coastal areas. For some areas, rural urbanization may be stimulated by commerce or transportation or tourism.

As the Pearl River Delta Goes

Thus the craze to establish special industrial zones in every county and every *xiang* or *qu* as is common throughout many areas of the country may represent misguided zeal. From what our team witnessed during our investigations, the nation should continue to focus on developing towns and small cities rather than follow the advice of some demographers and urban planners to concentrate resources on the large cities. These new towns and cities, however, must be integrated into a new urban/rural framework, one which takes into account the transformations of daily life and economy that the reform era unleashed nearly twenty years ago.

Comprehensive urban administrative reform is needed. Rural communities on city peripheries undergoing urbanization need to be integrated with cities into district-wide planning and administration. China is outgrowing its agricultural society-based administrative structure, and reform is needed just as surely as was the case in the United States as industrial and suburban economic and demographic shifts called for metropolitan and regional administrative readjustments. China's new towns and cities must be supported as part of a reordering of the old urban hierarchy of privileges and responsibilities.

The *hukou* system is of little aid in this process and should be severely curtailed or abolished. Too many townizing villages display divided management as they attempt to coordinate a population split between villagers' and residents' committees (*cunmin* vs. *zhumin weiyuanhui*). Add to this the ubiquitous presence of rural and urban *hukou* in the same village and same household, as well as the varying temporary and permanent *hukous* of migrants and locals, and we can see that the management of townizing Chinese villagers and citizing towns can be an administrator's nightmare of conflicting jurisdictions and responsibilities.

Two social problems must also be addressed forthrightly. As long as there are severe economic disparities between prosperous and poorer districts, migrants will continue to fill the labor demand of the industrializing and urbanizing areas. So far, however, the split and inattentive management system currently in place is not intervening consistently on behalf of an often exploited and ignored migrant labor force. This needs to be addressed in a comprehensive and just manner, looking towards both the labor needs of the host districts and the social, economic, and legal rights of the migrants.

Guo and Zhou also point to the potential of new social experiments such as the shareholders cooperative system which promises to surmount the anomalies of the dual *hukou* system. Rather than distribute benefits only to those with local rural *hukou*, the new system would distribute benefits according to labor and capital input regardless of *hukou*. Such an innovation could help decrease the gap between migrants and locals and also help keep people in the countryside even as peasants continue to leave agriculture. Ironically, of course, such an "innovation" also helps retain a socialist principle in the allocation of social benefits ("to each according [at least partially] to their labor").

What type of China have our investigations intimated the twenty-first century is bringing? If the Pearl River Delta is a harbinger of things to come, then peasant life is certainly marked for marginalization in the nation's life. Judging from food, clothing, employment structure, production, living conditions, and transportation, our authors have told us that the Delta is already an industrialized and urbanized society. In the mid-1980s, the Delta as a whole made the transition to majority non-agricultural status, and today some districts are 90 percent in non-agricultural occupations.

These districts, furthermore, are linking up. Humen Town, undergoing citization, will soon become a city, flanked by the newly designated "Baizha Town" towards its east, with that town itself the product of the administrative amalgamation of the townized villages of Longyan and Daning *Guanliqu*. As this process continues apace, the entire delta region, from Guangzhou to Macao to Hong Kong is becoming a great metropolis. Citization combined with townization is causing entire regions to undergo a comprehensive metropolitanization process.[2]

China will undoubtedly continue to townize, citicize, and metropolitanize in the next few decades. This urbanization, while similar to the kotadesasi process of rural-urban integration occurring elsewhere in Asia, displays some unique Chinese characteristics. First of all, migration's classic push and pull vectors are still restrained by the outdated *hukou* and dual urban-rural system. Secondly, the move to develop a socialist market economy has led to a peculiar and dynamic mix of private, collective and state economic forms which add to social fluidity. Finally and most significantly, Chinese urbanization is fed not by the collapse of rural agriculture but by rural prosperity. And the rural urbanization attendant on such prosperity is the linchpin of China's urbanization which is day by day bringing rural dwellers increasingly within an urban lifestyle nexus. As the twenty-first century dawns, we say farewell to peasant China!

Notes

1. Michelle Mood (1997) reports that in the Tianjin area privatization also leads to the local leadership cutting back on social welfare and the promise of full employment.

2. A macro-level study (Jones 1997) of regional trends in living standards and inequality indirectly confirms this hypothesis when it points to an "increased convergence between the coastal regions" and China's three autonomous municipalities of Beijing, Shanghai, and Tianjin. It is precisely those coastal regions which are undergoing the metropolitanization process (of combined townization and citization).

References Cited

Jones, Marion E. 1997. "Rising Inequality and Declining Living Standards in China Since 1983." Paper presented at Association for Asian Studies annual conference, Chicago, IL, March 13–16.

Mood, Michelle S. 1997. "Risks and Rewards: Effects of Rural Enterprises on Work and Welfare in Rural Tianjin." Paper presented at Association for Asian Studies annual conference, Chicago, IL, March 13–16.

Parrish, William, Xiaoye Zhe, and Fang Li. 1995. "Nonfarm Work and Marketization of the Chinese Countryside," *China Quarterly* 143:697–730.

Rozelle, Scott, Li Guo, Minggao Shen, John Giles, and Tuan Yee Low. 1997. "Poverty, Networks, Institutions, or Education: Testing among Competing Hypotheses on the Determinants of Migration in China." Paper presented at Association for Asian Studies annual conference, Chicago, IL, March 13–16.

Glossary

Pinyin	Chinese	English
bai cai	白菜	Chinese cabbage; bok choy
benke	本科	undergraduate
bieshu	别墅	villas
buqiu zuida, danqiu zui jia	不求最大，但求最佳	Don't strive to be the largest, but strive to be the best
(cheng)shi	城市	city
chengshi bianyuan qu	城市边缘区	the area on the edge of an urban zone
chengshihua biaozhun	城市化标准	urbanization criterion
chengxiang jiehebu	城乡接合部	where the rural and urban areas meet
chuzhong	初中	junior middle school
cunban qiye	村办企业	village-owned and managed enterprise
cunmin weiyuanhui	村民委员会	village committee
cunmin xiaozu	村民小组	village leadership group
cunzhang	村长	village head

dafoye	大佛爷	senior Buddhist monks
danwei	单位	work unit
dazhuan	大专	junior college degree
Dianshe Zhoubao	电视周报	TV Weekly
ditou she	地头蛇	"local snakes"
dushihua	都市化	urbanization or metropolitanization
duzi qiye	独资企业	independent foreign enterprise
feinongye hukou	非农业户口	non-agricultural household registration
fei zhuan nong	非转农	transferring from non-agricultural to agricultural household registration
feiShekouren	非蛇口人	non-Shekou people
getihu	个体户	individual enterprise/entrepreneur
gongye xiaoqu	工业小区	industrial small zones
guanbuliao	管不了	not able to control or watch over
guanliqu	管理区	management districts
hada (*Tibetan*)	哈达	kata; ceremonial scarf
hukou	户口	household registration
jianzhi zhen	建制镇	designated towns
jiaozi	饺子	Chinese dumplings
jing	精	smart; cunning
jingji hezuoshe	经济合作社	economic cooperative
jingji jishu kaifa (xiao) qu	经济技术开发(小)区	economic and technical development (small) zone
jishu rencai	技术人才	technical experts
jishu renyuan	技术人员	technical experts
jishu xuexiao	技术学校	technical school
jiti	集体	collective ownership/investment

jiti jingji	集体经济	collective economics
jituan	集团	a group company
jizhen	集镇	(market) town
jumin weiyuanhui	居民委员会	(urban) residents committee
lanpi hukou	蓝皮户口	blue (temporary) household registration
laoren jie	老人节	Old Folk's Day
laoxiang	老乡	home district people
liangpiao	粮票	food rationing coupons
lianheti qiye	联合体企业	multi-household (multi-family) cooperative enterprise
lianpian kaifa	联片开发	"coming together" development
linshi hukou	临时户口	temporary household registration
loufang	楼房	apartment buildings
luan	乱	chaos, chaotic
maai jujai (*Cantonese*)	卖猪仔	"selling piglets"
mangliu	盲流	"blind flow" migrants; vagabonds
mantou	馒头	steamed bread
mao	毛	one tenth of one chinese dollar (yuan)
mifen	米粉	vermicelli (rice-flour noodles)
mingong	民工	peasant worker
minzu (diqu)	民族地区	ethnic minority areas
moshi	模式	model
mu	亩	land measurement, equal to 0.0667 hectares
neilian	内联	domestic (enterprises) cooperation
nishuilao	泥水佬	"brickers"
nongcun jizhen	农村集镇	rural market towns
nongmin cheng	农民城	farmer's town

nongye hukou	农业户口	agricultural household registration
nongye gongren	农业工人	workers in agricultural industry
nong zhuan fei	农转非	transferring from agricultural to non-agricultural household registration
po-la (*Tibetan*)	波拉	paternal grandfather
qingke	青稞	highland barley
qiye	企业	enterprise
rencai	人才	talent; experts
rencai shichang	人才市场	talented person's labor market
sange zhua	三个抓	"grasps three tasks"
sanbao	三胞	"three compatriots" (from Hong Kong, Macao, and Taiwan)
sangong	散工	odd-job workers
sanlai yibu	三来一补	"three arrivals and one supply"
sanwu	三无	"three withouts"
sanzi qiye	三资企业	joint, cooperative or foreign venture
Shekouren	蛇口人	Shekou people
shenfen	身份	individual status; identity
shenzhou diyi lu	神州第一路	Number One Road of the Divine Land (Shenyang-Dalian Expressway)
shiyan	试验	experiment
shou nong men	守农门	holding on to the farm
shuishangren	水上人	"Boat People;" fisherfolk
tang baozi	糖包子	sugar buns
tiao nong men	跳农门	leaving the land
tongxiang	同乡	home district people
tongxianghui	同乡会	home district association

tsampa (*Tibetan*)	糌粑	roasted barley flour
tuqi	土气	"hickish"
waidi ren	外地人	outsiders, in-migrants
wailai renkou	外来人口	in-migrants
waishengren	外省人	out-of-province people
weixing chengzhen	卫星城镇	satellite town
wenming banshichu	文明办事处	"civilized office"
wenming cun	文明村	"civilized village"
wubaohu	五保户	five guarantee households
xian	县	county
xiang	乡	a subcounty district, formerly a commune
xiangcunlide dushi	乡村里的都市	countryside metropolis
xiangzhen qiye	乡镇企业	township (non-farmer) enterprise
xian jian zhi	县建制	designated county system
xianjin danwei	先进单位	advanced unit
xian zhen	县镇	county towns
xinde jingji fazhan qu	新的经济发展区	new economic development zones
xinshiqu	新市区	new city areas
youtiao	油条	fried fritters
zhaoshou ting	招手停	mini-van taxi
zhiye zhongxue	职业中学	vocational middle college
zhongdeng zhuanke xuexiao	中等专科学校	secondary specialized school
zili kouliang	自理口粮	supply own grain
ziran cun	自然村	natural village
zong fang	宗房	Buddhist temples
zong jingli	总经理	general manager

Index

Gregory Eliyu Guldin is an anthropological researcher, cross-cultural consultant, and development studies scholar. He is currently Professor of Anthropology and the chair of the Chinese Studies Program at Pacific Lutheran University in Tacoma, Washington. He has conducted fieldwork in Hong Kong, China, Southeast Asia, and the northwestern United States on migration, urbanization, social change, and ethnicity. He is the author/editor of *The Saga of Anthropology in China* (1994), *Urban Anthropology in China* (1993), *Urbanizing China* (1992), and *Anthropology in China: Defining the Discipline* (1990).